# THE COLLECTED POEMS OF LI HE

# THE
# COLLECTED POEMS
# OF LI HE

*Translated by J. D. Frodsham*
*Preface by Paul Rouzer*

THE CHINESE UNIVERSITY OF HONG KONG PRESS

NEW YORK REVIEW BOOKS

**Calligrams**
Series editor: Eliot Weinberger
Series designer: Leslie Miller

*The Collected Poems of Li He*
  Translated by J. D. Frodsham

Original edition © 1970 by Oxford University Press
Revised edition © 1983 by North Point Press
Calligrams edition © 2016 by The Chinese University of Hong Kong
Preface © 2016 by Paul Rouzer

Library of Congress Cataloging-in-Publication Data

Names: Li, He, 790-816, author. | Frodsham, J. D., translator. | Rouzer, Paul F.,
writer of preface.
Title: The collected poems of Li He / translated by J. D. Frodsham ; preface by
Paul Rouzer.
Other titles: Li Changji ge shi. English
Description: New York : New York Review Books, 2016. | Series: Calligrams |
Reissue of Goddesses, ghosts, and demons : the collected poems of Li He
(Li Chang-ji, 790-816)--London : Anvil Press Poetry, 1983 and San Francisco : North
Point Press, 1983. | Includes bibliographical references and index.
Identifiers: LCCN 2016012888 | ISBN 9789629966607 (paperback)
Subjects: LCSH: Li, Ho, 790-816--Translations into English. | BISAC: POETRY /
Ancient, Classical & Medieval.
Classification: LCC PL2677.L5 A2 2016 | DDC 895.11/3--dc23
LC record available at https://lccn.loc.gov/2016012888

ISBN: 978-962-996-660-7
Available as an electronic book; ISBN: 978-962-996-932-5

Published by:

**The Chinese University Press**
The Chinese University of Hong Kong
Sha Tin, N.T., Hong Kong
www.chineseupress.com

**New York Review Books**
435 Hudson Street, New York, NY 10014, U.S.A.
www.nyrb.com

Printed in Hong Kong
10  9  8  7  6  5  4  3  2  1

*For Simon, Stefan, Jonathan,*
*Myfanwy, and Julia*

The business is not alone to translate language into language, but poesie into poesie, and poesie is of so subtle a spirit that in the pouring out of one language into another it will all evaporate and if a new spirit is not added in the transfusion there will remain nothing but a *caput mortuum*.

—Sir John Denham
*Preface to the Second Book of the Aenied*


The work of the translator (and with all humility be it spoken) is one of some self-denial. Often he would avail himself of any special grace of his own idiom and epoch, if only his will belonged to him; often would some cadence serve him but for his author's structure—some structure but for his author's cadence.... Now he would slight the matter for the music and now the music for the matter but no, he must deal with each alike. Sometimes too a flaw in the work galls him and he would fain remove it, doing for the poet that which his age denied him; but no, it is not in the bond.

—D. G. Rossetti

# Contents

# Preface to the Calligrams Edition

❧

Reading poetry in translation is an exploration born of restlessness, a search for something that will add new colors to our own experience. Yet the poetry we read and appreciate from outside the comfort zone of our own culture inevitably has a resonance with our own traditions and views. The "world literature" we choose is a reflection of our tastes—one that often does not precisely coincide with the tastes of the readers in the original language.

The translation of classical Chinese poetry in the English-speaking world is intimately connected to the history of modernism (especially through the efforts of Ezra Pound and Kenneth Rexroth as well as the Bloomsbury scholar Arthur Waley). But not only does our enthusiasm for Chinese poetry sometimes empha-size qualities traditionally of lesser interest to Chinese readers—and ignore aspects they would consider quite important—our versions of Chinese poetry do not exhibit merely one form of modernism.

The dean of Chinese translators in America, Burton Watson, operates very much in the tradition of American verse defined by William Carlos Williams—he prefers to work with straightfor-ward, allusion-free poetry that conveys its charms directly, whether it is the flamboyant rhyme-prose of the Han and post-Han eras, or the genial directness of the great Song poet Su Dongpo. Eminent Chinese literature translators who worked in Great Britain or in the Commonwealth have often been attracted by more difficult as-pects of modernism; they are the descendants of William Empson, with his erudite mastery of the English literary tradition and his fascination with the difficult. Although Waley was attracted to the relatively transparent Bai Juyi, A. C. Graham, David Hawkes, and J. D. Frodsham turned to denser and more allusive texts: *The Songs of Chu*, late Tang verse, aristocratic court poetry—and, of course, one of the great eccentrics of the Tang, Li He (790–816).

Many American fans of Chinese poetry first encountered Li He as I did—in the renderings of twenty-two poems by A. C. Graham in his *Poems of the Late T'ang* (1967; republished by NYRB books). Graham, like Frodsham, described Li He as a modern rediscovery, seemingly popular because of his resemblance to the symbolists (Frodsham explicitly terms him a *poète maudit*). He was heady stuff for a college freshman drunk on Rimbaud and Patti Smith: I loved his anguish, his visionary nihilism, and, above all, his tragic early death (probably from that most romantic illness, tuberculosis). Yet Li's poetry, though it does bear some resemblance to the nineteenth-century decadents and to the work of some difficult modernists, deserves appreciation for its own sake. Frodsham's complete translation of the poems first appeared first in 1970, and then in revised form in 1983 (the version reprinted here). It enables us to get a fuller sense of the poet, beyond Graham's immediately accessible selections.

And we gain from having Li He complete, as opposed to the other major Tang poets. For most educated men in the Tang era, verse was a social skill that demanded social response—we have poems requesting patronage, poems praising the emperor or this or that official, casual letter-poems, parting poems written at banquets for people whom the poet barely knew. These are all fairly conventional and not terribly interesting, and even someone as original as Du Fu has dozens of them. This is why Chinese poetry

lovers tend to read anthologies of selected poems, and most trans-
lators have followed suit. But Li He was temperamentally unable
to write a conventional social poem, and consequently he is very
rarely dull. Take, for example, the poem *Song for the Boy Tang Son of
Du, Duke of Bin*, a rather fawning effort in praise of the infant son
of a powerful aristocrat (and which ends with the cringe-worthy
"May he never forget the man called Li / Who wrote this song!").
It begins:

> Skull like jade, hard as stone,
> Blue-black eyelashes.
> Master Du has certainly begotten
> A very fine boy.
> Serious of face, pure of spirit,
> A temple-vessel,
> With a pair of eyes that can see through men
> Like autumn water.

This is almost as strange in the Chinese as it is in the English. A
precocious toddler has been turned into something from *The
Village of the Damned*.

An even better example can be found in *Song of the Old Jade-
Hunter*, a rare attempt on Li's part to write the kind of bland politi-
cal poem known as a "New Ballad" (*xin yuefu*). Here, Li protests
government labor in the jade fields in northwest China, where
peasants were compelled to leave their crops and engage in the
dangerous work of jade extraction. To appreciate the poem's dis-
tinctive qualities, it is worthwhile translating an earlier verse on the
same theme by the talented but highly conventional Wei Yingwu
(737–792):

> The government has drafted the common folk
> To go hunting for Indigo River jade.
> On steep peaks they have no homes at night;
> In remote hazel-wood groves they sleep in the rain.
> They return to bring a ration of grain to their lonely wives;
> Their fields desolate—they sob south of their huts.

Li He probably knew Wei's effort and its description of sad workers spending the night in their hazel-wood groves; he adapts it for the anguished middle stanza of his own poem:

> On rainy nights, on the ridge of a hill,
> He sups on hazel-nuts,
> Blood that wells from a cuckoo's maw
> The old man's tears.
> The waters of Indigo River are gorged
> With human lives;
> Men dead a thousand years
> Still loathe these torrents.

The poem transforms conventional suffering into something horrific and ghostly; as the jade-miner attempts to nourish himself with paltry nuts, he is surrounded by a landscape inhabited by the spirits of dead workers, whose corpses now replace the jade as the area's distinctive product. The subject is also haunted by another presence as he weeps, one that emerges through allusion. In his notes, Frodsham mentions the folk belief asserting that the cuckoo is the soul of a banished emperor, who would weep blood in his distress. In fact, the ancient emperor mentioned here (an Emperor Wang) abdicated his throne to his chief minister and later died of shame because he slept with the minister's wife. The cuckoo's cry is said to sound like the phrase "You should go home" (*bu ru gui qu*) and so evokes homesickness in its hearer. All of this is just a passing allusion in Li He's line, which compares the man's bloody tears to that of the cuckoo's; but it creates a certain resonance in the reader's awareness that brings a greater poignancy and clothes the lowly peasant with a classical grandeur. This is different from Eliot's ironic use of allusion; rather, it creates a sort of tragic distancing, as if the phrase "so rudely forc'd" was inserted into a Woody Guthrie song. In this case, I cannot quite agree with Professor Frodsham that "the poem makes its point dramatically and effectively and must certainly be ranked as a ballad of social protest squarely in the tradition." It is too self-consciously gothic.

But if Li He was unconventional by the standards of his own tradition, it is also not quite true that he is a modern rediscovery (*pace* Graham and Frodsham). He may have seemed peculiar to his contemporaries and to later Chinese readers, but he was not without influence. As we learn from the preface (dated 831) by the great late Tang poet Du Mu (803–853), Li He's friend Shen Ziming sat on the sole manuscript of the poems for fifteen years before rediscovering it in one of his trunks. Du Mu's imprimatur likely resulted in the copying and extensive circulation of the poems among the literary community beginning in the 830s (the only way to spread literary fame before the introduction of inexpensive wood-block printing in the eleventh century). Almost immediately his influence can be detected in lines by that generation's major poets (Du Mu himself, Li Shangyin [812–858], Wen Tingyun [c. 801–c.866]), as well as by a host of minor ones. And this influence continued in the centuries that followed, often emerging more strongly in periods of poetic innovation and revolution.

A number of qualities in Li's work struck later poets as fascinating and imitable; and each of these also challenged the traditional aesthetic and moral concerns of mainstream Chinese verse. Professor Frodsham discusses the most important of these: Li's habit of stringing together images in a montage that often cannot be reconstituted into a clear narrative from the perspective of one authorial consciousness. Chinese poetry was made readable through a series of shared assumptions, including the belief in an autobiographical voice: a poem was meant to re-enact lived experience. However, no one could have seen what Li saw— the poetic persona seemed to transcend ordinary boundaries of time and space (as well as the boundaries of the human and spirit world), as if he were not quite mortal. In the very first poem of his collection (*Song: Li Ping at the Vertical Harp*), Li praises the performance of a musician friend. This was a conventional theme. But Li strings together a series of unconnected images that illustrate the cosmic scope of Li Ping's music—images that are filled with gods and monsters:

> Jade from Mount Kun is shattered,
> Phoenixes shriek,
> Lotuses are weeping dew,
> Fragrant orchids smile....

> Where Nü Gua smelted stones
> To weld the sky,
> Stones split asunder, sky startles,
> Autumn rains gush forth.

He goes in dreams to the Spirit Mountain
To teach the Weird Crone,
Old fishes leap above the waves,
Gaunt dragons dance.

Traditional Chinese commentators attempt to put the pieces of Li He's mind together in various ways, not always convincingly; they know more than the unschooled Western reader, but still do not have all the answers. For a younger generation of poets, this incoherence must have seemed unnerving but exciting. It influenced the style of the greatest ninth century poet, Li Shangyin, who is famous for his obscure hermeticism. The opening poem of *his* collection, *The Brocade Zither*, is a similar string of allusions that seem to have nothing to do with each other (two of these allusions can also be found in Li He's jade-hunter poem):

... Master Zhuang's morning dream confuses the butterfly;
Emperor Wang's lascivious heart is entrusted to the cuckoo;
Bright moon over the gray sea; pearls weep tears.
The sun is warm on Indigo River fields; jade emits smoke....

One soon imagines that these mysterious poems are not concealing a secret narrative; rather, mystery itself *is* the narrative.

Another novel aspect of Li He's poetry was its fictional imagination. It was common for poets to reminisce about important historical events, especially when visiting the site of an ancient battlefield or an old palace. This usually gave them an opportunity to deliver a moral lecture, or to dwell on the ephemerality of human accomplishments. However, it was quite another matter to visualize scenes from the past, or to ventriloquize dead poets—something Li He attempts most obviously in *Song: Returning from Guei-ji, The King of Qin Drinks Wine, Song: Do Not Dance, Sir!, Qing Gong, Reflections on the Ancient Terrace of Liang*, and more subtly in other verse. He may be the first Chinese poet to ever compose a poem in the voice of an inanimate object, as he does in "Songs of the Brazen Immortal Bidding Farewell to Han." And when he does write a site-visiting poem, he discovers that the places are animated with the quite literal ghosts of the past (as in *Su Xiao Xiao's Tomb* and *Song of an Arrowhead from Chang-ping*). This identification with the past also resulted in his resurrection of the dense and hyper-aesthetic diction of the court poets of the sixth century. This brought a sort of archaic flavor to his writing, as well as romanticizing the refined and pampered lives of doomed aristocrats of those past ages. The effect is not unlike that produced by the pre-Raphaelites, and by the early poetry of Ezra Pound.

These attractive though somewhat questionable techniques (lyrical fragmentation, fictional imagination, and use of archaic diction for aesthetic purposes) kept emerging at various points in later Chinese poetry as a sort of counter-narrative to the mainstream. Everybody read Li He, and he influenced many; but he was a disreputable model, a poet who was somehow unhealthy. The founding text of Chinese poetics, the second century CE "Great Preface" to the ancient *Classic of Poetry*, had clearly linked poetic style with the well-being of the state: "The sounds of a well-governed age are peaceful and joyous; its administration is harmonious. The sounds of a chaotic age are resentful and angry; its administration is perverse. The sounds of a doomed state are lamenting and brooding. Its people are in hard straits." No one wanted to be famous for sounding like Li He. If he was not included in the standard school anthology *Three Hundred Tang Poems* (as Graham and Frodsham both note), it wasn't because no one knew about him; it was because you didn't want your kids to read him.

Li He was thus very much a product of his own poetic tradition—eccentric and unique, but a product nonetheless. However, even if we as English-language readers bring our own baggage when we read him, the analogies between our cultural inheritance and his are close enough to be appropriate. If we react positively to his strangeness and acknowledge his originality, we are not completely different from pre-modern Chinese readers (though we may be less bothered by the moral problems his work provoked). When I read him, I still think what I thought as a college freshman: I see a doomed young artist like Dowson or Rimbaud or Trakl (or Hendrix or Cobain). And it is maybe not so anachronistic to see a sort of post-romantic sensibility beneath the famous story told in Li Shangyin's short biography of the poet, one that was repeated in the official *New Tang History*: "His mother used to have her maid rummage through the bag [of verse he had written during the day] and when she saw that he had written so much she would exclaim angrily: 'This boy of mine won't be content until he has vomited out his heart.'" For younger readers—ones perhaps less inclined to know poetry—there might be something Goth as well as Gothic in him; a combination of adolescent moodiness with a Lovecraftian paranoia directed at the alien world he unwillingly inhabits:

> Though I have a horse to ride,
> I cannot go home,
> For the waves that drowned Li-yang

Loom large as mountains.
Poisonous, horned dragons glaring,
Rattling their brazen rings.
Lions and griffons drooling
From slavering jaws....

*Paul Rouzer,*
*University of Minnesota*

# Preface

Since the first edition of this work appeared some years ago under the title *The Poems of Li Ho* (Oxford, 1970) there have been considerable advances in scholarship which made it imperative to augment and revise the original. After years of comparative neglect, Li He suddenly became the focus of critical attention in the late sixties. Since then several new editions of his work have been published, among them the splendid *Tang Li He Xie Lü Gou Yuan* (Hong Kong, 1973) and the invaluable photolithographic reproduction of a fine Northern Sung edition, *Li He Ge Shi Bian* (Taibei, 1971). Recent events in China have even permitted a new edition of selections from He's poems to appear there, though this work, the *Li He Shi Xuan* (Shanghai, 1978), cannot be regarded as a serious contribution to studies of our poet.

In Japan, a great deal of critical attention has recently been devoted to Li He, notably by Kusamori Shinichi, whose lengthy and definitive biography of the poet has been appearing serially since 1965, and by Harada Kenyu, whose journal devoted to studies of Li He first came out in 1971. Chinese scholars from Hong Kong and Taiwan have also added to our knowledge of Li He, among them Zhou Cheng-zhen, whose *Li He Luan* (Hong Kong, 1972) typifies much current research in this area, and Ye Qing-ping.

In addition, we have benefited from four excellent dissertations on Li He by Maureen Robertson (1970); Yang Zhong-ji (1970); Michael Fish (1973); and Du Guo-jing (1974), all of whom have made further valuable contributions to our understanding of this difficult poet.

This edition has therefore incorporated many augmentations and revisions to both the poems and the introduction which have been suggested by such recent scholarship, full details of which appear in the bibliography. Though annotation of the poems has been cut to a minimum, it may still appear excessive to some readers. I can only plead that Li He is such a recondite poet that the Chinese assert that "his work cannot be read without a commentary." If even Chinese readers need explanatory notes, then Western readers can hardly be expected to understand this poet without some assistance.

Finally, since *pin-yin* romanization has now been generally adopted in Western publications, I have used this system throughout.

*J. D. Frodsham*
*Murdoch University,*
*Perth, Western Australia*

# Du Mu's Preface to the
# Songs and Poems of Li Chang-ji

In the tenth month of the fifth year of the Tai-he period (A.D. 831) there came a sudden shout outside my house at midnight from someone bearing me a letter. "This must be something out of the ordinary," I exclaimed, as I hurriedly took a torch and went outside. When I opened it, it turned out to be a letter from the Scholar of the Hall of Assembled Sages, Shen Zi-ming, which read:

> During the Yüan-he period my dead friend Li He and I were very loyal and affectionate to each other. Day and night we rose and rested, ate and drank together. When He was dying, he gave me all the songs and poems he had written during his lifetime. These were divided into four sections, numbering 233 pieces altogether. For several years now I have been wandering all over the place, till I had begun to think these poems were already lost. Tonight as the wine wore off me, I found I could not get to sleep again, so I decided to go through my trunks and set things in order. Suddenly I came across the poems which He had given me and my thoughts turned to days gone by. I recollected all my conversations and pleasant outings with him. Every place, every season, every day, every night, every goblet, every meal came back to me with such clarity, no detail forgotten, that I found myself shedding tears.
>
> Since He no longer has a family or children that I can support or sympathize with, I regret that all I have done up to now has been to think of him and enjoy his words as I recited them. You have always been very good to me. Would you now somewhat

solace my thoughts by writing a preface to He's works for me, explaining their worth?

I was unable that night to send him a letter saying I could not do this, but went to see him next day to excuse myself from this task, remarking that people considered that He's genius surpassed those of his predecessors.

For several days after this refusal I pondered this matter, reflecting that Shen had a profoundly subtle and extraordinarily comprehensive knowledge of poetry as well as a thorough understanding of both He's poetic abilities and his shortcomings. Hence if I did not definitely decline to write this preface I would certainly leave him dissatisfied. What could I do then but go and make my excuses to him once more, explaining to him in detail why I did not dare write a preface to He's works? However, he insisted that I must write it or he would feel humiliated, so that I did not dare refuse again. I have tried my best to write this preface but am still very much ashamed of it.

He was a descendant of the Tang imperial house. He was styled Chang-ji. During the *Yüan-he* period, Han Yü, the President of the Ministry of Civil Office, praised his songs and poems. Clouds and mist gently intermingling cannot describe his manner; limitless waters cannot describe his feelings; the verdure of spring cannot describe his warmth; the clarity of autumn cannot describe his style; a mast in the wind, a horse in the battle-line cannot describe his courage; earthenware coffins and tripods with seal-characters cannot describe his antiquity; seasonal blossoms and lovely girls cannot describe his ardour; fallen kingdoms and ruined palaces, thorny thickets and gravemounds cannot describe his resentment and sorrow; whales yawning, turtles spurting, ox-ghosts, and serpent-spirits cannot describe his wildness and extravagance.

He is in the tradition of the *Li Sao*. Even though he does not come up to it in high seriousness he sometimes surpasses it in expression. The *Li Sao* is full of resentment and criticism of the rule and misrule of princes and ministers. Often it goads men into thought; though this quality is sometimes lacking in He's work. He has the ability to delve into the past. Heaving deep sighs, he would grieve over things which nobody had ever recounted either now or in days gone by. We may instance his *Song of the Brazen Immortal Bidding Farewell to Han*, or the songs in which he supplemented the Palace Poetry of Yü Chian-wu of Liang. In hunting out facts and collecting material he broke with tradition and went far into the distance along paths of the brush and ink. We cannot really claim to understand him.

He died when he was twenty-seven. We, his contemporaries, all believe that if he had added a little more high seriousness to his work and had not died when he did, he could have treated the *Li Sao* itself as his servant.

I, Du Mu of Jing-zhao, write this preface some fifteen years after He's death.

# Introduction

Li He, styled Chang-ji, a native of Fu-chang country, Henan, was born in A.D. 790, the year of the Horse, to a minor branch of the imperial house of Tang. There has been some dispute about the precise year of his birth, some scholars arguing that it took place in A.D. 791. But the weight of the evidence suggests that he was born in a Horse year, since he wrote no less than twenty-three poems in which the horse stands as a symbol for himself. Though his connection with the imperial family is well established, we have no precise details about his relationship to them, for his name is missing from the Genealogical Tables of the Imperial House as set out in the *New Tang History*. Several sources assert that he was a descendant of a certain Prince Zheng: but since there were no less than three princes of that name in the Tang royal house we cannot be sure with which one he was connected, though it is likely that the prince in question was the thirteenth son of the founder of the dynasty.

Though several of He's relatives held offices of great distinction in the mid-Tang period, his immediate family gained very little besides respect from his kinship with royalty, for neither wealth nor honors accrued to it from this connection. He's father, Li Jin-su, never rose high in the official hierarchy, attaining only the magistrateship of a county, a post of the fifth rank. His sole claim to fame lies in his friendship with the great poet Du Fu (712–70), to whom he was distantly related as a twenty-ninth younger cousin, and who once wrote a farewell poem to him. Jinsu died before He was eighteen, leaving the boy to make his own way in the world with nothing but his admittedly extraordinary talents to recommend him. The family's lack of status and consequent neglect by the official historians and local gazetteers involves the historian in considerable difficulties when it comes to finding out something about He himself, since very little information can be obtained from any reliable sources. What we do know is all too often fragmentary and tantalizingly vague. We are aware, for example, that He's mother, née Zheng, came in all probability from the Zhengs of Henan, who were one of the most distinguished families of the period. We know also that he had an elder sister who married into the Wang clan, as well as a younger brother, whom he mentions several times in his poems. But apart from these, he and his widowed mother, to whom he was devoted, would appear to have had no other immediate family.

Several commentators have maintained however that He had several elder brothers and a wife. The first assertion is based merely on a misunderstanding of the term *Xiung*, which is often used in the sense of "elder kinsman of the same generation" and does not necessarily mean "elder brother." If He had really had fourteen elder brothers, as some critics would have us believe, it is likely that some of them at least would have survived him. But in fact, his friend, Shen Zi-ming, writing only fifteen years after He's death, says explicitly that He had no brothers, sisters, or children left alive.

The question of whether he had a wife or not is more difficult to resolve. It seems highly unlikely that he would have been married, since during this period it was unusual for any scholar to take a wife until after he had gained his doctorate and been given an official post. Moreover marriage was an expensive business since the bridegroom had both to provide a dowry and pay for the wedding. He could hardly have afforded to do this since he was supporting both his widowed mother and his younger brother. Furthermore, the case for his having had a wife rests on nothing more substantial than his use of the term qing-qing ("my dear one") in one of his poems. This is very flimsy evidence indeed. We should note, also, that Li Shang-yin (812–58), one of his earliest biographers, makes no mention of any wife of He's being present at his death bed and has to rely on the testimony of his elder sister. The scholars—most of them Chinese—who naively insist that He must have been married, simply because he wrote numerous love poems, would seem to be merely over-anxious to assure us that he was a respectable citizen who did not squander his substance on singing girls. It seems to me that the Qing commentator, Yao Wen-xie, who asserted that He's death was brought about by "sexual dissipation," as with the protagonists of so many Chinese novels, was possibly nearer the truth of the matter, in the light of evidence provided by the poems, than those who would make our poet into a pillar of domestic sobriety. Perhaps the main obstacle encountered by the historian is the fact that He's collected works, which might have been a valuable source of information about the writer's life, consist only of poems, songs, and ballads—some 242 in all—while prose works, invariably a much richer digging-ground for the biographer, are totally lacking. (Two of the poems are held to be forgeries, thus reducing the number to 240.) Since Du Fu has some 1,500 poems extant, Bo Ju-yi 2,900, Li Bo 1,400, and Han Yu 400, this is a very small number indeed. The Tang writer, Zhang Gu, has a story which explains this. He alleges that Li Pan, a Vice-President of the Ministry of Rites, was a great admirer of He's work. After He's death Li Pan handed over all his songs and poems to an elder cousin of He's and asked him to correct them. This cousin, who had often been slighted by He, took revenge by throwing the lot down the privy. This dearth of biographical material means that He is all poet; the man himself has become almost as shadowy a figure as Qu Yuan, reputed author of the *Li Sao* from which He drew so much of his own inspiration. The faded picture can at best only be restored a little through a perusal of his poems; the lineaments of that vanished face conjured up again through such brief biographies and anecdotes as have come down to us. Consider for a moment He's official biography as recorded in the *New Tang History* (*Xin Tang-shu*), written some 250 years after his death:

> Li He, styled Chang-ji, was a descendant of Prince Zheng. When only seven years old he could write verse. When Han Yu and Huang-fu Shi first heard of this, they could not believe it, so they called at his house and asked him to write a poem. He picked up his writing brush and dashed one off as though he were merely copying it out, giving it the title: *The Tall Official Carriage Comes on a Visit*. Both men were flabbergasted. From this time on he was famous. Li He was frail and thin, with eyebrows that met together and long fingernails. He wrote at great speed. Every day at dawn he would leave the house riding a colt, followed by a servant-lad with an antique tapestry bag on his back. When inspiration struck him, he would write the verses down and drop them in the bag. He never wrote poems on a given topic, forcing his verses to conform to the theme, as others do. At nightfall he would go home and work these verses into a finished poem. If he was not blind drunk or in mourning, every day was spent like this. Once he had written a poem he did not greatly care what became of it. His mother used to have her maid rummage through the bag and when she saw that he had written so much she would exclaim angrily: "This boy of mine won't be content until he has vomited out his heart." Because his father's name was Jin-su, he was not allowed to sit for the Doctoral examination. Han Yu wrote his *Essay on Taboo Names* on his behalf; but he was never ac-

cepted as a candidate. His verse delights in the extraordinary. Everything he wrote was startlingly outstanding, breaking with accepted literary tradition. None of his contemporaries could follow him in this. He wrote dozens of ballads which the Yun-shao musicians set to music. He became a Harmoniser of Pitch-pipes, dying when he was twenty-seven *sui*.

His friends Quan Qu, Yang Jing-zhi and Wang Gong-yuan frequently made off with what he wrote. This fact, coupled with his premature death, has resulted in very few of his poems and songs coming down to us.

This account, which is largely based on the short biographies which the poets Du Mu (803–52) and Li Shang-yin wrote for He's collected poems, tells us very little indeed. The lack of a solidly based biography means that He has been romanticised more than most Chinese poets of his stature. The Li He of literary legend is the demon-talented (*guei-cai*) poet, tall and cadaverous, his hair white as snow round his haggard face, who on his deathbed is summoned to heaven by a spirit-messenger riding a red dragon. Such legends have their uses, for they direct us to an important truth about the poet; namely, that his verse and his personality alike were considered odd both by his contemporaries and by later critics. He is, in fact, close to the Western idea of the *poète maudit*—and this is not a stock type of literary man at all in China. Chinese poets were almost invariably members of the bureaucracy, cultivated officials who yet secreted poetry as naturally as oysters produce pearls. For the Chinese, the poetic vocation and the official career have never been at variance. To attain a post at all one had of necessity to be something of a poet, since the passing of the government examinations demanded considerable poetic proficiency of all aspirants to office. This was true of most periods of Chinese history, but never more so than during the Tang dynasty, when poetic talent alone could steer one through the examinations, though the poet Meng Jiao (751–814) once wrote sardonically: "Bad poetry makes you an official. Good poetry leaves you on a lonely hill." In short, Flaubert's dictum: "Les honneurs déshonorent, le titre dégrade, la fonction abrutit" ("Honours dishonour, titles degrade, office brutalises"), would have been quite incomprehensible in China to anyone but a Taoist hermit. The Chinese gentleman sought office, first and foremost: everything else—fame, riches, literary renown—was subordinate to this great aim, could hardly indeed be won without the fulfillment of it.

It was Li He's great misfortune never to have attained high office. His failure to do so was all the more humiliating since he was not only renowned for his literary talents but had for his patron one of the most eminent literary men of the time, the great Confucian scholar, Han Yu (768–824). To understand the importance of this, one must realize that to be sure of success in the examination system of the time, it was not enough to be merely talented. One had in addition to secure the support of a powerful patron who would act as a guarantor and later on further one's official career. To be sure, Han Yu was not as highly esteemed by his contemporaries as he was by later generations, but he was nevertheless a most eminent, if controversial, writer. One story of He's first encounter with Han Yu has already been mentioned in the brief biography given above. Another and rather more likely version, given by the Tang writer, Zhang Gu, has He visiting Yu, not at seven years of age but on the eve of his sitting for the examinations, when he was nineteen or so: "Li He went to visit Han Yu, taking with him his songs and poems. Han Yu at that time held the post of Doctoral Professor at the Luo-yang branch of the University of Sons of State. He had just returned home exhausted after seeing off some guests when his gatekeeper presented the scrolls to him. He loosened his girdle and began to read the first poem: *Ballad of the Grand Warden of Goose Gate*, which begins:

> Black clouds whelm on the city,
> Till it seems the city must yield.
> Our chain-mail glitters under the sun,
> Metal scales agape.

Having read these lines, he immediately fastened his girdle again and gave orders to invite He in.

Whatever the truth of such stories, there can be no doubt that He did succeed at an early age in attracting the attention of two influential patrons, Han Yu and Huang-fu Shi, the latter being one of the brighter stars of Han Yu's literary coterie. He seems to have been on especially intimate terms with Huang-fu Shi—a surprising fact, in view of the latter's notorious irascibility—and wrote at least four poems in his honour. However, since Shi had become involved in an examination scandal in 808, He found himself solely dependent on the good offices of Han Yu, whose support was especially valuable since practically every candidate who had enlisted his backing had succeeded brilliantly.

It must have been with high hopes, then, that He secured Yu's sponsorship for the Henan Provincial Examinations of 809, which he must have passed effortlessly. Candidates successful in this examination were eligible to sit for the Doctoral (*ju*) examination held in the capital under the auspices of the Ministry of Rites. There were several types of Doctoral examination in Tang times varying from law, calligraphy, and mathematics to knowledge of the classics (the *ming-jing* degree). However, the most difficult and the most highly regarded was the Literary examination, which rigorously tested both a candidate's literary abilities and his grounding in the classics. To succeed in this, He would have to answer questions on current affairs, write exegetical essays on passages from classical texts, and—most important of all—compose long poems of a type called *fu* ("rhyme-prose") as well as *shi* ("lyric verse"). Once he had gained his doctorate, he was entitled to sit for the Selection (*xuan*) examination, which determined whether or not he could be appointed to office. The Selection examination was very like the country-house interviews which were once so much a feature of British Civil Service examinations. The candidate was judged by his bearing, ability to express himself, calligraphy, and wisdom in making judgements. Only when he had satisfied the examiners in all these qualities was he judged to be both a scholar and a gentleman (*jun-zi*) and therefore fit to govern.

It is hardly surprising to learn that the road to office was long and early, with many falling by the wayside. Han Yu once pointed out that of every 3,000 distinguished candidates who emerged from the great crowd of aspirants, fewer than 200 finally attained the Selection examination. This means that fourteen out of every fifteen candidates failed even to reach the last hurdle. Add to this the fact that only a modest percentage of the final 200 could be allotted a post, and the heart-breaking nature of the Tang examination system becomes only too apparent. As Han Yu remarked, since a candidate might well spend twenty years or more in reaching the Selection examination, half of those who succeeded were already grey-haired old men.

With the stakes so high and the course so difficult it is not too surprising to find that every sort of unscrupulous practice was adopted to advance oneself and eliminate one's rivals. This was a free-for-all, with no holds barred, as He himself was soon to discover to his cost. To a casual observer, however, his success must have seemed a foregone conclusion. Dazzlingly talented, scion of a branch of the royal house, and supported by a prominent literary man, he must have already been marked down as the most outstanding candidate of his year. Yet it was almost certainly this very fame which was to prove his undoing, making him too conspicuous a target to avoid the shafts levelled at him. Shortly after arriving in the capital, Chang-an, he was stunned to hear that he was not even to be allowed to sit for the *jin-shi* examination at which he should have carried all before him. The excuse put forward was that since his deceased father's name had been Jin-su, the word *jin* in the term *jin-shi* violated a family taboo.

To understand what occurred, some explanation is necessary. The Chinese have always been scrupulously careful to avoid using the personal names of certain people—one's father or the emperor, for example—either in speech or in writing. When such a word was met it had to be avoided, either by pronouncing it *mou* (so-and-so) or by substituting another character in its place. Now the Chinese spoken during Tang times, though differing markedly from the Mandarin (*putonghua*) of today, similarly abounded in homophones. Hence official regulations concerning these taboos had shown common sense in asserting that only the word itself had to be avoided, while its homophones could be pronounced or written with impunity. Since the *Jin* of He's father's name is quite a different word from the *jin* ("to advance") of the term *jin-shi*, though closely related to it etymologically, it might have been supposed that no taboo was therefore violated. Unfortunately, official regulations have never owned the force in China that they have enjoyed in Europe. What mattered was customary law, not bureaucratic rulings: and customary law insisted that homophones be considered taboo.

Tradition has it that it was Bo Ju-yi's friend, the poet Yuan Zhen (779–831), who brought this matter to the notice of the authorities because He had once insulted him. If this is true, the situation would have been ironic, since Bo himself had once been attacked on the ground that he had infringed a taboo by writing poems about a well and plum blossom, though it was known his mother had died by falling into a well while admiring some blossom. However, Han Yu's account of the affair is less specific, designating the informer as simply "one who was contending with He for fame"—a description which leads one to suspect one of He's fellow-candidates and rivals. Since Yuan passed his Selection examination in 803, when He was only thirteen or so, the traditional story is perhaps inaccurate.

However, one writer has suggested that the informer was in fact Yuan, who at that time held the post of Censor and had made a good many enemies, among them Fang Shi, governor of Luoyang, the man responsible for authorizing He's candidature. So Yuan is held to have acted in this way not so much to obtain revenge on Li He as to discomfort Fang Shi, since the authorizer of an unworthy candidate was himself liable for severe penalties.

Political struggle for control of the middle and upper echelons of the bureaucracy was rife during this period. If entry into the Tang bureaucracy was difficult, then promotion within its ranks was no less so. To make the jump from the career grade of the sixth rank to the senior positions of the fifth rank and above was arduous enough. But to cross the gap from the fourth rank to the third rank, where most effective power resided, was given only to a gifted and ruthless few. The financial and social privileges that went with positions of the fifth rank and above, including the right to have one son enter officialdom without passing the usual examinations, were considerable. Little wonder then that the struggle for power was so ferocious. In this internecine strife the examination candidates were just so many pawns on the political chessboard. In 821, a mere four years after Li He's death, a major scandal blew up when it was discovered that the examiners had been guilty of flagrant partiality and favouritism towards the close relatives of powerful courtiers. The fact is that the examination system during Tang was still in its infancy and as such open to abuse in a way that would have been impossible under later dynasties, when the most stringent precautions were taken to hide the identity of the candidates from the examiners. We may conclude, therefore, that Li He was probably sacrificed either because he had incurred the animosity of an examiner or, more likely, because some powerful bureaucrat wished to strike a blow at a rival who happened to be He's patron.

It seems probable that some faction (*dang*) hostile to Han Yu was involved in this questionable maneuver, since Yu, as He's guarantor, stood to lose a great deal by his protégé's disgrace. This would explain why Yu rushed in to intercede for He with his famous essay on taboo-names, as Yu himself points out:

> He's candidature for the Doctorate degree has become a *cause célèbre*. Somebody who was contending with He for fame slandered him, saying: "He's father's name was Jin-su. It would be bad form for He to sit for the Literary examination. Those who sponsored him are in the wrong!"... Hence Huang-fu Shi said to me: "If you do not explain matters, both you and He will find yourselves in trouble."

Yu then goes on to ridicule the accusations made against He by pointing out that to apply the homophone taboo in this way would result in ridiculous excesses. If, for example, the father bore the personal name Ren (love) then the son would be unable to call himself a man (*ren*)! Yu's essay was successful insofar as it ensured that neither he nor He was involved in any further trouble. But even Yu's persuasive prose could not prevail upon the authorities to let He sit for the examination. The imbecilic misuse of the taboo regulation had barred him from this forever.

From then on until his untimely death seven years later, a death which was very likely hastened by the dashing of all his hopes for a brilliant official career, He was a man ravaged by sickness and disappointment. He seems to have suffered a severe illness—perhaps a nervous breakdown—consequent upon his failure to gain his degree.

> I came back home, all skin and bones,
> A fleshless face,
> A murrain lighted on my head,
> My hair fell out.
>
> Mournfully chanting, I study the sighs of Chu,
> My sick bones ache in lonely poverty.
> Autumnal in aspect with hair turning white,
> A tree whose leaves lament in wind and rain.

From this time on, the melancholy and despair which is the hallmark of so much Tang poetry stamped itself ever more deeply on his verse.

In Chang-an city lives a lad of twenty
Whose heart's already so much rotten wood…
He knows by now the way is blocked to him,
No need to wait until his hair turns white.

Sparse cassia blossom under snow,
A crying crow, struck by a bolt came home…
The woman he loved asked him no questions—
Her face in the mirror bore two streams of tears.

Your elder brother is now turned twenty.
The mirror tells him how his beard is growing.
Three years ago he left our home—to come to this!
Begging rice at princes' gates,
An utter failure.

Who can he be, this sad and lonely man,
Who's come to suffer autumn in Chang-an?
Young as I am, brooding on stifled sorrows,
Weeping in dreams until my hair turns white.

Though I have reached my twentieth year
I've missed my goal,
My whole heart sad and withered
As a dying orchid.

The king of Qin is nowhere to be seen,
So dawn and dusk fever burns in me…
Because I cannot roam round with the moon,
My hair's grown white before I end my song.

The melancholy of the Southern Mountains,
Ghostly rain drizzling on desolate grass!

In one respect, however, He was more fortunate than the countless other young men of his time who were unsuccessful in the examinations. As the son of an official of the fifth degree he was entitled to avail himself of the so-called *yin* privilege. This meant he was allowed to sit for the Selection examination without having first to pass the Doctoral examination. Of course, his lack of a Doctorate meant that he could never hope for promotion or even for a job worthy of his talents. But beggars cannot be choosers. He was, after all, a man with a widowed mother and a younger brother to support, as he reminds us in his verse:

My whole family welcomes me with joy,
Counting on me to fill their empty bellies.
Born into this world, I have to feed myself,
So out of my gate I go, with burdened back.

In the tenth month of 810, he set out from Luo-yang to take the Selection examination in the capital:

I'm going to play around with words
For the Office of Heaven,
For who would pity a royal scion
Left unemployed?

For a man of his abilities and background such an examination could have presented few problems. In the following year he was back in Chang-an again, this time as Supervisor of Ceremonies in the Court of Imperial Sacrifices. In spite of its high-sounding title, this was a low-ranking post whose duties were of the dullest. The two Supervisors were officials of the ninth degree, third class, a rank well down in the official hierarchy. Li He was in fact little more than a glorified usher, who had to see that the ceremonial vessels were set out correctly in the imperial ancestral temple, attend to seating arrangements at court audiences, and give the requisite signals which indicated when to bow, kneel, kowtow, or rise during ceremonies. Such a post called for neither literary talent nor administrative ability. To place a man of his genius in this position was like using a racehorse to draw a plough, as he never wearied of reminding his friends.

> This steed is no ordinary horse
> But the very spirit of the Fang star.
> Stand in front, rap on its slender bones,
> They'll ring out like bronze.

> The Office of Rites has forced me from my true nature,
> I look haggard and worn, like a straw dog cast aside.
> In wind and snow I serve at the Altar of Fasting,
> My black belt threaded through a brazen seal.
> The work I do is fit only for slaves and bondmaids
> Who want no more than to wield dustpan and brush.

> The warm sun leaves me lonely and depressed,
> Blossoms only sadden this Bei-guo Sao.

The reference in the last line to Bei-guo Sao, who, though a man of genius, supported his widowed mother by weaving nets and making sandals, sums up succinctly enough what He thought of his own position. We do not know for certain whether he ever succeeded in rising from this post. Both the Tang histories state that he was given the rank of Harmonizer of Pitch-pipes, a post of the eighth rank and thus one step above his position as Supervisor of Ceremonies. In view of his high reputation as a writer of songs, I am inclined to believe that he was in fact eventually promoted to this position, though precisely when must remain uncertain. What is certain is that he was highly dissatisfied with whatever post he held in the Court of Imperial Sacrifices and expressed his longing to be away from it all, time and time again in his verse, as for example in *After Days of Rain in the Chong-yi District*.

> Who can he be, this sad and lonely man,
> Who's come to suffer autumn in Chang-an?
> Young as I am, brooding on stifled sorrows
> Weeping in dreams until my hair turns white.
> I feed my skinny nag on mouldy hay,
> As gusts of rain splash in the chilly gutters.
> The Southern Palace is darkened by ancient blinds,
> Its sundials blank beneath a watery sun.
> My mountain home's a thousand leagues away,
> East of here, at the very foot of the clouds.
> Sleeping in sorrow, my sword-case as my pillow,
> In bed at an inn I dream of a marquisate.

The Chong-yi district referred to in the title was a busy quarter of Chang-an, close to the Ministry of Civil Office. The cost of living in the capital was very high and He's salary regrettably low. Furthermore, though his elder sister was married and hence off his hands, he still had to support his mother and young brother back in Chang-gu, which must have made considerable inroads on his income. Nevertheless, pleading poverty is a convention of Chinese verse and I find it difficult to believe that he was so destitute he could not afford a servant ("Back from the office, I must shut the gates myself"), still less find himself unable even to buy wine, as he alleges on at least one occasion. What probably did gall him, as it has vexed many another young bachelor in his position, was to live among all the delights provided by a great city without being able to afford to enjoy them. For Chang-an was a metropolis, populous even by modern standards, with close to a million inhabitants. It was, in fact, the largest city in the world at that time, rivalled in size and splendour only by Haroun Al-Rashid's Baghdad, which was then approaching its apogee. In this sophisticated and highly cosmopolitan city a young official on a meagre salary might very well feel that life was passing him by for sheer lack of money, especially if he had a taste for wine and women, as He undoubtedly did.

We have already mentioned that a Qing critic alleged that Li He died of sexual exhaustion, basing his statement partly on the numerous allusions to courtesans which abound throughout his verse. One might perhaps conceivably be persuaded to agree to the assertion that He was married: but not even the most casual reader of his poems could reasonably claim that he was monogamous. One of his longest poems, "She Steals My Heart," is an account of his unhappy affair with a singing-girl who was clearly a good deal too expensive for him to maintain a permanent liaison with her. For the courtesans of Chang-an, many of them exotic blond, blue-eyed foreigners, made heavy demands on both the purse and the constitution, as we know from the short stories (quan-qi) of the period—demands which He was ill-equipped to withstand, both financially and physically. Furthermore, his reputation as the most brilliant songwriter in the empire put him in great demand, exposing him to temptations he might otherwise have avoided. In the preface to his *Outing Among Blossoms*, he states that he went off on a picnic with various princes and singing-girls, for whom he wrote a song.

> This morning, drunk outside the city walls,
> Rubbing our mirrors we brush on our rich brows.
> In drizzling mist we fret in clumsy carriages.
> Red oil-cloth covers up our painted clothes.
> These dancing-skirts, though perfumed, are not warm,
> Our faces flush but slowly from the wine.

Such outings, where his genius admitted him briefly to the company of rich young playboys and their lovely companions, must have tantalized him with a taste of pleasures just beyond his reach. For He, like Keats whom he so much resembles, was a great sensualist delighting in tastes, sounds, and colours. Fine food and wine, music, rich silks and brocades, jewels, and beautiful women figure prominently in his verse, so much so that at times we feel we are closer to the languid, erotic world of the later *ci* poets than to the lyric verse of mid-Tang. The pity of it was that—again like Keats—he could not afford the delights he savoured most. So he swings abruptly from contemplation of these joys to sharp condemnation of them; from eulogies of the flesh to graveyard poetry; from *vers de société* to social satire; from the ballad to something close to the *ci*. This dichotomy is vividly illustrated by his imagery which alternates between vivid colour—with special prominence given to gold, red, blue, green, and yellow—and stark black and white. All this, I believe, reflects the tensions engendered in him by living in Chang-an, that fascinating, decadent city whose evanescent pleasures and fugitive splendours mocked him like life itself.

In 814 he gave up his post—whether voluntarily or not we do not know—and returned to his estate in Chang-gu (modern Yi-yang), a place to which he was deeply attached. Chang-gu has never found its way into the gazetteers; but all commentators agree that it was located in Fu-chang county, some fifty miles west of Luo-yang. Its proximity to the Eastern capital, still a major centre of intellectual life, explains how he managed to acquire his early education. The district was mountainous, thickly wooded, and fertile. He's family estate, though run-down and dilapidated, could not have been quite as poor as his sense of literary convention would have us believe, nor limited to "a weed-grown patch of stony ground." In his long poem, *Chang-gu*, he celebrates the tranquil beauty of the countryside and the honest simplicity of its people in some of his most delicately-wrought verse:

Paddy fields at Chang-gu, in the fifth month,
A shimmer of green covers the level water.
Distant hills rise towering, crag on crag.
Precarious greenery, fearful of falling.
Dazzling and pure, no thoughts of autumn yet,
A cool wind from afar ruffles this beauty.
The bamboos' fragrance fills this lonely place,
Each powdered node is streaked with emerald.
The long-haired grass lets fall its mournful tresses,
A bright dew weeps, shedding its secret tears.
Tall trees from a bright and winding tunnel,
A scented track where fading reds sway drunkenly.

Swarms of insects etch the ancient willows,
Cicadas cry from high sequestered spots.
Long sashes of yellow arrowroot trail the ground,
Purple rushes criss-cross narrow shores.
Stones coined with moss lie strewn about in heaps,
Plump leaves are growing in glossy clusters.
Level and white are the wave-washed sands,
Where horses stand, printing dark characters.
At evening, fishes dart around joyfully,
A lone, lean crane stands stock-still in the dusk.
Down in their damp, mole-crickets chirp away.
A muted spring wells up with startled splash…

Reed-shoots are peering from the cinnabar pond.
Ripples and eddies sport with sky's reflection,
The hands of ancient junipers grasp the clouds.
The mournful moon is curtained with red roses,
Thorns of fragrant creeper catch the clouds.
The bearded wheat lies level for hundreds of leagues,
On the untilled acres stand a thousand shops.
This man from Cheng-ji, restless and fretful,
Would like to emulate Master Wine-sack's ways.

The last couplet in this long nostalgic poem, which he wrote while in Chang-an, means simply that he would like nothing better than to emulate Fan Li, the great statesman who retired into obscurity after saving the state of Yueh from its enemies. He, however, had no hope of ever rising to any office even remotely approaching Fan Li's. Furthermore, however alluring the idea of a life in the country may have seemed from the capital, he soon found that the prospect of retirement for life as an invalid at the age of twenty-three was not to be seriously contemplated, in spite of the idyllic days he would seem to have spent in his rural retreat:

> Lying on river sand softly sleeping
> Two ducks in the sun.
> l punt my little skiff slowly past
> The winding shores.
> Magnolias steeped in wine
> Covered with pepper-leaves.
> Friends help the sick man to his feet
> To plant water-chestnut.

Living among the crumbling splendours of this ruined, noble estate must have been unbearable for him, as was the knowledge that the household depended largely on his efforts to maintain them. So after some months of sickness and enforced idleness in Chang-gu, he was once again in search of an official post. For some time past he had been seriously contemplating abandoning a civil career for a military one, as is apparent from several of the verses in his *Thirteen Poems from My Southern Garden*:

> Better to go and buy a sword
> From Ruo-ye river,
> Come back at dawn next day to serve
> The Monkey Duke.

> Why shouldn't a young man wear a Wu sword?
> He could win back fifty provinces in pass and mountain.

Over twenty years of incessant study had brought him nothing except hardship and disappointment. What use was a poet in such a war-torn age?

Seeking a style, culling my phrases,
Grown old carving grubs!
At dawn the moon hangs in my blinds,
A bow of jade.
Can't you see what is going on, year after year,
By the sea of Liao-dong?
Whatever can a writer do
But weep in the autumn wind?

These lines reveal his dilemma only too clearly. As a disciple of Han Yu's he shared his master's firm conviction that literature ought to play an important social role, that the poet was the guardian of the conscience of society. Yet all his endeavours to aid his country with his poetic talents had come to nothing. In fact, his outspoken, satirical poems attacking the abuses of the time had almost certainly blocked his chances of promotion if not actually removed him from office. What then was left to him except to seek service with some military governor or other in an outlying province? He could then both serve his country and at the same time further his own ambitions. Once he had established his reputation in such a post, he could return to work for the central government again, just as Han Yu himself had done in his youth. Far better to take office under the roughest of military commands in some distant border region than to starve in aristocratic poverty and idleness in Chang-gu:

Not yet thirty but still turned twenty,
Hungry in bright sunshine, living on leaves.
Old man on the bridge! Feel sorry for *me*
And give me a book on the art of war!

Fortunately for He, his friend Zhang Che, pupil and relative
of Han Yu, was at that time in the service of Xi Shi-mei, a general
still loyal to the emperor and commanding an army in Lu-zhou
(Shanxi). Since the rebellion of An Lu-shan (A.D. 755) the central
government had been gradually losing power to the provincial
military governors. The Emperor Xian-zong (*regnet* 805–20) had
attempted to arrest the decline of the dynasty by bringing these
military satraps under the rule of the Chang-an regime. This in-
volved the launching of a number of costly punitive expeditions
against those governors who flatly refused to come to heel when
called. The most notable of these was Wang Cheng-zong, who
could not be compelled to return to allegiance until 818, in spite
of the numerous campaigns directed against him. Xi Shi-mei's
army, along with those of five other commanders, was at that time
(814) all set to wage a protracted struggle against Wang's forces in
Hebei. Hence He must have felt that by putting himself at the
service of this general he was directly contributing to the restora-
tion of dynastic greatness. In the autumn of 814 He set out from
Chang-gu, heading northeast as he made for Lu-zhou. Several of
the poems he wrote while on this journey have been preserved,
among them the magnificent *Song of an Arrowhead from Chang-
ping,* a poem which proves that poverty, sickness, and misfortune
had, if anything, enhanced his poetic powers:

Flakes of lacquer, dust of bones,
Red cinnabar,
The ancient blood once spurted forth
And bore bronze flowers.
White feathers and its metal stems
Have rotted in the rain,
Only the three spines still remain,
Broken teeth of a wolf.
I searched this plain of battle
With a pair of nags,
In stony fields east of the post-station,
On a weed-grown hill.
An endless wind, the day short,
Desolate stars,
Black banners of damp clouds,
Hung in void night.
Souls to the left, spirits to the right,
Gaunt with hunger, wailing,
I poured curds from my tilted flask,
Offered roast mutton.
Insects silent, the wild geese sick,
Reed shoots reddening.
A whirlwind came to see me off,
Blowing the ghost fires...

This poem with its insistent images of death and war, ghosts and sickness, gives us a disquieting glimpse of He's state of mind as he pushed north through that bitter autumn towards the garrison town that was to be his home for the next three years.

We know nothing of his life in Lu-zhou, but can only guess at what it must have been like from the few poems written during this period that have come down to us. From the length of time he was there, it is clear that he must have found a post on Xi Shi-mei's staff. Xi's forces were very active in the campaign against Wang Cheng-zong, so it seems likely that He saw something of the actual fighting. Life in a military border-town, in the thick of a campaign, must have made both the hectic pleasures of Chang-an and the quiet happiness of Chang-gu seem as remote as a fading dream. Two of his poems written at this time draw a vivid picture of life in a northern frontier post:

> Barbarian horns have summoned the north wind,
> Thistle Gate is whiter than a stream!
> The road to Green Sea vanishes into the sky,
> Along the Wall, a thousand moonlit miles.
> While dew falls drizzling on our flags,
> Cold metal clangs the watches of the night,
> Barbarian armour meshes serpent scales,
> Horses whinny where Green Grave gleams white…

Even more powerful than these evocative verses is the poem *Under the Walls of Ping City*:

> Hungry and cold, under Ping City's walls,
> Night after night we guard the shining moon.
> Our farewell swords have lost their sheen,
> The Gobi wind cuts through our temple-hair.
>
> Endless desert merges with white void,
> But see—far off—the red of Chinese banners,
> In their black tents they're blowing short flutes,
> Mist and haze soaking their painted dragons.

At twilight, up there on the city walls,
We stare into the shadows of those walls,
The wind is blowing, stirring dead tumbleweed,
Our starving horses whinny within the walls.

"Just ask the builders of these walls
How many thousand leagues from the Pass we are?
Rather than go home as bundled corpses
We'll turn our lances on ourselves and die."

Verse like this, sober, taut and bare, harking back to the ballad tradition and the concept of poetry as a vehicle for social criticism, is a long way removed from the ornate verse He had composed in Chang-an. Yet in what may well be his last poem, written as he lay sick in Chang Che's house in Lu-zhou, he evokes once again the strangeness which so distinguished his earlier verse, marries it to the simplicity of his Lu-zhou poems, and achieves a deeply moving masterpiece which must rank among his finest creations.

Only when autumn comes to Zhao-guan,
Will you know how cold it is up here in Zhao.
I tied this letter to a short-feathered summons,
Cut out a long screed for a recital of woes.
Through the clear dawn I slumbered in my sickness,
While the sparse plane-trees cast fresh emeralds down.
The city crows cried from white battlements,
Military bugles saddened the mist in the reeds.
With turban askew, I lifted the silken curtains,
In dried-up pools the broken lotus lay.
On the wooden window, traces of silver pictures,
On the stone steps, water had left its coins.

The traveller's wine caught at my ailing lungs,
While songs of parting rose from languid strings.
I sealed this poem with a double string of tears,
And culled a single orchid wet with dew.
The sedge is growing old, the cricket weeping.
While broken gargoyles peer from withered pines.
Waking, I sit astride a horse from Yan,
Dreaming, I voyage on a boat through Chu.
Pepper and cinnamon poured above long mats!
Perch and bream sliced up on tortoise-shell!
Surely you can't forget the homeward road,
To spend your youth on river-girdled isles?

Verse of this quality, written when he was only twenty-five
or so, makes one realize just how great a loss literature sustained
by his untimely death. For at this juncture he was very near the
end. We do not know precisely from what disease he was suffer-
ing, though repeated references to his emaciated condition in his
verse, combined with other symptoms—his prematurely white
hair, his fever, and his weakness—would seem to indicate pulmo-
nary tuberculosis. An ancient source (*Yun xian za ji*) carries the
story of a visitor who saw our poet "spit on the floor three times"
while composing three poems, which is perhaps another indication
that he was suffering from consumption. In any case, the disease
that had haunted him for years was now pressing the attack home
for the last time. He gave up his post in Lu-zhou and returned to
Chang-gu, where he died sometime during the year 816, at the age
of 26 or so. He left behind him a corpus of verse which, strangely
enough, has not enjoyed widespread popularity in China since the
Song dynasty. The standard anthology of Tang verse, *Tang shi san-
bai shou* (*Three Hundred Tang Poems*), which was compiled in Qing

times and is familiar to every Chinese schoolboy, does not include a single poem of his. Until quite recently he was comparatively little read, though modern critics, Chinese, Japanese, and European, are paying him increasing attention. So the last twenty years or so have witnessed the appearance of several important new editions of his poems in Chinese, as well as three Japanese translations. In addition, there have been numerous Japanese studies of He's life and poetry as well as no less than five doctoral theses on him submitted to American or Australian universities.

The reason for the comparative neglect of He evinced by traditional Chinese scholarship—a couple of dozen studies in twelve hundred years—is not difficult to ascertain. If Chinese culture—to borrow Nietzsche's terminology—is essentially Apollonian, He's verse is essentially Dionysian. The only other poet writing in Chinese whose verse seems at all akin to He's is, significantly enough, the Manchu poet Singde (1655–1685), who had been shaped by a shamanistic culture. There is a wild, exotic air about He's poetry which the Chinese mind finds distasteful, an air which has only sporadically made its appearance in Chinese literature since the *Chu Ci*, those *Songs of the South* from which He so clearly drew his inspiration. There is an air of romantic extravagance about his lines which is quite unmistakable.

> Straddling a tiger, the Prince of Qin
> Roams the Eight Poles.
> His glittering sword lights up the sky,
> Heaven turns sapphire.
> Ix and He whip up the sun
> With the sound of glass....

Jade from Mount Kun is shattered,
Phoenixes shriek.
Lotuses are weeping dew,
Fragrant orchids smile....

The West's White King was struck with fear
When it was drawn,
His demon Mother wailing loudly
In the autumn wilds.

Lines like these carry the imprint of He's unique style, bearing a strangeness of tone which led an eleventh-century critic to dub him "the demon-poet." "Weird," "astonishing," and "demonic" are all adjectives frequently applied to his verse. Zhou Chi-zhi remarked: "Li Chang-ji's language is astonishing, verging on the weird," while Yen Yu, a Song dynasty critic, asserted that He "used the language of a demonic immortal." One does not have to search very far before coming across scores of lines which bear out this remark.

The Blue Lion kowtows and calls
To the Palace Spirits.
With a fearful howl the Dog of Jade
Opens Heaven's gates....

On an autumn grave a ghost sits chanting
That poem of Bao's.
A thousand years in earth makes emerald jade
That rancorous blood.

Blue racoons are weeping blood
As shivering foxes die....
Owls that have lived a hundred years,
Turned forest demons,
Laugh wildly as an emerald fire
Leaps from their nests.

A white fox barking at the moon,
The mountain wind....

No wonder that one ancient critic remarked that "His ideas are original and his language extravagantly beautiful."

The quality of imagination displayed in the stanzas just quoted is rare in any poetic tradition, let alone in Chinese verse where what one might call the "shamanistic style" has only sporadically appeared.

...In the west are the Moving Sands stretching
endlessly on and on,
And beasts with heads like swine, slanting
eyes and shaggy hair,
Long claws and serrated teeth and
wild, mad laughter....

...I lashed the Wind God and made him
ride before me
Imprisoned the Dark Spirit in the Pit of Night

Verses like these last—selected almost at random from David Hawkes's fine translation of the *Chu Ci*—had their origin in a culture where shamans were employed to call down spirits by means of music, dancing, and incantations.

Female shamans—or "witches," as we might call them today —were widely employed during Tang, not only by the gentry but by the royal house. Exorcism was generally carried out by shamans, who were considered to have greater powers in these rites than Taoist priests, who for their part often assumed the role of shamans. He has several poems describing shamanistic ceremonies, written with an immediacy which indicates his personal experience with such ritual.

> The witch pours out a libation of wine
> And clouds cover the sky,
> In a jade brazier charcoal burns—
> The incense booms.
> Gods of the sea and mountain demons
> Flock to her seat....

Exorcism often involved the eradication of zoomorphic demons, dangerous spirits masquerading as animals which could only be destroyed by magical practices:

> Blue racoons are weeping blood
> As shivering foxes die.

The shaman's role, however, was not limited to exorcism, rain-making, or other goetic practices. As in other shamanistic cultures, the shaman's power lay in the ability to call down a number of supernatural entities, some of them demonic:

> She calls down stars and summons demons
> To savour meat and drink,
> When mountain-goblins come to eat
> Men are breathless and hushed.

Sometimes the shaman could summon a higher entity who would take possession of her and speak through her mouth before returning:

> The Spirit's anger, the Spirit's delight
> Shows in her face
> Ten thousand riders escort her back
> To the emerald hills.

Li He's verse abounds with references to the *Chu Ci*, which he may well have understood as shamanistic in inspiration, even though traditionally Chinese poets have interpreted its romantic and erotic verses as political allegories rather than as the longing of the shaman for the embrace of the god. The wild, ecstatic cries of the shaman are echoed in He's verse time and time again, leading one to believe that he may well have been a shaman by temperament. Certain critics, ever eager to invest our poet with a temperament they would find congenial, have seen him as a sceptical rationalist, believing passionately in social reform but far too Confucian to lend a credulous ear to the supernatural. This represents a flagrant, modernistic misreading of He's character. Everything about him, from his lifelong preoccupation with gods, ghosts, and demons to his final deathbed vision indicated that he possessed a highly psychic nature, perfectly at home in the world of shamanistic and Taoist ritual in which he appears actively to have participated.

Unusual as He's work undoubtedly is, he is nevertheless very much of his time. He does not stand apart from it in the way, say, Blake and Smart stand apart from the eighteenth century. In a sense, his verse simply carries to an extraordinary degree qualities of intensity, floridity and deep-grained pessimism already highly characteristic of Tang verse. Only in his development of *Chu Ci* tradition, especially that of the *Nine Songs* and *The Summons of the Soul*, can he really be called unique. Take for example the prevailing pessimistic tone of his verse. From the Han dynasty onwards Chinese poetry is on the whole deeply melancholic in tone. Tang poetry was no exception to this, and even poets like Du Fu and Li Bo (699–762) write verse steeped in sadness. It was not until the Song dynasty (960–1279) that Chinese poets rid themselves of the burden of sorrow, as the great Japanese critic Yoshikawa Kōjirō has pointed out. In this respect He is typical of his age, for much of his verse is so imbued with melancholy that the pages seem to darken as one reads. As Ryosuke Kamio avers, He was "essentially, a poet of night" whose true poetic genius blossomed to the full only in the darkness.

Any thorough study of He's verse would attempt to explain this fully. In doing so, it would have to account for the whole shift in outlook which took place in the poetry of the ninth century, the movement away from the outgoing, assertive verse of Du Fu to the esoteric, withdrawn poetry of Li Shang-yin. This introduction is no place to attempt such a feat. But I should hazard a guess that the basic factors involved were the decline of the empire after the rebellion of An Lu-shan, the weakening of the central government, the increasing dominance of the eunuchs, and the dissociation of literary men from political power. All of these—and especially the last—resulted in what Toynbee would call "a failure of nerve on the part of the creative minority." This would account for the pervading sense of melancholia, nostalgia, and regret that so characterizes most of the poetry of the Yuan-he period (806–21). Furthermore, this was an age when none of the traditional remedies seemed to make sense any more. Taoism had degenerated into superstition; Buddhism was on the verge of collapse—the persecution of 845 finally struck it a mortal blow; and even the most ardent Confucian reformers found that the time was not yet ripe for revival of the Master's teachings.

What is peculiar, then, about He's verse is not his melancholy but the extent of it; not the sentiment itself but the symbols he used to express it. Wada Toshio has analysed He's verse statistically and found that expressions hinting at death occur 198 times, expressions of sadness 131 times and expressions of anxiety and fear 262 times—a total of 665 in all. On an average there are three expressions concerned with death or unhappiness in every poem. Wada's analysis simply lends statistical support to what the reader had already felt in his senses; namely that He's verse is extraordinarily melancholy even by Tang standards. Furthermore, the images he persistently draws on, those of ghosts, demons, spirits, bones, blood, tombs, corpses, will-o'-the-wisps, and so on, are normally studiously avoided by Chinese poets, as they are avoided by ordinary Chinese, on the grounds that they are unlucky. Admittedly, during Tang the weird tale or ghost story (quan-qi) enjoyed a great vogue; but these stories are certainly not obsessed with death and decay as is He's verse.

He's "death-wish," as we should style it today, has been noted by the contemporary writer, Hong Wei-fa, who remarked that He was afraid of death, yet longed for it, for since he was sick of the world of men, he yearned for heaven. He's longing for death is certainly understandable. For a start, he stemmed from that most pessimistic of classes, impoverished aristocracy—people for whom the past recedes ever further in a golden haze. Secondly, he was unlucky in not being allowed to take an examination which would almost certainly have led to fame and fortune—and for a Chinese to think himself unlucky is to have lost all hope. Finally, he was a man ravaged by disease, constantly in failing health and—to cap all this—poor, at least in comparison with his friends. Small wonder then that he found life a burden which he would gladly shake off. He would fain have fled the world—but to what?

Classical Confucianism admits of no life beyond the grave, beyond the squeaking and gibbering of ghosts. In this it is as comfortless as the religion of the ancient Greeks. Hong Wei-fa's assertion that He "longed for heaven" must therefore refer to his belief in either Buddhism, or Taoism, or both. Ostensibly He was no Taoist, at least in the conventional sense, for many of his satirical poems are attacks upon Emperor Xian-zong, who spent a great deal of time and money which could have been better employed in the business of government in seeking for elixirs of eternal life. On the other hand, there can be no denying that He was fascinated with the concept of Heaven, which recurs constantly in his poems as a place of exquisite beauty, where immortals dwell.

> Là, tout n'est qu'ordre et beauté,
> Luxe, calme et volupté.

It seems to me highly probable that at one level of belief He was convinced of the reality of the Taoist heaven. This would help to explain the stories about his deathbed:

> When Chang-ji was at death's door, suddenly, in broad daylight, he saw a man in purple raiment driving a red dragon and

carrying a tablet with characters on it like ancient seal script
or "peal of thunder" inscriptions....who said: "I am here to
summon Chang-ji"...He could not read the inscription. He at
once got out of his bed and kowtowed saying:

"Mama is old and ill. I don't want to leave her." The man in
purple raiment said with a smile: "The Emperor (of Heaven)
has just built the White Jade Tower and summons you to
come at once and write a description of it. Life up in Heaven is
delightful; there is no hardship there." Chang-ji only wept the
more. All those attending him witnessed this. In a little while
He drew his last breath. From the window where he was wont
to sit, a mist rose into the air and the sounds of flutes and car-
riages were heard.

Li Shang-yin goes on to state that this story was narrated to him by
Mrs. Wang, He's sister, who was present at his death, adding that
her veracity was undoubted.

Now if, in fact, He really believed in Heaven, then it is highly
likely that during his final moments he actually saw and described
the events that his sister spoke of. What we have here, indeed, is
a graphic account of He's deathbed vision—a consoling truth as
touching and as vividly colourful as many of his poems. But how
can this Taoist belief be reconciled with He's avowed Buddhism,
for he states quite plainly in his poem *Presented to Chen Shang* that
the *Laṅkāvatāra-sūtra* is his constant companion, along with the
*Chu Ci*? The importance of this statement, which must be taken in
conjunction with another verse in which he refers to "listening to a
sutra" can hardly be overestimated. The *Laṅkāvatāra-sūtra*, a work
of notorious difficulty and profundity which had been translated
into Chinese three times by the eighth century A.D., was the prin-
cipal sutra favoured by the Chan (*Zen*) school during the Tang. He
probably read Śikshānanda's translation of 700–04, which had been

sponsored by Empress Wu and revised by the monk Mi-to-shan and the great master Fa-zang.

There were no less than ten major schools of Buddhism flourishing in China during Tang, six of which were Mahayana (Great Vehicle) schools. Of these the most important were the Lotus, or Tian-tai, whose basic scripture was the *Saddharmapundiarīka-sūtra* (*Sutra of the Lotus of the Wonderful Law*); the Flower Garland or Hua-yan school, whose basic scripture was the magnificent *Avataṁsaka-sūtra*; the Pure Land or Jing-tu school, which emphasized salvation through faith and ejaculatory prayer to Amitabha Buddha; and the Meditation or Chan school, which relied not on the scriptures but on direct transmission of teaching from master to disciple and the development of intuitive wisdom (*prajñā*).

A Japanese authority on the *Laṅkāvatāra-sūtra*, Daisetz Teitaro Suzuki, has pointed out that though this sutra is a veritable compendium of Buddhist doctrine, noting down "in a somewhat sketchy fashion almost all the ideas belonging to the different schools of Mahayana Buddhism," it has always had a very special relationship to the Chan school. We are therefore immediately confronted with the question as to whether Li He was an adherent of the Chan school. If he were, this would help to explain the otherwise puzzling lack of overt Buddhist allusions in his verse, since this school attached only secondary importance to the scriptures. But even if he were not a devotee of Chan, the very fact that he was accustomed to read the *Laṅkāvatāra* indicates the seriousness of his interest in Buddhism. Some critics have denied that He was a Buddhist at all, on the ground that his poetry is sensuous and worldly and abounds in Taoist and shamanistic references. Against this we may point out that he mentions the *Laṅkāvatāra* in conjunction with the *Chu Ci*, a work which all critics admit to be of the first importance as an influence on his thought and sensibility.

The *Laṅkāvatāra*, being mentioned in the same breath as the *Chu Ci*, can therefore reasonably be considered as a work to which he attached the highest value. Furthermore, his attachment to this sutra indicates a real seriousness in his attitude towards Buddhism, for it is arguably the most difficult in the whole Buddhist canon. As another great poet, Su Shi (1036–1101), also an admirer of this scripture, remarked in his preface to the edition of 1085: "The *Laṅkāvatāra* is deep and unfathomable in meaning, while in style it is so terse and archaic that the reader finds it troublesome even to punctuate the sentences correctly, let alone understand their ultimate spirit and purport...."

Suzuki confirms this verdict, pointing out in his *Studies in the Laṅkāvatāra-sūtra* (London and Boston, 1930), that "the sūtra requires a great deal of learning as well as an insight to understand all the details thoroughly." In fact Suzuki himself was driven to give an interpretation rather than a translation at times, since the latter "reproduced as it stands in the original" would be quite unintelligible to the average reader. Consider, for example, the following representative passage, translated from Śikshānanda's Chinese version of the Sanskrit original:

> [The wise] too see the aspect of [self-nature] in all things, for it manifests itself as if characterised with false attachment. They do not talk about causation and no-causation, they fall into the view of [self-] aspect in all things. World-honoured One, [thus they say that] this belongs to another realm, and is not like such [as is maintained by others]. If so, this is the fault of non-finality. Who can then have a clear understanding as regards the aspect of [self-] nature in all things? World-honoured One, the aspect of [self-] nature in all things is not dependent on discrimination; why do you say that all things exist because of discrimination?

Since the sutra abounds in passages of such difficulty it is clear that He's attitude to Buddhism could hardly have been that of a dilettante. If he was prepared to grapple with the *Laṅkāvatāra* he must have had a very serious commitment to Buddhist doctrine, serious enough to induce him to wrestle with a text which even in the best of the Chinese translations is still one of quite extraordinary difficulty.

But what was it that drove this young and unhappy poet to delve into such a scripture? The principal theme of the *Laṅkāvatāra* is that "all things have no self-substance, they are like a cloud, like a circle traced out by a revolving fire-brand...like māyā, or mirage, or the moon in the water or a dream." Thus the universe is essentially only an illusion formed by the false discrimination (*vikalpa*) of the mind.

The doctrine of "Mind-only" forms the very heart of the sutra. Again and again we are told that "The triple world is Mind itself" and "All is Mind." As Suzuki points out, "The doctrine of 'Mind-only' runs through the *Laṅkāvatāra* as if it were warp and weft....To understand it is to realise the ultimate truth and not to understand it is to transmigrate through many a birth-and-death." The pure idealism of the sutra insists that the entire universe, the whole fabric of the space-time continuum, and even Nirvana itself, which is by definition beyond Being as we know it, are no more than the creation of our own mind. "O Mahāmati, when a man sees into the abode of reality where all things are, he enters upon the truth that what appears to him is not other than mind itself."

The essential purport of the sutra is that enlightenment is reached when we realise that the universe is unreal and uncreated. What we take for reality is due to false discrimination (*vikalpa*), which in turn arises from impressions (*vāsāna*) inherited from all the thoughts, words, and deeds of countless past incarnations. As long as we cannot free ourselves from such impressions we are cut off from Reality (*dharmatā*) and condemned to revolve endlessly on the Wheel of Birth and Death. But once we have cleansed out Intellect (*prajñā*) freeing ourselves from hate, anger, greed, lust, and other passions, then a revulsion (*parāvṛitti*) takes place in our minds, enabling us instinctively to grasp the truth that there is nothing but Mind. This is what the sutra calls "inner realisation" (*pratyātmāryajñānagocara*), the direct presentation of truth to the mind.

Such pure monistic idealism contrasts oddly with Li He's passionate interest in the world of colour, sense, and form. His sensuous apprehension of reality stands in vivid contrast to the *Laṅkāvatāra* insistence on the delusory nature of the senses. Most important of all, his poetic genius found itself at complete variance with the sutra's insistence on the inadequacies of language itself.

> Language, O Mahāmati, is not the ultimate truth; what is attainable by language is not the ultimate truth. Why? Because the ultimate truth is what is enjoyed by the wise; by means of speech one can enter into the truth, but words themselves are not the truth. It is the self-realisation inwardly experienced by the wise through their supreme wisdom, and does not belong to the domain of words, discrimination, or intelligence; and, therefore, discrimination does not reveal the ultimate truth itself. Moreover, O Mahāmati, language is subject to birth and destruction, is unsteady, mutually conditioning, and produced according to the law of causation; and what is mutually conditioning and produced according to the law of causation is not the ultimate truth, nor does it come out of such conditions, for truth is above aspects of relativity, and word are incapable of producing it....

In view of his attachment to this sutra, it seems clear that He must have realised the ultimately hallucinatory nature of the world on which he lavished so much of his art, as well as the limitation of the world of words to which he had devoted his short life. Knowing as he did that "the truth (*tattvaṃ*) is beyond words," he must have been ironically conscious of the ultimate futility of his efforts to seek to paint a mirage on the mists of an illusion.

To understand He's passionate concern with social and political issues one must realize that China was then going through a period of great turbulence involving nothing less than the restoration of the imperial sway. Since the rebellion of An Lu-shan (A.D. 755) the central government had been losing power to the provincial military governor, who had been steadily encroaching on the prerogatives of the emperor. When Emperor Xian-zong (*regnet* 805–20) came to the throne he was determined to restore the power of the imperial house and demonstrate the strength of the government in Chang-an. In this he was to evince remarkable success. In the fifteen years of his reign he brought his rebellious satraps to order by launching punitive expeditions against them whenever they refused to come to heel when called. In 806 he defeated Liu Pi, a rebellious general who had attempted to seize the vital region of Sichuan. The following year he overthrew Li Qi, a recalcitrant governor of a southern province and then, emboldened by his victories, decided to challenge the powerful Wang Cheng-zong, military governor of Cheng-de, Hebei, who had long been a thorn in his flesh. Unfortunately, Xian-zong made the mistake of appointing a eunuch, Tu-tu Cheng-cui (d. 820), as commander-in-chief of the imperial armies, probably to placate the powerful eunuchs at court, and was eventually compelled to call off the campaign in 810. In an early poem Li He attacked this singularly incompetent general in biting, satirical verse.

A lady-general leads our Chinese soldiers.
A dainty kerchief tucked into her quiver.
She's not ashamed of her heavy, gold seal,
Mincing along with bow-case at her waist.
Simple old men, just honest villagers,
Tested the teeth of arrow-barbs last night,
But she sent her courier to cry victory—
Must powder and mascara blind us all!

Such satire must have caused a minor sensation in Chang-an and perhaps even played a part in finally forcing the emperor to dismiss Tu-tu Cheng-cui from his command of the Armies of the Divine Plan on charges of bribery.

Xian-zong's restoration of the empire was highly successful. By the end of his reign he had not only subdued the rebellious provinces of Huai-xi and Ping-lu but had firmly established the imperial power throughout China in a way that had not been seen since the dynasty was at its height. But such successes were accomplished at considerable cost. Not only was the country in turmoil, with prominent officials falling victim to hired assassins in the capital itself, but the extensive military campaigns necessary to restore order placed a heavy burden of taxation on the peasantry, while conscription into the army added to their hardships.

Li He was deeply concerned at the abuses he saw around him and wrote a number of poems to record his indignation. It is difficult at this remove for us to estimate just how many of the poems are to be understood as satires. The commentator Yao Wen-xie ascribes satirical intent to almost every verse He wrote, but this, of course, is an exaggeration. However, it is fair to assume that a great many poems which appear innocuous enough now would have been read as satires by He's contemporaries. Perhaps some-thing like 20 percent of the verse, at a conservative estimate, can even now reasonably be labelled satirical, though half the time we can never be sure just what target he is aiming at. In any case, it is certain that his involvement with the New Ballad Movement must not be underestimated. Bo Ju-yi (772–846) and Yuan Zhen had both come to the conclusion that "the duty of literature is to be of service to the writer's generation: that of poetry to influence public affairs." This conviction was a revival of an ancient belief, dating back to *The Classic of Poetry* and the *Songs of Chu*, that the poet was the social conscience of his time. To ensure the widest possible circulation for their work, Bo and Yuan cast their criticisms of existing abuses into ballad form. These ballads, which enjoyed as much vogue as the popular songs of our own time, were songs with a message. As Bo puts it in the preface to his own collection of fifty ballads:

> [These songs] are concerned with ideas, not with fine phrases....
> This was the principle behind the three hundred poems [of *The Classic of Poetry*]....Their style is smooth and flowing, so they can easily be played and sung. In short, they have been written for the emperor, for his ministers, for the people....They have not been written simply for art's sake.

This manifesto of Bo's may be considered as the inception of the New Ballad Movement. Bo and Yuan were soon joined by a number of other writers—Li Shen, Meng Jiao, Zhang Ji, and Han Yu among them—who were all concerned in some degree with the use of verse as a vehicle for social criticism. Strictly speaking, the New Ballad had to conform to the criteria Bo Ju-yi himself adopted. It had to be simple in expression—Bo is said to have tried out all his poems on an old maidservant, deleting anything she could not understand—and conform to the ballad form, while revealing sympathy for the plight of the common people. The poetry, in fact, was in the pity. He has comparatively few ballads which meet all these requirements, for he was influenced more by the *Li Sao* tradition (the greatest poem of the *Songs of Chu*) than by *The Classic of Poetry*, and the *Li Sao*, though critical of governmental abuses, was ornate and highly obscure. Nevertheless, he would certainly have subscribed to Empson's dictum:

> Politics are what verse should
> Not fly from, or it goes all wrong.

Furthermore, he did write a few ballads which fulfill all the criteria laid down by Bo Ju-yi and yet carry his own inimitable stamp, as in the following song describing the miseries of the jade-gatherers, who had taken to this dangerous work to save themselves and their families from starvation:

> On rainy nights, on the ridge of a hill,
> He sups on hazel-nuts,
> Like blood that wells from a cuckoo's maw
> The old man's tears.
> The waters of Indigo River are gorged
> With human lives;
> Men dead a thousand years
> Still loathe these torrents.

Though apparently simple, analysis reveals this to be a far more complex and intricately structured poem than anything Bo Ju-yi ever wrote. In modern terms, we can discern within this verse something of that peculiar tension between symbolism and naturalism manifest in the work of so many writers of our own century. But I shall come back to this point later. For the moment we shall simply note that the poem makes its point dramatically and effectively and must certainly be ranked as a ballad of social protest squarely in the tradition.

In another poem he satirizes greedy officials whose depredations have stripped whole districts of their natural resources.

> He-pu has no more shining pearls,
> Lung-zhou has no more "wooden slaves."
> Enough to show us that the powers of Nature
> Can never meet officialdom's demands.
> The wives of Yue had not begun their weaving,
> Silkworms of Wu had just started wriggling about,
> When a district official came riding on his horse,
> He'd a wicked face, a curly purple beard.
> Now in his robe he carried a square tablet,
> And on this tablet several lines were written.
> "If it were not for the Magistrate's anger,
> Would I have come in person to your house?"

More dangerous than his attacks on governmental oppression were his scarcely veiled satires on Emperor Xian-zong's quest for immortality through Taoist arts—a quest which was eventually to result in his death. Taoists believed that with the aid of the proper drugs, life could be lengthened almost indefinitely. Since most of these drugs were highly toxic preparations of gold, arsenic, lead, mercury, and like substances, it is hardly surprising to learn that those who sought immortality the most assiduously were frequently those who departed this life the most precipitately. As early as 810, the Emperor had evinced considerable interest in elixirs of immortality, much to the disapproval of his minister, Li Fan, who had given him a stern lecture on the folly of putting one's faith in Taoist magicians. This seems to have had little effect on Xian-zong's ardour, for by 819 we find him swallowing drugs daily and so becoming more and more bad-tempered and thirsty, as well as showing increasing signs of mental instability, a process which continued until his demise the following year. It is still unclear as to whether he died of an overdose of elixir or was poisoned by Chen Hong-zhi, one of the palace eunuchs, for reasons which still remain obscure.

Several writers attempted to remonstrate with the emperor on this subject, though to do so was really "to run up against the dragon's scales," since this was a topic on which he was notoriously short-tempered. Han Yu himself, who had merely alluded indirectly to the subject in his well-known memorial on the Buddha's bone, only narrowly escaped death for his indiscretion. Bo Ju-yi, Meng Jiao, and other poets preferred to couch their protests in the form of verse gibing at the vain quest for immortality undertaken by previous emperors such as Qin Shi Huang-di, Emperor Wu of Han, and Emperor Wen of Wei. He himself has a large number of poems on this subject, so many in fact that one wonders how he escaped punishment, for he was undoubtedly running a risk by circulating songs dealing with such a topic.

> Why should we swallow yellow gold,
> Or eat white jade?
> Who is Ren Gong-zi
> Riding a white donkey through the clouds?
> Liu Che lies in the Mao-ling tomb,

Just a pile of bones.
Ying Zheng lies in his catalpa coffin—
What a waste of abalone!

By eating cinnabar you may become
A serpent riding a white mist,
A thousand-year-old turtle in a well of jade.
Can't you see yourself transformed to snake or turtle
For twenty centuries,
Dragging your life out, year after year,
On the grass-green dikes of Wu?
Eight trigrams on your back,
Blazoned "Immortal,"
Your cunning scales,
Your stubborn armour
Slimed with a fishy spittle!

The bizarre imagery of the second poem which transforms
an emperor into a stubborn and cunning reptile, "slimed with a
fishy spittle," reminds us that He was a disciple not just of Han
Yu, whose style resembles that displayed in this poem, but of the
great Du Fu, who once remarked: "Not even death would stop me
from trying to startle my readers." We should remember that the
period in which He was writing was one of literary reform based
on the principle of "return to antiquity" (*fu gu*). Han Yu, who was
Li He's patron, had already established a reputation for verse in the
"antique" style, so it is hardly surprising to find that He avoids the
Regulated Verse, with its fixed lengths and rigid tone-patterns, and
writes most of his poems either in the freer Ancient Verse, in both
its five-syllable and seven-syllable forms, or in Irregular Verse with

lines of mixed length. He did this because of the greater freedom to express himself and "startle his readers" afforded by these verse forms. As Wang Shi-zhen (1526–90) observed: "Li Chang-ji follows the dictates of his heart so that his poems often sound strange, while he also has lines that surprise his readers."

Such poetic power springs from great artifice. As one Chinese critic remarked: "Li He's poetry is like the art of jade-carving; not a single word but has been refined a hundred times. This is really the product of work that made him 'vomit out his heart.'" His insistent craftsmanship is reminiscent of the French Parnassiens for whom:

> L'oeuvre sort plus belle
> D'une forme au travail rebelle,
> Vers, marbre, onyx, émail.

His language often possesses a Keatsian sumptuousness, every rift loaded with ore, a Keatsian "devotion to the intensity imbedded within the concrete," giving his lines "a heavy richness, a slow, clogged—almost drugged—movement, a choked-in fullness… which gives him strength with all his luxury and keeps his sensuousness firm and vital." These lines, originally written of Keats, are applicable to a great deal of He's concinnous verse.

Comparatively few of He's poems have the directness and simplicity of the poems quoted above. In fact, his verse on the whole is notoriously difficult and enigmatic. If, as Hugo Friedrich maintains, one of the chief characteristics of modern Western poetry is its obscurity, then Li He is in this respect a very modern poet. It has been alleged that Browning was the first poet to have been criticised for his obscurity, though surely *Sordello* is a much less recondite work than Shakespeare's *The Phoenix and the Turtle*. But Li He was criticised for his wilful obscurity over a thousand years before Browning first set pen to paper. "Li He's poems cannot be read without a commentary" is an old literary saw which may help to explain why, even in this translation, I have been compelled to include copious notes. His poems, like those of his younger contemporary, Li Shang-yin (813–858) present special difficulties, above those normally occurring in Tang verse, for a number of reasons. Firstly, his poems have an innate logic of their own which, to the unsuspecting reader, often appears lacking of logic. Take, for example, the song *Gossamer*:

> In the aging leaves of weeping-willows,
> Orioles feed their young,
> The gossamer is vanishing,
> Yellow bees go home.
>
> Black-haired young men, and girls
> With golden hairpins,
> From goblets, powder-blue, are quaffing
> A liquid amber.
>
> Twilight over flower-decked terraces,
> Spring says goodbye,
> Fallen blossoms rise and dance
> To eddying airs.
> Elm-tree seeds now lie so thick
> They can't be counted,
> Young Shen's green money strewn along
> Our city roads!

This seems, at first glance, to be no more than a loosely-linked collection of images illustrating spring. However, as one critic, Lin Guo-yuan, has astutely pointed out, the poem actually renders the feelings of an aging courtesan for whom the spring is but a reminder of another passing year. The weeping-willow is an accepted symbol for a prostitute in Chinese verse. Its "aging leaves," coupled with the images of an oriole feeding its young, suggest that she is lamenting that she has no child of her own although she is growing old. "Gossamer" again suggests her vanishing youth, here contrasted with the "black-haired young men" who have now found younger company. As spring fades, so does her youth. Try as she may to hold back the years, she is but a fallen blossom, now discarded, dancing vainly in the twilight. She has squandered her youth as recklessly as the elm-tree seeds which litter the ground, seeds which suggest the money she has earned and spent in her prodigal pursuit of pleasure. This is a delicately subtle poem which achieves its effects with economy. At one level it may be read simply as an impressionistic picture of a late spring day; its deeper meaning only emerges on careful examination. Hence its apparent lack of structure and logic is illusory, for the poem is tightly organised and structurally compact, to the point of density.

He's imagination is neither rhetorical nor yet dramatic; it is purely visual. He sees things in flashes, apparently disconnectedly, so that in this respect his work may be less puzzling to modern readers, whose eyes have been trained by years of television and cinema, than it was to his traditional audience. His technique is undoubtedly connected with the method of composition described in his biographies, in which he would jot down lines and phrases as they occurred to him and then piece them together like a mosaic on his return home. As a result of this, some of his long poems, like *Chang-gu* and *She Steals My Heart* tend to break down into disparate shots in which the inner unity that should bind them has been lost. In cinematic terms, He's camera—work—whether black-and-white or colour—is always brilliant. It is his montages that sometimes fail him.

It is this technique that has led some of his modern commentators like Arai Ken and Seto Yasuo to complain that He jumps about in time and space, keeps changing his subject, and in general lacks unity. Seto objects that the lines of some of the poems are disjointed and quite lacking in temporal, spatial, or logical connections. Quite often, as in the poem quoted above, He's critics are wrong, for they have failed to descry the innate logic of his verse. Even when their criticisms are just, however, we should note that this disconnectedness, allied as it is to the crossfade technique of our cinematic arts, is yet another instance of He's modernity, being characteristic of much modern verse, an anticipation of the Bergsonian flux of twentieth-century art. It is this disparateness which has led Qian Zhong-shu to remark that He's poetry resembles the shifting sands of the desert—a desert which, I might add, has deterred many who might have wished to cross it.

Other difficulties confront the reader, not least among them the density of the verse. He's favourite measure is the seven-syllable line, which he packs with subjects and verbs, often in compound form, and crams with attributives. This syntactical density, taken in conjunction with a use of trope hitherto unparalleled in Chinese poetry—metonymy, synecdoche, hyperbole, periphrasis, personification, simile, metaphors, and conceit—at times renders his verse peculiarly recalcitrant to both the reader and the translator. Yet, paradoxically, in spite of its density, his verse gives an impression of swiftness and lightness, as Qian Zhong-shu has pointed out: "Though each individual element of his poetry is stagnant, weighty, hard and solid, the movement of the verse as a whole is swift, speedy and volatile. Individually, each word seems stagnant and heavy, while collectively they float airily...." Classical Chinese, whether poetry or prose, is characterised by parataxis, a figure of rhetoric which signifies the placing of two terms in juxtaposition without expressing a grammatical or logical connection between them. Like all Chinese poets Li He is fond of employing this device, generally in the form of metaphor. C. Day Lewis's epigram: "We find poetic truth struck out by the collision rather than the collusion of images" (*The Poetic Image,* 1947) is certainly applicable to Li He, whose high poetic energy expresses itself characteristically through brilliant parataxis.

> "Leaves on the lotus pool, numberless green coins:
> The fragrant sweat that soaks them, jewels of grain."
> "Windy *tong* trees, lutes in jasper cases,
> Fire-flies' stars, envoys to Brocade City."
> "Bamboo quiver, short flutes playing."
> "Blood that wells from a cuckoo's maw,
> The old man's tears."
> "Tamarisk faces half-asleep,
> The Premier's trees."

When one half of the metaphor is suppressed, we are left with something close to a kenning. Thus autumn flowers are "cold reds"; wine is "liquid amber"; a sword is "jade dragon," "a sash of white satin," or simply "three feet of water"; jujubes are "hanging pearls," or "hanging reds"; the moon is a "cold hare," a "jade wheel," an "emerald flower," or a "cold toad"; moss is "purple coins," or "emerald earth-flowers"; a river is a "dragon-bone," or a "duck-head," the latter because it is soft and green. He's originality, his penchant for coining strange metaphors or reformulating tired metaphors in new ways, made him unpopular with orthodox Chinese critics who were repelled by his strangeness. As a modern critic, Ye Cong-qi, has pointed out, He "rigorously avoids clichés and is unwilling to follow ordinary conventions and practices... transforming clichés such as 'the silver River' and 'the silver Han' [terms for the Milky Way] into 'the cloudy banks.' "

The originality of his metaphors is often a source of perplexity, for his imagery is often difficult to follow until one has grasped its innate logic.

> Xi and He whip up the sun
> With the sound of glass.

This borders on the synaesthesia of the Symbolists, whom He so much resembles. The sun is like glass, because both are white and shining (glass was an exotic substance for Tang Chinese). The sun is being shattered by time so it sounds like breaking glass as Xi and He, who drive the chariot of the sun, apply the whip. He's verse abounds in images of this nature which are reminiscent of the conceit of the Metaphysicals and quite as difficult to grasp at first reading. The difficulty and density of most of He's verse vanishes when we turn to his love poetry, largely because he is here writing in imitation of an older tradition which antedated Tang, namely the Palace Poetry of the Southern Qi and Ziang dynasties (479–556 A.D.). He has over forty poems dealing with women, a surprisingly high proportion for a poet of the Yuan-zhao period. In a very real sense this verse not only looks backward to an earlier era but also looks forward, anticipating the languid, incense-laden atmosphere of the *ci*, a kind of song lyric composed to fixed melodic patterns which was to come into being some fifty years or so after his death.

> Clouds tumbling over her jewelled pillow,
> She seeks a spring dream,
> In caskets cold with inlaid sapphires
> The dragon-brain grows chill.

> She lies resentful in her net of pearls
> Unable to sleep,
> Beneath a robe ornate with golden phoenix
> Her body is chill,…

> Drowsy with wine, idle all the white day
> In a moored boat,
> In a plum-breeze by the ferry she waves
> Her singing-fan.

> Butterflies lighting on China pinks—
> Hinges of silver,
> Frozen water, duck-head green—
> Coins of glass.
> Its six-fold curves enclose a lamp
> Burning orchid-oil.
> She lets down her tresses before the mirror,
> Sheds her gold cicadas,
> Perfume of aloes from a warm fire,
> Smoke of dogwood.

A single skein of perfumed silk,
Clouds cast on the floor,
Noiseless, the jade comb lights upon
Her lustrous hair.

Delicate fingers push up the coils—
Colour of an old rook's plumes
Blue-black so sleek—the jewelled pins
Cannot hold it up.

Flowers bow down beneath light dew,
Melilote's breath,
Windlass of jade and rope of silk
Draw the dawn water,
Her powdered face, like rose carnelian,
Hot and fragrant.

Part of this verse—like the last example—is undoubtedly satiric. But in any case, even when He's intentions were to mock, he lingered to admire. This world of black-haired, jade-skinned beauties, blushing cheeks, perfumed silks, gauze bed-curtains, flickering tapers, carved screens, golden censers fuming with rare incense, and the mournful drip of rain on the kolaunut trees, was to become the sole poetic province of *ci* writers like Wen Ting-yun (812?–70?), Wei Zhuang (836–910), Li Yu (937–78), and others. He's natural sensuality could not resist the appeal of this glittering kingdom of pearl and aloes-wood, jasper and cassia, though he invested it with a significance lacking in later writers. Not only does He anticipate the great poets of the *ci*: he also looks forward to the two outstanding romantics of the ninth century, Du Mu and Li Shang-yin. Like them he delights in wine and spring flowers, beautiful women and the moon on the water. He takes love as seriously as the Confucian poet took friendship. Li Shang-yin, one of the greatest poets of love writing in Chinese, was a devoted admirer of He's and must have found support for his passionate affairs of the heart in He's verse:

> What sort of love am I seeking?
> That of Xun Feng-qian.
> O sun above the city wall,
> Forever stay above the city wall!
> Let a single day be as a thousand years,
> And never sink to rest.

Certain critics give the impression that He's love of beauty was somehow incompatible with the Confucian gravity and sense of purpose associated with the New Ballad Movement: that aestheticism and naturalism could not go together. This is a misleading dichotomy. Tang poetry, even the best of it, is inclined to be florid: but one should never mistake this for a lack of high seriousness. One has only to look at Han Yu's own verse to see that it abounds in quaint conceits and odd expressions, breaks many of the time-hallowed rules of composition, and deals with subjects which no earlier poet would have thought fit to mention in verse. I hazard the opinion that both the intricate nature of He's own poetry and his choice of subjects were in fact partly the result of a deliberate attempt to please his patrons. There is certainly nothing in He's verse which Yu or his fellows would have thought frivolous. Some critics have failed to see that there is a difference between He's verse and the effete, palace poetry against which Yu fulminated. Palace poetry was largely mere empty rhetoric; once penetrate its glossy surface and there was little or nothing underneath. But He's verse, even when concerned with the very subjects that formed the sole staple of the palace poets, never wavered from the *Li Sao* tradition. Beneath the intricately patterned surface lay solid layers of meaning. Ultimately, Yu waged war on the poetry of Qi and Liang not because of its decadent subject-matter but because it was void of social content. He praised He's verse because it came to grips with reality, whether it dealt with soldiers starving in a frontier-post or a princess getting drunk at a banquet. Yu was astute enough to realize, as so many later critics have not, that if verse was to mirror the complex, sophisticated, and disintegrating fabric of Tang society it could not confine itself to simple ballads. It is only because He possessed this poetic range that he could so successfully hold up the mirror to his age: and it was precisely for this quality that Yu admired him. His verse in its own way reflects the realities of Tang life just as faithfully as the poems of Du Fu and Bo Ju-yi. The parallel with our own times, when naturalism and symbolism, aesthete and realist flourish together, is quite striking. One is reminded of Mallarmé congratulating Zola on the publication of *L'Assommoir*, both having, as Durkheim pointed out, a common need to destroy the real or escape from it.

The contention that the main difference between He's poetry and the verse of Qi and Liang, which it sometimes superficially resembles, lies in their content, brings us directly to the problems of meaning in Chinese verse. He was brought up in a poetic tradition which laid great stress on metaphor (*bi*) and allegory (*xing*): "The parables employed in the *xing* appear subtle, but they are so apparent!" wrote the critic Liu Xie (c. 465–522) in the chapter on metaphor and allegory of his *Wenxin diaolong* (*The Literary Mind and the Carving of Dragons*). Subtle they certainly are; but they are not always as apparent as they might be. Thus the first song of *The Classic Songs* begins with the line:

*Guan-guan* cry the fish-hawks.

The commentators point out here that fish-hawks are a symbol of virtue, because male and female do not mix promiscuously; hence the poem is a eulogy of the virtue of Queen Wen, wife of Wen of the Zhou. So Liu Xie adds sagely: "Do not let these birds of prey distract your mind, because the important thing is the virtue of sexual separation. Such parables are like the first rays of light before the break of dawn, still enveloped in ambiguity. This is the reason why commentators are required to make the meaning clear." Liu then goes on to deal with the difference of metaphor, whose most important function, he implies, is to act as a further means of remonstration. "Thus gold and pewter are used to stand for illustrious virtue, a jade tally signifies an outstanding man, a caterpillar means education, cicadas and grasshoppers denote howling and shouting, washing clothes symbolises sadness of the heart and the rolling up of a mat denotes firmness of will."

Now He's style is admittedly based not on the *Songs*, from which all the above examples are drawn, but on the *Chu Ci*. Yet ultimately this makes no difference to our argument, for as Liu points out, the *Sao* was created in the spirit of the *Songs* and has "adopted its formal remonstrations." We may protest, of course, that the *Chu Ci* is not really like that; for its dragons do not always betoken men of virtue any more than its clouds and rainbows invariably stand for flatterers and sycophants. But this is after all rather to miss the point. What matters in this context is that He's views on the nature of the *Chu Ci* must have been essentially those of Liu Xie.

Western sinologists have very much inclined to ignore the part played by *bi* and *xing* in Chinese verse, largely because the tradition of a work possessing several levels of meaning died out in Europe during the seventeenth century and has only recently been revived. I. A. Richards's "multiple definition," Kenneth Burke's "multiple causation," William Tray's attempt to revive the medieval "four levels of meaning" are all of them relevant to any attempt to read Chinese literature in depth. Unfortunately, very little, if anything, has as yet been done towards applying modern critical methods to the study of Chinese poetry. A. C. Graham's recent excursions into this field in his *Poems of the Late Tang* have the distinction of being the first serious attempt of its kind. In general, due credit has not been given to traditional Chinese explanations of the meanings hidden in verse. Hence in my own annotations to He's poems, I have attempted to bring out this aspect of the verse wherever possible, while attempting to avoid falling into the pitfall that Yao Wen-xie tumbled into in his anxiety to suppose every bush a bear.

A point closely connected with this is the question of plurisignation (a better term than "ambiguity") in He's verse. Lack of literary professionalism among sinologists has all too often led to a concern with outmoded, pre-Empsonian ideas about the meaning of a poem. The notion has persisted that the denotative aspect of language is more important than the connotative: that a line—or a whole poem—must mean one thing and one thing only. In fact, Chinese poetry has consciously employed plurisignation since the Six Dynasties period; by late Tang times, when Tang was writing, multiple meanings had become quite as involved as those of Shakespearian verse. This poses special difficulties for the translator, who is in any case forced by the very nature of the English language to be precise where Chinese is vague and suggestive. At times, he may be lucky enough to hit upon a rendering which will convey something of the ambiguity of the original; but most of the time he can only labouriously spell out the other possible meanings of the line in a footnote.

A reluctance to annotate poems copiously has been one of the main reasons, I think, why He has not received the attention that is his due from Western translators. From the end of the eighth century onwards, Chinese poetry becomes steadily more complex and allusive. The Chinese poet has always relied heavily for his effect on allusions. Pound's characterization of a poem as a form that should be able to do as much in a line as a whole page of prose, is strikingly true of Chinese verse, which can sum up a situation, draw an analogy, or reveal a contrast in the minimum of words through the use of the shorthand of allusion. As the corpus of literature increased there was a tendency on the part of poets to refer not only to the Confucian and Taoist classics but to the whole ever-growing body of earlier writings. This means that the later Tang poets tend to be rather more difficult to read than their predecessors, if only because they have incorporated so much into their verse. This is not to say that there is a great deal of purely literary allusion in He's verse; on the contrary, there is far less of this than in, say, the fifth-century poet Xie Ling-yun. But there is enough general use of allusion to ensure that there are very few poems in He's collected works that can be understood without at least some notes and a good many poems that require a great deal of annotation indeed.

Here the Western reader is at a considerable disadvantage compared with even the Chinese reader who has received no formal classical education; for the latter has acquired, by cultural osmosis as it were, a great deal of information which the unfortunate Westerner has painstakingly to imbibe. All this goes to swell the already excessive volume of footnotes, until the translator half begins to wonder, with Pound, whether he is not "obscuring the text with philology." Nevertheless, I myself am convinced for one that this is the only way in which Chinese verse can be made intelligible to the European reader, without fobbing him off with mere *chinoiserie*. A belief in the essential untranslatability of a text, particularly a poetic work, has ancient roots in Western society, going back at least as far as St. Jerome. It was reiterated by Dante, Du Bellay, Dr. Johnson, Diderot, and Heine. In our own time Rilke and Nabokov have both insisted that poetry is untranslatable, the latter voicing his objections, with characteristic vividness, in verse:

> What is translation? On a platter
> A poet's pale and glaring head,
> A parrot's speech, a monkey's chatter
> And profanation of the dead.

In his memorable treatise on translation (*After Babel*, 1975), George Steven has convincingly refuted such arguments, pointing out that they are "only a weak form of an attack on language itself," and insisting that "to dismiss the validity of translation because it is not always possible and never perfect is absurd."

Nevertheless the translator must concede that a great deal of the essential poetry of the original may be spilt in translation. As Mallarmé put it, since "poetry is made with words not ideas" it must evaporate like spilt perfume when poured into the alien flask of another language. On the other hand, it can be argued that this contention has come up against some very sharp and perceptive criticism in recent years, the most telling onslaught on this cherished doctrine coming from the Chicago critics. They reject the doctrine that literature is only a question of particular arrangements of words on a page, as Leavis puts it, in favor of the view that we are moved not only by the words but by the things the words stand for. One can test this for oneself. Flecker's lines:

A ship, an isle, a sickle moon—
With few, but with how splendid stars

lose little when rendered into any language. The quality of the imagery here is such that it passes unscathed through the refining fires of translation. It is precisely this characteristic of He's verse, the giving of sharp perceptions in images of extraordinary colour and clarity, that makes him a peculiarly translatable poet. Whatever else may be lost, this at least is not.

But He has other advantages for the translator besides the vividness of his imagery. Chinese poets, on the whole, are impersonal, self-effacing, and inclined to generalize in a way which sometimes muffles the impact of their verse on the Western reader, who is accustomed to as forceful a display of individualism in his poetry as in his culture. The Western poet, at least since the Romantics, has almost invariably been endowed with a personality which makes itself strongly felt through his verse. In this respect, He is an aberration from the Chinese standard; for though he very seldom consciously intrudes himself into his verse, rarely using the personal pronoun, the stress of his personality is there all the same. One is continually aware of a sort of controlled violence in his poems, informing even the most casual-sounding lines. He is a poet of exaggerated gestures and moods, swinging between despair and exultation in a way that leads one to guess that he must have been something of a manic-depressive. It is, I suspect, this violence of gesture that has made him so irritate many of his Chinese readers, who are vaguely conscious all the time that the proprieties are being offended. An image like the following illustrates what I mean:

Blood that wells from a cuckoo's maw
The old man's tears.

Occurring as it does in a poem of social protest, which we are accustomed to think of in terms of the gentle, conversational ironies of Bo Ju-ji, this image brings one up with a start. It is altogether too vehement. What is more, it has a peculiar tellingness about it which is hard to explain. The educated Chinese reader would at once link this with the story of the Emperor of Shu who abdicated his throne, fled into the wilds, and was changed into a cuckoo. But what has this allusion to the weeping emperor to do with an old peasant? The most likely explanation is that the blood the old man weeps (another exaggeration) makes him kin to the cuckoo and hence an animal; at the same time, the cuckoo is an emperor, so the old man's grief is imperial. Linking cuckoo, peasant, and emperor in this way through the highly unpleasant image of blood flowing from the eyes and mouth, works on the reader powerfully and upsettingly. For a Chinese, the implied social confusion of man with animal, peasant with Son of Heaven, would have been not the least disturbing thing about this comparison.

Another factor which is not lost in translation but can be brought over unscathed is He's evocative use of colour to symbolize emotion. As the critic Fan Xi-wen remarked: "Li He's words are like a coat of many colours, a hundred embroidered patches dazzling the eye." White, gold, silver, black, red, green, yellow, blue-green, emerald, vermilion, scarlet, purple, turquoise, and cinnabar run riot through his work. Furthermore, his palette is a highly idio-syncratic one in which certain colours, notably white, red, and blue-green, are dominant, with white standing far above the rest. The table below shows the frequency with which the principal colours are distributed through He's poems. They fall neatly into six groups:

| COLOUR | NUMBER OF OCCURRENCES IN POEMS |
|---|---|
| White (*bai*) + ecru (*su*) | 93 |
| Jade or jade-white (*yu*) | 79 |
| Gold or metal (*jin*) | 73 |
| Red (*hong*) | 69 |
| Blue-green (*ching*) | 68 |
| True-green or emerald (*lu*) | 48 |
| Yellow (*huang*) | 45 |
| Luminescent blue-green or sapphire (*bi*) | 26 |
| Silver (*yin*) | 21 |
| Purple (*zi*) | 25 |
| Turquoise or kingfisher-blue (*cui*) | 21 |
| Black (*hei*) | 11 |
| Vermilion (*zhu*) | 9 |
| Azure (*cang*) | 9 |
| Russet or dark red (*chi*) | 3 |
| Cinnabar (*dan*) | 3 |
| Deep red (*jiang*) | 3 |
| Reddish-brown (*zhe*) | 2 |
| Greenish-white (*piao*) | 2 |
| Indigo (*lan*) | 2 |
| Powder-blue (*piao-fen*) | 1 |
| Rosy-red (*cheng*) | 1 |
| Blood-red (*xue se*) | 1 |
| Jet-black (*dai*) | 1 |

He's liking for white, a colour associated in China not with purity and virginity but with mourning and misfortune, is highly significant. To the Chinese, white is an unlucky colour, suggesting death and old age. In the Han system of correspondences it was linked with autumn, the west (and hence the setting sun), and the element metal, which interestingly enough ranks second in He's list. Moreover, since "jade" as an adjective always means "jade-white" in Chinese and never "jade green," the combination of white and jade—172 instances in all out of 615—represents a quite extraordinary preference for white. Even in the West, psychologists tend to associate a strong liking for white with psychic abnormality: in China, where white has many of the emotional overtones that in Europe would be carried by black, such a predilection would be considered morbid and ill-omened.

He's landscapes, drenched in this white radiance, shine with an unearthly pallor.

In the ninth month, the great wilderness is white.
The entire mountain bathed in a white dawn.
Horses' hooves trampling in white.
Autumn whitens the infinite heavens.
White grasses, dead beneath invading mist.
A white sky, water like raw silk.
Where endless desert merges with white sky.
Vast autumn gleamed white.
Jade mist on green water
Like pennants of white.
To an islet where white duckweed grows...
The cloud-towers are half-revealed,
Walls slant and white.

Above cold gardens, deserted courtyards,
A limpid, white void.
The white light returns to the Western Hills.

It is possible that He's obsession with white was in some way connected with the premature and sinister whitening of his own hair, a physiological quirk which he refers to several times in his poems. He was haunted by the mystery of whiteness as another great poet, Lorca, was haunted by the spell of green.

Against this pallid background the other colours burn with a brilliant flame:

Under massing clouds red nets darken,
Over broken stones slant purple coins.

Beyond the frontiers like rouge from Yen,
Night's purple congeals.

Who is this girl shedding vermilion tears?

Cold candles, kingfisher-green…

Smoky yellow mantles the willows.

A thousand hills of darkest emerald.

A flame-red mirror opens in the east.

His glittering sword lights up the sky,
Heaven turns sapphire.

On the scarlet walls hang girdle-gems of jade.

Under the white sun, a thousand hills
Look darkest green.

Black waters of the Pine Stream
Spawn new dragon-eggs.

Emerald smoke swirling...

Cold reds weeping dew...

What hungry beetles would not eat
Piles up in broken yellows.

Twilight purple freezes in the dappled sky.

Only black waters' waves sobbivng at dawn.

Pattern of golden snakes on her dancing-rug.

Along with this striking use of colour goes a wholly personal imagery which, again, is unique in Chinese if not in world literature. The following images all occur in He's verse, some of them several times: shrieking phoenixes; lonely simurghs; aging simurghs; shivering hares; old fishes; gaunt dragons; crying mole-crickets; weeping raccoons; dying foxes; white foxes barking; snarling dogs; wailing crickets; drooling lions; slavering griffons; whinnying and half-starved horses; crying crows; serpents riding a white mist; old turtles in jade wells; poisonous, horned dragons; demon-owls, and weeping bronze camels. The last figure leads us to the next class of imagery, that of normally inanimate objects which in He's verse become endowed with a mysterious life of their own. This is the world of Tang ghost stories: swords that roar, swords that fly, painted dragons ridden by rain-elves, haggard straw-dogs, weeping statues and gargoyles peering out of stunted trees. It is but a step away from the realm of gods and spirits proper, ranging from cave-dwelling demons, mountain trolls, witches and Weird Crones to Nü Gua, the Purple King and the Mother who is Queen in the West. Against the flickering background of a hallucinatory universe, where mountains crumble away in the wind and land lurches out of the sea only to disappear again, He's phantasmagoria dances wildly past. The only constant here is the inexorable passing of time: the dripping water-clock and the booming drum mark men's progress towards the graves where the fireflies dance like corpse-fires, and lonely candles bum. Nor are men alone in their predicament. In the Buddhist vision of things, even the gods must perish; and He's heaven is a place of funerals where the blessed themselves are borne in never-ending procession to the tomb.

Ultimately, He was at heart a mystic, as we might have guessed from his preoccupation with the *Lankāvatāra*, the central theme of which is the doctrine of self-realization (*svasiddhānta*) and inner enlightenment (*pratyātmagati*). Many of his poems are clearly records, not of hallucinations, but of genuine, if elementary, visions, in which he transcends the world of egoistic experience, the illusions of Māyā, entering a realm in which he contemplates a higher state of being than our own. Today, we have so completely lost touch with inner reality that very few of us can believe in its existence, a fact that makes it difficult for us to respond adequately to He's greatest poems, where the vision shines the most resplendently. Nevertheless, we must realize that the world of his visions was not a mere fantasy into which he retreated from the miseries of "reality." Rather, his Buddhist training enabled him to journey to places far removed from "the weariness, the fever, and the fret" of his existence without losing his orientation, while his poetic genius enabled him to describe vividly what he had seen.

He's grasp of universal principles, his intuitive Knowledge, his sense of the ultimate identity (*samatā*) of the world-of-birth-and-death (*saṁsāra*) and Nirvana, is central, not peripheral, to his poetic art. He wrote verse ultimately not for aesthetic pleasure but to express what the *Laṅkāvatāra* calls *pratyātmāryajñānagocara*— the state of intuitive awareness of inner truth. It is perhaps this which makes the perceptive Western reader want to link him with that great sapiential tradition which includes Norwid and Blake, Rimbaud and Yeats. Though his visions are admittedly never more than two-fold (to use Blake's term) they are intensely felt and realized, even if they do lapse at times when the spirit fails him into mere fantasy. His moments of epiphany occur when he realizes—to quote his favorite sutra—that "this world of error is eternity itself, truth itself" ("*Bhrāntih śāśvata, bhrāntis tattvam*"); when he glimpses as Yeats puts it, "the uncontrollable mystery on the bestial floor."

To say this is not to overlook the fact that He's poetry lacks the serene assurance of the mystic who has achieved realization and enlightenment. Since for much of his life he was a sick man, a great deal of his verse betrays all the feverish and heightened sensibility of the consumptive. In this he is very much of his age. As Yoshikawa Kōjirō remarks: "Tang poetry burns with intensity. The moment in which the poem is born is one of the most vital instants in a man's life in his headlong plunge towards death. He must fix his eyes upon the instant and pour his feelings into it. The emotion must cohere, it must jet forth, it must explode."

Never was this truer than of the poetry of Li He. In his sensuality and the despairing intensity with which he strives to hold the passing moment burning eternally in his art, like a frozen flame, he is akin to Keats: and like Keats—or Trakl, whom he also resembles—he is half in love at times with easeful death. He wrote in the shadow of the grave: and no philosophy, no religion, no consoling belief could quite keep out its ineluctable cold. Only at the white radiance of his own poetic visions could he warm himself for a while before making his final journey to those cypress-shadowed tombs where he had wandered so often during his brief lifetime like some pallid and melancholy ghost. Yet it would have been some consolation to him, I feel, to learn that now "after a thousand years in earth," his "rancorous blood" shines forth in the light of day as emerald-jade.

# Translator's Note

The poems in this collection are arranged according to the order of their appearance in the Zhong-hua Shu-ju edition of the *San-jia Li Chang-ji ge-shi* (1760) of Wang Qi (Shanghai, 1959).

Most of the poems translated were originally written in either the five-character or the seven-character line. The former comes over well into English; but the latter tends to produce lines too long to be handled without clumsiness. In the seven-character line, the caesura normally falls after the fourth syllable thus:

Chui yan ye lao / / ying bu er
Weeping willow leaves old / / Orioles feed young.

I have therefore tried to resolve this problem by breaking the line into two at the caesure:

In the aging leaves of weeping willows
Orioles feed their young.

Change of rhyme occurs frequently in his poetry and has been indicated by beginning another stanza wherever a new rhyme occurs.

Classical Chinese poetry must take account of tone in its rhymes. Our poet was especially fond of level tone rhymes (447 rhyme-words) with oblique tone (240 words) and entering tone (125 words) rhymes, often in difficult rhyming categories, lagging not far behind. The "startling abrupt" musical qualities of his verse are famous. None of this, of course, can be brought over by the translator, but it is as well for the reader to know something of what he is missing. Finally, we should remember that over half of his poems are modelled after *yüeh-fu* ballads and were meant to be sung, not just chanted. Here our loss is doubly great, for we have been bereft of both the subtle music of the setting and the subtler music of the lyrics themselves.

# POEMS

## Song: Li Ping at the Vertical Harp

❧

Silk from Wu, paulownia from Shu,
Strummed in high autumn,[1]
In the white sky the frozen clouds
Falling, not floating.
Ladies of the River weeping among bamboos,
The White Girl mournful[2]
As Li Ping plays his harp
In the centre of the Kingdom.

Jade from Mount Kun is shattered,
Phoenixes shriek,[3]
Lotuses are weeping dew,
Fragrant orchids smile.

Before the twelve gates of the city
The cold light melts,[4]
The twenty-three strings can move
The Purple Emperor.[5]

Where Nü Gua smelted stones
To weld the sky,[6]
Stones split asunder, sky startles,
Autumn rains gush forth.
He goes in dreams to the Spirit Mountain
To teach the Weird Crone,[7]
Old fishes leap above the waves,
Gaunt dragons dance.[8]

Wu Zhi, unsleeping still,
Leans on his cassia tree,[9]
As wing-foot dew aslant
Drenches the shivering hare.[10]

## Song: Gossamer

In the aging leaves of weeping-willows,
Orioles feed their young,
The gossamer is vanishing,
Yellow bees go home.

Black-haired young men, and girls
With golden hairpins,
From goblets, powder-blue, are quaffing
A liquid amber.

Twilight over flower-decked terraces,
Spring says goodbye,
Fallen blossoms rise and dance
To eddying airs.
Elm-tree seeds now lie so thick
They can't be counted,
Young Shen's green money strewn along
Our city roads![1]

# Song: Returning from Guei-ji

When Yu Jian-wu was living, during the Liang dynasty (A.D. 502–57) he used to writes songs in the palace poetry style to harmonize with those of the Crown Prince. When the state was subverted, Jian-wu fled to hide from the danger in Guei-ji. Later, he was able to return home. I thought that he would have left some poems on this subject but none of them has been found. So I myself wrote this song after his return from Guei-ji to express his sadness for him.

Wilderness crumbles the yellow walls of pepper,[1]
Wet fireflies fill the palaces of Liang.[2]
Once poet to a prince in the Tai-cheng palace,[3]
I dream of bronze carriages under an autumn quilt.
Home again, Wu frost whitens my hair,[4]
My body grown old, like rushes in the pools.
Sleeplessly staring, his Golden Fish now lost,[5]
This wandering courtier must live in poverty.

## Sent to Quan Qu and Yang Jing-zhi
## When I Left the City

Warm grasses, darkening clouds, compose
Ten thousand leagues of spring.
The palace flowers bid me farewell,
Caress my face.
I tell myself that a sword of Han
Should fly away.
Why does this homeward carriage bear
Only an ailing man?[1]

## To Be Shown to My Younger Brother

Three years ago, I left my younger brother,
Already I've been home ten days or so.
Tonight we have the good wine of Lu-ling,[1]
And our yellow-covered books of long-ago.
I've managed to keep my ailing bones alive.
But in this world our troubles come in packs.
Why bother to ask who's ox and who is horse?[2]
You throw your dice, then take your "owls" or "blacks."[3]

## Bamboo

Its patterns of light ripple over water,
Thrusting into air, it greenly shadows spring.
Flowers of dew beget the young bamboo,
Its frosty roots caressed by coloured moss.
Woven into mats, it's damp with fragrant sweat,[1]
Cut into rods, it catches ornate scales.
Once it was used to make three-layered caps,
One section I present to you, my prince.[2]

## Harmonizing with a Poem Written by Shen, the Imperial Son-in-Law, Entitled: "The Waters of the Royal Canal"

Flowing through the park, white water broad and deep,
Palace ladies put on their yellow patches.[1]
Winding round hills, its dragon-bones are cold,[2]
Brushing the banks, its duck-head green is fragrant.[3]
It startles concubines from fading dreams,
Cups stop circling, little goblets float.[4]
I was lucky enough to wander for a while
Beside this wavy stream with Master He.[5]

# On First Taking up My Post as Supervisor of Ceremonies My Thoughts Turn to My House in the Mountains of Chang-gu.

Horses' hoof-prints have been brushed away,
Back from the office, I must shut the gates myself.[1]
In the long saucepan, River rice is cooking,
On little trees the jujubes flower in spring.
Up on the wall I hang my lotus-sceptre.[2]
Inspect my pointed turban by the screen.[3]
I sent my dog to carry a letter to Luo,[4]
The crane fell sick, regretting its wanderings in Qin.[5]
The tea is sealed away in earthen jars,
My mountain wine locked up with the bamboo stumps.
Nothing so fine as moonlight on a boat...
But who is punting on that cloud-filled stream?

# Seventh Night

The Shores of Parting are dark this morning,[1]
The silken bed-hangings mournful at midnight.[2]
Magpies leave the moon of threaded silk,
Flowers fill the towers where clothes are aired.[3]
Up in the sky, half of a golden mirror,[4]
Down among men, we gaze at a jade hook.
In Qian-tang city, Su Xiao-xiao
Endures the autumn of yet one more year.[5]

## Passing by the Hua-qing Palace

Spring moon, crows crying at night,
Palace screens shutting out royal flowers.
Under massing clouds red nets darken,[1]
Over broken stones slant purple coins.[2]
Jade bowls now filled with fallen dew,
Silver lamps have blackened antique silk.[3]
No news of late about the Prince of Shu,[4]
Around the springs young parsley grows.[5]

## Song: Seeing off Shen Ya-zhi
(Together with an Introduction)

In the seventh year of the Yuan-he period (812) the poet and writer, Shen Ya-zhi,[1] failed his Doctoral Examination in Calligraphy and went back to the River Wu. I was sad at his going, but had not the money to buy wine to console him. Furthermore, I was moved by his pleas. So I sang these stanzas as I escorted him on his way.

This talented man from Wu-xing[2]
Resents the winds of spring.
Peach blossom burgeons over the roads—
A thousand leagues of red!
With purple reins and a snapped bamboo[3]
On a small piebald nag,

He's riding home to Qian-tang[4]—
East, then east again.

From criss-cross shoots of white rattan,
His book-basket was woven.
Short bamboo-slips, all of a length,
Like Buddhist texts.
His flashing strength, his precious ore,
Offered to Spring Officials.[5]
He skimmed the waves beneath the mist,
Riding a single leaf.[6]

The Spring Officials garner talent
Wherever the white sun shines,
But threw away this yellow gold,
Let slip this dragon horse.
So satchel in hand, here turned to the River,
Back through his gates,
Weary and worn—yet who was there
To give him sympathy?

I hear a brave man always treasures
His heart and his bones.
Three times that ancient ran away,
Yet never lost his head.[7]
I beg you now to wait till dawn
Before you ply your whip.
Your carriage will come back one day
To the tune of autumn pipes.[8]

# Expressing My Feelings

❧

## 1

Chang-qing[1] was deep in thought at Mao-ling,
Where emerald grasses dropped by a stone well.
As he played his zither, he watched Wen-jun,
The spring breeze stirring her shadow-dappling hair.
The Prince of Liang and Emperor Wu
Had cast him aside like a snapped-off flower.[2]
All that he left was a single memorial,
Buried in liquid gold on top of Mount Tai.[3]

## 2

At dusk, when I have done with writing,
Surprised by frost, my white silk starts to fall.[4]
I laugh at myself in the mirror for a while,
How can I live as long as the Southern Hill?
I wear not urban wrapped around my head,[5]
The bitter-cork has already dyed my clothes.[6]
Cannot you see the fish in the clear stream
That drink its water and do just as they please?

# Written after the Style of a Poem by Liu Yun

To an islet where white duck weed grows,
Liu Yun comes home, riding upon his horse.
The head of the river is fragrant with quince,
Over its shores butterflies flutter about.

Wine in the cups like dew from bamboo-leaves,
Her jade-pegged lute of hollow paulownia from Shu.[1]
A waterway runs past the scarlet tower,[2]
Where the sand is warm, you'll find a pair of fish.[3]

# Song of the Sword of the Collator in the Spring Office

༄༅

Elder, within your casket glints
Three feet of water,[1]
That once plunged into a lake in Wu
To behead a dragon.[2]
A slash of brightly slanting moonlight,
Polished, cold dew.
A slash of white satin, smooth and level,
Unruffled by wind.
Its hilt of ancient shark-womb skin
Bristles with caltrops,[3]
Damasked blade, tempered with sea-bird's grease,
A white pheasant's tail.

It is, in short, a sliver
Of Jing Ke's heart.[4]
May it never shine on the characters
In the Spring Office!
Twisted sashes, whorls of gold
Hang from its hilt.
Its magic beams can cut clean through
A Blue-field jade.[5]
The West's White King was struck with fear
When it was drawn,
His demon mother wailing loudly
In the autumn wilds.[6]

## Song: A Nobleman at the End of the Night

Smoke of aloeswood curls and swirls,[1]
Crows cry the worn-out night.
Lotus among ripples in a curving pool—
White jades around the waist strike cold.[2]

## Ballad of the Grand Warden of Goose Gate

Black clouds whelm on the city,
Till it seems the city must yield.
Our chain-mail glitters under the moon,
Metal scales agape.

Clangour of horns fills the sky
With colours of fall.
Beyond the frontiers, like rouge from Yan
Night's purple congeals.
Our scarlet banners, half unfurled,
Withdraw to the river Yi,
So cold the drums, in the heavy frost,
Their sound is dulled.
We requite the king for his favours to us
At Yellow Gold Tower,[1]
Clutching our Dragons of Jade
We die for our lord.[2]

## Song: Great Dike

In Heng-tang is my home,
Red, sendal curtains redolent with cassia.
Black clouds have taught me
To pile up my hair,
Bright moons have made me
Ear-rings of pearl.[1]

A lotus wind stirs
On the spring river-bank.
Down in Great Dike
Girls linger with northerners.
"You will eat tails of carp,
While I eat gibbons' lips."[2]

Oh, do not point to
The road to Xiang-yang!
Down the river's green reaches
Few sails return.
Flowering sweet-flag today,
Withered maple tomorrow.

# Music for Strings from Shu

Maples' fragrance, twilight flowers are tranquil,[1]
In Brocade River, southern hills' reflection,[2]
Fearsome rocks are falling, gibbons wailing,
Bamboos and clouds sadden half the peaks.

Cold moon rises over autumn shores,
Jade sand glistens through translucent waves.
Who is this girl shedding scarlet tears?
She cannot bear his journey through Qu-tang Gorge.[3]

## Su Xiao Xiao's Tomb

Dew upon lonely orchids
Like tear-brimmed eyes.
No twining of love-knots,
Mist-wreathed flowers I cannot bear to cut.

Grass for her cushions,
Pines for her awning,
Wind as her skirts,
Water as girdle-jades.
In her varnished carriage[1]
She is waiting at dusk.
Cold candles, kingfisher-green,
Weary with shining.[2]

Over the Western Grave-mound
Wind-blown rain.[3]

# A Dream of Heaven

❧

The ancient hare, the shivering toad,[1]
Weep sky-blue tears,
The cloud-towers are half-revealed,
Walls slant and white.[2]
Jade wheel crushes the dew,
Wet globe of light,
Pendants of phoenix jade I meet
On cassia-scented roads.[3]

Now yellow dust, now clear water,
Below the Three Hills,[4]
Sudden the changes of a thousand years
As a galloping horse.
From far above, the Middle Kingdom
Is just nine wisps of cloud,[5]
All the clear waters of the sea
A spilt cup.

## Song for the Boy Tang
## Son of Du, Duke of Bin

Skull like jade, hard as stone,
Blue-black eyelashes.
Master Du has certainly begotten
A very fine boy.
Serious of face, pure of spirit,
A temple-vessel,[1]
With a pair of eyes that can see through men
Like autumn water.
His bamboo horse shakes its green tail
In the wind,[2]
On his short sleeves, simurghs of silver
Prance glittering.
His eastern neighbour's pretty daughter
Is in search of a husband,
With a dazzling smile he writes on air
The character "Tang."[3]
Ambitious eyes, a hero's heart
Foretell his future,
May he never forget the man called Li
Who wrote this song!

## Sealing up Green Prayers
## A Sacrifice Performed at Night by the Taoist Master, Wu

The Blue Lion kowtows and calls
To the Palace Spirits.
With a fearful howl the Dog of Jade[1]
Opens Heaven's gates.
Pomegranate-blossom in full bloom
Covers the ford.
Maidens bathe blossoms in the stream,
Dyeing white clouds.[2]

Sealing up the green prayers
We pray to the Primal Father.[3]
On the six highways horses' hooves
Run wild and masterless.[4]
From an empty sky the wind's breath comes,
Hot and impure.
Short robes and little hats
Huddle in dust.

In perfumed lanes of the Jin family,[5]
Noise of a thousand wheels,
But no one mentions the autumn rooms
Of poor Yang Xiang.[6]

I want to call up his bookish ghost
With a halberd of Han.[7]
May his rancorous bones not be interred
In a weed-grown grave!

# Twelve Lyrics for Music on the Theme of the Twelve Months of the Year (together with an Intercalary Month) Composed While Taking the Examinations in Henan-fu.

## *First Moon*

We climb a tower to greet the spring,
As spring returns newly,[1]
Smoky yellow mantles the willows,
The palace-clock drips slowly.[2]
A scant veil of lightest cloud
Stirs on the face of the wilds,
Through chill greens the desolate wind
Raises silk stubble.[3]

Asleep in her rich bed at dawn
Her jade flesh cool,
Her dewy lids, not yet in bloom,
Turned to dawn's pallor.

You cannot yet cut willow-sashes
On the public roads,
When will the leaves of the sweet-flag
Belong enough to tie?[4]

## *Second Moon*

Drinking wine in the second month
By Gather-mulberries ford.[1]
Day-lilies bloom there.
Smiling orchids too.
Like crossed swords the rushes,
Wind like incense,
Northern swallows, hard at work,
Chide the heightened spring.[2]
Curtains of roses in lingering mist
Gather green dust,[3]
Golden hairpins, high-piled tresses,
Shame the evening clouds,
With billowing dresses, they dance
In skirts of pearl.

They bid us farewell at the ferry
Singing "Water flows."
The drunkards' spines grow cold,
South Mountain dies.[4]

## Third Moon

A wind comes blowing from the east,
Filling our eyes with spring,
Willows darken in this city of blossoms,
Breaking our hearts.

Through deep halls of the storied palace
Stirs a bamboo breeze,
We dance in new collars of emerald-green,
Translucent as water.
A sunny wind bends the melilotus
Over a hundred leagues,[1]
A genial mist urges on the clouds,
Caressing heaven and earth.

Adorned like warriors, palace-girls
Closely brush on their brows,[2]
Embroidered banners wave their state
Along the warm, walled road.[3]
The wind-borne fragrance wafts away
Across the Serpentine,[4]
Pear-blossom scattered everywhere
Brings autumn to the park.[5]

## *Fourth Moon*

Cool at dawn and cool at dusk,
Trees like a canopy,
A thousand hills of darkest emerald
Beyond the clouds.

Vaguely a scented rain is falling
Through a haze of green,[1]
Glossy leaves and curls of blossom
Shining through side-gates.

Water in its golden pools,
Jade-green ripples trembling.
Vistas heavy with aging spring,
No startled petals fly.
Faded pinks and fallen calyx
Dappled in the shade.

## *Fifth Moon*

Carved jade heavy on screen-lintels,
Light gauze veils the open gates.
From leaden wells we draw the flowering water,[1]
Our fans ornate with mandarin ducks and drakes.[2]

Whirling snow dances through the Hall of Coolness,[3]
Sweet dew washes the emerald air,
Silken sleeves are wheeling and hovering,
The fragrant sweat that soaks them, jewels of grain.[4]

## Sixth Moon

We snip raw silk,
Hew speckled bamboo,
Sleeveless robes dusted with light frost,
Mats of autumn jade.[1]

A flame-red mirror opens in the east,
A haloed cartwheel journeying on high,
With a roar of flames comes the Scarlet Emperor[2]
Riding his dragons.

## Seventh Moon

Cold glint of starlight round the Cloudy Island,[1]
Upon the plate the beaded dew-drops fall.[2]
Fine flowers are born out of the tips of the twigs,[3]
Deserted gardens grieve for dying orchids.
The night-sky turns to terraces of jade,[4]
Leaves in the lotus-pool, numberless, green coins.
Vexed at the thinness of her dancing-gown

She feels a chill creep through her flowery mat.
A wind wakes sighing just at break of day,
The Northern Dipper glitters down the heavens.

## Eighth Moon

The widowed wife must dread these weary nights,
The lonely traveller dreams he's back at home.[1]
Beside the eaves insects twist their silk,[2]
Along the wall a lamp lets fall its flowers.[3]
Outside the screens, the room exhales its light,
Inside the screens, slant shadows of the trees.
Leisurely flies the dew in loveliness,
Adorning even the lotus in its pool.

## Ninth Moon

In the summer palace scattered fireflies—
A sky like water.
Bamboos turn yellow, pools grow chill,
The lotus dies.

Moonlight glints on golden door-rings,
Purposeful beams.[1]
Above cold gardens, deserted courtyards,
A limpid, white void.

Flowers of dew are flying, flying
On an unhurried wind.[2]
Kingfisher brocades in gorgeous hues
Strewn along galleries.[3]

The Cock-herald chants no longer—
Refulgence of dawn![4]
Ravens cry by the brazen well
As kola-leaves flutter down.[5]

## Tenth Moon

❧

The jade vase with its silver arrows
Can scarcely pour,[1]
Lamp-flowers smile upon the night
Where light and dark congeal.[2]

Slivers of frost dance slantingly
Across gauze curtains,
Two rows of candle-dragons shine[3]
In her winged pavilion.[4]

She lies resentful in her net of pearls,
Unable to sleep,
Beneath a robe ornate with golden phoenix
Her body is chill,
She stares at the moon, her long brows
Vie with its curved jade.[5]

## Eleventh Moon

The palace walls lie coiled and shivering,[1]
In the cold, stark light.
The white sky, shattered in pieces,
Drops diamantine fragrance.[2]

Strike the bells! Drink your fill
Of this thousand-day wine![3]
Fight to conquer the freezing cold!
Quaff the lord's health!

The royal canal is locked in ice,
Like a circle of silk.
Where is the Well of Fire?
Where are the Warm Springs?[4]

## Twelfth Moon

From the sun's feet a wan light[1]
Is shining redly.
The thin frost does not melt at all
Beneath the cassia branches.
Rarely a warmer air will try to banish
The bitter winter.
For now we run to longer days—
Farewell to the long nights.

## *Intercalary Month*

When emperors display their glory,
The years display their due seasons.
Seventy-two periods wheel about
Urging each other on.[1]
From the astronomer's jade tubes
The ashes fly.[2]
Why must this year be so long,
The coming year so late?

The Western Mother plucks her peaches,
To give to the Emperor.[3]
Xi and He let their bridled dragons
Go far astray.[4]

# A Ballad of Heaven

The River of Heaven wheels round at night
Drifting the circling stars,
At Silver Bank, the floating clouds
Mimic the murmur of water.[1]
By the Palace of Jade the cassia blossoms
Have not yet fallen,
Fairy maidens gather their fragrance
For their dangling girdle-sachets.[2]

The Princess from Qin rolls up her blinds,
Dawn at the north casement.[3]
In front of the window, a planted kolanut
Dwarfs the blue phoenix.
The King's son plays his pipes
Long as goose-quills,[4]
Summoning dragons to plough the mist
And plant Jade Grass.[5]

Sashes of pink as clouds at dawn.
Skirts of lotus-root silk,
They walk on Blue Island,[6] gathering
Fresh orchids in spring.

She points to Xi He in the east,
Deftly urging his steeds,
While land begins to rise from the sea
And stone hills wear away.[7]

# A Wild Song

The south wind blows upon the mountains,
Levelling them flat,[1]
God sends Tian Wu to sweep away
The waters of the sea.[2]
As the Queen Mother's peach-blossoms redden again
The thousandth time,
How often have Grandfather Peng and Wizard Xian
Come to their deaths?[3]

The blue-black hair of my piebald horse
Dappled with coins,
Willows of the graceful spring
Wreathed in light mist.

A girl with a zither coaxing me
To a golden goblet,
Before blood and spirit had yet congealed,
Who then was I?[4]

No point in drinking ocean-deep,
Or singing mournful songs,[5]
The finest men in this world of ours
Have owned no master.
Let me buy silk to embroider the image
Of the Lord of Ping-yuan.[6]
And then pour out a libation of wine
On the soil of Zhao.[7]

Hurrying drops of the water-dock
Choke the jade toad,[8]
The Wei girl's tresses grow so thin
She cannot bear the comb.[9]

Since autumn eyebrows in an instant
Replace fresh green!
Why must a lad of twenty
Fret life away?[10]

## Coming of Autumn

Wind in the plane-trees startles my heart
To a man's bitter grief
In guttering lamplight, spinners cry
Their cold, white silk.[1]
Who will ever read these slips
Of green bamboo,[2]
Or forbid the ornate worm[3]
To pierce its powdery holes?

Such thoughts tonight must disentwine
My knotted heart.
In the cold rain comes a fragrant spirit[4]
To console this poet.
On autumn graves the ghosts sit chanting
That poem of Bao's[5]
A thousand years in earth makes emerald jade
That rancorous blood.[6]

# Song to the Goddess

Bright moon light over Dong-ting lake
A thousand leagues around.
In the chill wind wild geese are crying,
Heaven within the water
Nine-jointed calamus lies dead
Upon the stones.[1]
Spirits of Xiang are playing their lutes,
To welcome the Goddess.

On the mountain-top, old cinnamon-trees
Waft antique scent.
A Dragon Lady chants her sorrow,
Water glints cold.
By the sandy shores where fishes swim
The Lord of White Stone[2]
Idly casts a precious pearl
To the dragon-hall.

## The King of Qin Drinks Wine

Straddling a tiger, the King of Qin
Roams the Eight Poles,[1]
His glittering sword lights up the sky,
Heaven turns sapphire.[2]

Xi and He whip up the sun[3]
With the sound of glass,
The ashes of kalpas have flown away,
Past and present at peace.[4]

From a dragon's head spouts wine
Inviting the Wine-Stars,[5]
All night the gold-groove zithers
Twang and sing.[6]
The feet of rain on Dong-ting lake
Come blown on the pipes.[7]
Flushed with wine, he shouts at the moon—
It runs back in its course.
Beneath dense drifts of silver clouds
The jasper hall glows.

The Keepers of the Palace Gate
Cry out the first watch.
In the ornate tower, a jade phoenix sings,
Faltering and sweet.[8]
From ocean-pongee, patterned in crimson,
A faint, cool scent.[9]

The yellow beauties reel in their dance.
A thousand years with each cup![10]

As fairy candle sticks waft on high[11]
A light, waxy smoke,
Eyes rapt with wine, those Emerald Lutes[12]
Shed seas of tears.

## Pearl—A Luo-yang Beauty

My Lady Pearl came down to earth
From the blue void.[1]
To a Luo-yang park on a scented wind
She flew slowly down.

Hairpins aslant in her cool tresses,
Sheen of jade swallows,[2]
Singing to the moon in her tall tower,
Beating time on a pendant.

Orchid breezes and cassia dew
Sprinkle dark, blue leaves.
Red-string music writes to the clouds,
As she sobs out her grief.[3]
Flowered jacket and white horse—
He has not come back.
Dark moth-eyebrows, double willows,
Lips fragrant with wine.[4]

Gold geese screen her from the wind,
She dreams of Shu mountain,[5]
Simurgh skirt and phoenix sash
Heavy with mist.[6]
As sunlight dazzles at all eight windows,
Her eyelids stir.

Rays of the setting sun are pouring
Through gauzy curtains.
"In the gay quarters, south of the city,
The fall is not cold.[7]
Waists of Chu, hair-styles of Wei,
Fragrant all year.
Crystal voices from throats of jade
Brush the lights of heaven.
Pulling at clouds, tugging at snow,
They detain Master Lu."[8]

# The Lady Li

Where the Purple Emperor's halls and towers
Rear their storeyed heights,[1]
Among those towers of chalcedony
The Lady has flown away.

When will the emerald incense fade
From her broidered hangings?
Blue, so blue and lustreless the clouds
Over sobbing palace waters.
Cassia flowers come fluttering down
From the autumn moon.
The lonely simurgh gives a startled cry,
As a *shang* note sounds from the strings.[2]

On the scarlet walls hang girdle-gems of jade,
Abandoned now.
Singing in the tower, the dancing-girls
Gaze into the distance.[3]
From out of the Jade Toad water drips,
The Cock-herald chants.[4]
Dewy flowers and orchid leaves
In dazzling disarray.[5]

## Song of the Horseman

I left my village with a sword
Whose edge of jade could shear a cloud.
Among the horsemen of Xiang-yang,[1]
My spirits were as spring itself
At dawn I grieved the sword's fair blade was clean,
At dusk I grieved the sword's bright gleam was cold.[2]
I hold a sword that's meant for other men:
A sword is not conducive to reflection.

# The Royal Ladies of the Xiang

Spotted bamboo lasts a thousand years,
Growing old, yet not dying.
Antique companion of these spirit ladies
It covers Xiang's waters.

Southern maidens' singing and playing
Fill the cold sky.[1]
On the Nine Mountains, tranquil and green,
Red-tear flowers.[2]
Departure of simurgh, farewell of phoenix,
In mist-hung Cang-wu,[3]
Clouds of Wu and rain of Shu,
Love reaching afar.[4]
Drearily, sadly, the spirit of autumn
Mounts the green maples.[5]
In the icy night among those waves,
The ancient dragon roars.

# Thirteen Poems from My Southern Garden

≈≈≈

### 1

Budding branches, stems of flowers,
Blossom while I watch.
Touched with white and streaked with crimson—
Cheeks of a girl from Yue,[1]
Sad to say, once dusk has come,
Their wanton fragrance falls.
They have eloped with the spring wind,
Without a go-between.[2]

### 2

North of the palace over the furrows
Full flush of dawn,[3]
Yellow mulberries, drinking dew,
Rustle on palace blinds.
Tall girls, sturdy girls stealthily
Breaking branches,
Feeding the eight-fold silkworms,
Of the King of Wu.[4]

### 3

The spinner in the bamboos
Turns his spinning wheel.[5]
A green cicada sings alone
In the setting sun.
Amber fragrant, peach-tree sap
Welcomes the summer,

I order my native gardener
To plant out melons.[6]

4
"Not yet thirty but still turned twenty,
Hungry in bright sunshine, living on leaves.
Old man on the bridge! Feel sorry for me
And give me a book on the art of war!"[7]

5
Why shouldn't a young man wear a Wu sword?[8]
He could win back fifty provinces in pass and mountain,[9]
I wish you would visit the Ling-yan pavilion,[10]
How can a student ever become a rich marquis?[11]

6
Seeking a style, culling my phrases,
Grown old carving grubs!
At dawn the moon hangs in my blinds,
A bow of jade.
Can't you see what is going on, year after year,
By the sea of Liao-dong?
Whatever can a writer do
But weep in the autumn wind?[12]

7
Chang-qing was lonely and wretched
In his empty house.[13]
Man-chian was always joking—
Too anxious to please.[14]
Better to go and buy a sword
From Ruo-ye river,[15]

Come back at dawn next day to serve
The Monkey Duke.[16]

8
First flush of waters,
Swallows with fledglings flying.
Small-tailed yellow bees come home
From flying round the flowers.
The window brings a distant scene
To my study curtains.
Fish throng round my scented hook
By river-washed stones.

9
Lying on rivers and softly sleeping
Two ducks in the sun.
I punt my little skiff slowly past
The winding shores.
Magnolias steeped in wine,
Covered with pepper-leaves.[17]
Friends help the sick man to his feet
To plant water-chestnut.

10
Bian Rang this morning was thinking
Of Cai Yong,[18]
Lying down in the spring breeze,
No heart to chant songs.
South of my house there grow bamboos[19]
For writing-slips.
When old, I'll go up-river and live
As an ancient fisherman.

11

Xi's house stands near a little peak,
By a valley-mouth.[20]
Under the white sun, a thousand hills
Look darkest green.
Roaming around in cane sandals,
Gathering honey from stones,
I pull away strands of moss
From long water-plants.

12

Black waters of the Pine Stream
Spawn new dragon-eggs.[21]
The Cassia Cave bears sulphate—
Old horses' teeth.[22]
Who has tailored Taoist robes
For this Yu Qing,[23]
Out of a length of light chiffon
Dyed with pink, mists of dawn?

13

Under small trees a path opens at dawn—
Long, thick grasses soaked by the night mist.
Willow catkins startle the snowy banks,
Wheat-rains flood the fields down by the stream![24]
Occasional boom of a bell from the old monastery,
Distant storm-clouds hang from a shattered moon.
I light a fire on the sandy shores, striking stones together—
Burning bamboo flares on the fisherman's boat.

# Song of the Brazen Immortal Bidding Farewell to Han

❦

In the Mao-ling tomb lies the lad named Liu,
Guest of the autumn wind.[1]
At night we hear his whinnying horse—
At dawn not a hoof-print there.
From painted balustrades, the cassia trees
Cast down autumnal fragrance.[2]
Over six-and-thirty palaces grow
Emerald earth-flowers.[3]

The courtiers of Wei harnessed their chariots
To travel a thousand leagues.
The vinegar wind from the eastern passes
Arrowed their eyes.
Vainly bearing the moon of Han
I went out of the palace gates.[4]
Remembering the emperor, my pure tears
Dropped down like molten lead.

Withering orchids bade them farewell
On the Xian-yang road.[5]
If God could suffer as we do
God too would grow old.[6]
Bearing my dew-plate, I journeyed alone
By the light of the cold, wild moon,
Already Wei-cheng lay far behind
And its waters faintly calling.[7]

## Ballad: Time Goes on Forever

❦

The white light returns to the Western Hills,
The jasper flower soars into the sky.[1]
When will past and present ever end?
Thousands of years have whirled away on the wind.
Sands of the sea have turned into stone,
Fish blow bubbles at the bridge of Qin.[2]
The lights in the void drift far, far off,
Pillars of bronze melt away with the years.[3]

## The Young Man with a Yellow Hat

❦

Young man with a yellow hat,
You've rowed away, not to return.
Lotus shadow by south shore,[1]
Sad, red petals drooping alone.

Water murmurs,
Lady of Xiang's girdle-jades,[2]
Bamboos weep, moon over dew-drenched hills.
On a jade zither she plays "Green Gates,"[3]
Hill-clouds drenching yellow arrowroot.[4]

Deer-parsley flowers on sand,
Autumn wind already rises.[5]
With loving care, she sweeps fine, silken mats,
Perfume wafting from warm mandarin-ducks.[6]

# Twenty-Three Poems about Horses

❧

### 1

Dragon-spine marked with strings of cash,
Silver hooves whitely trampling the mist.
No one can weave brocade caparisons.
Who will make a golden whip for him?

### 2

In the twelfth month, grass roots are sweet,
In the capital's streets, snow looks like salt.
Has he a hard-mouth or a tender?
Let's try him out with a caltrops bit![1]

### 3

Suddenly I remember that Emperor of Zhou,[2]
Urging his chariot on, up Jade Hill at a gallop.
Rattle of horse and chariot out of Phoenix Park—
Red Bayard was his favourite horse of all.

### 4

This steed is no ordinary horse
But the very spirit of the Fang star,[3]
Come forward, rap on its slender bones,
They'll ring out like bronze.

### 5

On the mighty desert, sand seems snow,[4]
Over Mount Yan, a moon like a hook.[5]

When will he ever wear a gold-headstall
Running swiftly, pure autumn under his hooves?

6

He lies there starving, a huddle of bones,
Rough coat branded with broken flowers.
From his burnt mane the red is fading,
His jagged forelock hacked by the long rope.[6]

7

The Western Mother's party is almost over,
The Eastern King is finishing his meal.[7]
Should Your Majesty want to attend the banquet
What would you harness to your carriage-shafts?[8]

8

No other man could straddle Russet Hare,
It had to be Lü Bu who rode him.[9]
But I have heard that fruit-tree ponies[10]
Can be haltered and whipped even by native boys.

9

Shu of Liao died suddenly,
So no one knows how to rear dragons.[11]
At nightfall, frost thick on the stable,
The west wind splits the thoroughbred's bones.

10

With rapid pole he crossed the River Wu,
Divine Dapple wept, breasting the wind.

"My lord has taken his sword and slain himself.
Where will I find another hero now?"[12]

11
A royal horse given to a palace lady,
Silver trappings embroidered with unicorns,
At midday, on that hill of salt,
A foundering steed is struggling through wind and dust.[13]

12
Ears like bamboo-slivers, close together,
No peach-blossom showing on its coat,
In a few years' time, it will smash a battle-line,
So take this horse and lend him to a general.[14]

13
What house owns this be-ringed young gallant?
I've heard a dead knight's bones are fragrant,
Bu he bought a bayard's bones for a heap of gold
Just to present them to King Xiang of Chu.[15]

14
Perfumed saddle-cover of fresh, scarlet sendal.
Coiled dragons' scales around his stirrups,
As he gazes all around the southern road,
How can you say he has not met with spring?[16]

15
If it hadn't gone hunting with Duke Huan,
It could never have frightened tigers![17]

One morning it will leave its fields and dikes—
Just watch it soar to brush against the clouds!

16
When Tang swords beheaded the Dukes of Sui,
Chuan-mao was the horse Tai-zong loved best.
No one gave a thought to its heavy armour,
For it was fleet enough to catch a whirlwind.[18]

17
White steel cuts down green grain,
Between mortar-stones drop tiny leaves,[19]
Nowadays people want dainty-necked ponies,
Wealthy owners fear long-toothed steeds.[20]

18
Once Bo-luo looked at this horse,
Saw its hair grow in whorls on its belly.[21]
So far they've fed it on white grass—
When will it leap across the emerald hills?

19
This horse, whose native land is India,
Brought back scriptures to Xiao temple.[22]
We know this is a noble animal
That does not want to run round Zhang-tai street.[23]

20
Your double baldric, like a swallow-tail,
Your jewelled sword like Fish-gut itself.[24]

You want a horse can run a thousand leagues?
First try looking for the gleam in its eye.[25]

21

Tying up Prancing Yellow for a while,
The Fairy climbs his coloured tower.
The groom who waits with jade bridle and whip—
Why must he be banished to Gao-zhou?[26]

22

Blood-sweating steeds came to the royal house,[27]
Following the bells, shaking jade bridle-gems.[28]
Shao-jun rode one by the sea,
Yet in men's eyes it was only a black mule.[29]

23

Emperor Wu longed to be god or immortal,
Smelting gold, he got nothing but purple mist,[30]
In his stables nothing but horses of flesh,
Not knowing how to mount the blue heavens.[31]

# Song: Bearded Shen Playing His Tartar Horn

Preface:

Bearded Shen was the servant of a northern friend of mine. This northerner, who belonged to an old and honourable branch of the Li family, was entitled to offer sacrifice in the temple of the Prince of Jiang-xia.[1] He had once committed some small offence or other, lost rank and been posted to a commandery in the north. He claims to be highly proficient in 5-word and 7-word verse: yet fame has for long eluded him. In the fourth month of this year, when I was a neighbour of his in the Chong-yi quarter of Chang-an, after pawning his clothes to buy wine, he invited me to join him in a drinking party. When our spirits were high and all of us well in our cups, he said to me: "Li Chang-ji! You can only write 7-word poems. You can't handles 5-word poems. You may force the tip of your brush to write something, but you'll never come with in miles of the verse of Tao Yuan-ming and Xie Ling-yun." [2] After I had replied to this I asked if I could write a *Song for Bearded Shen Playing His Tartar Horn*. When I'd finished my song, all the guests started shouting for us to sing it together. My northern friend was quite delighted. He stood up, raised his goblet to toast me, and then called for his concubine, Hua-niang, to come out from behind the curtain and walk up and down paying her respects to the guests. I asked her which type of music she was best at. She replied that "Peaceful and Slow" was the mode she preferred. Then we sang my verses together, while Shen accompanied us, wishing me long life with his music.

Faces glowing from your wine, sir,
We savour the sound of the reeds,
Hua-niang, her hair in careful disarray,
Wakes from her sleep behind the screen.
Who cut the flute of Perfect Peace,[3]
Bored these holes like stars in the sky?
Piercing and sudden, a wind opening blossoms,
It sends the clouds scudding through the heavens.
Tonight the flowers of our years are falling,
Breaking my heart for days beyond recall.
My passions surge as wild as waves,
I sit here startled time and time again.
The northerner rides on a white horse,
Grasping his sword with orchid-tasselled haft.
He is strong and quick as a wild monkey,
Yet catches fireflies in tumbleweed.[4]

## Song of the Old Jade-Hunter

Hunting for jade! Hunting for jade!
Only crystal-emeralds will do,[1]
For cutting into Shake-as-she-walks,[2]
Only to please the eye.
For an old man hungry and cold,
Even dragons must grieve,
The mist-hung waters of Indigo River[3]
Not clear, nor white.

On rainy nights, on the ridge of a hill,
He sups on hazel-nuts,
Blood that wells from a cuckoo's maw
The old man's tears.[4]
The waters of Indigo River are gorged
With human lives;
Men dead a thousand years
Still loathe these torrents.[5]

A steep hillside, wind in the cypress,
Whistle of rain—
On spring-dripping rocks he hangs from a rope,
Green curling and swirling,
Cold village, white thatched hut—
He frets for the children he loves,
On ancient terraces, steps of stone,
The Heartbreak grass.[6]

## Ballad of an Aching Heart

Mournfully chanting, I study the sighs of Chu,[1]
My sick bones ache in lonely poverty.
Autumnal in aspect with hair turning white,
A tree whose leaves lament in wind and rain.
The lamp burns blue, its orchid-oil run dry,
Round its fading glow the flying moths are dancing,
On ancient walls the dust grows thicker still,
The vagrant spirit mutters through its dreams.[2]

# Song: On the Lake

Girl with long eye brows crosses the sands,
Gathering orchids and iris.
Cassia leaves and smartweed spread
An ambient fragrance.
Drowsy with wine, idle all the white day
In a moored boat,
In a plum-breeze by the ferry she waves
Her singing-fan.[1]

Jade forks of her swallow-hairpins gleam
In the clear canal,
The king of Yue's handsome son
Sends her a delicate letter.[2]

Paper from Shu, wrapped in a kerchief,
Tells this cloud-haired girl,[3]
They will meet tonight when the water-clock
Has stilled its drops.

# The Caves of the Yellow Clan

Treading like sparrows, they kick up the sand
With sibilant feet,
Horn-trimmed bows a yard in length,
Arrowheads of green stone,
Jet-black banners dip three times,
Bronze drums calling,[1]
High-pitched voices shrilling like apes,
They shake their quivers.

Coloured cloth around theirs hanks, half-slanting,
On river banks their war-bands muster
Gorgeous as arrowroot,[2]
In mist-wreathed mountain tarns at dusk
White alligators boom,[3]
Bamboo snakes and flying crawlers,
Spurters of golden sand.[4]
Quietly trundling their bamboo-horses,[5]
They slowly go home,
Leaving the government armies to kill
The natives of Rong-zhou.[6]

## Song: The Screen

Butterflies lighting on China pinks—
Hinges of silver,
Frozen water, duck-head green—
Coins of glass,[1]
Its six-fold curves enclose a lamp
Burning orchid-oil.[2]
She lets down her tresses before the mirror,
Sheds her gold cicadas,[3]
Perfume of aloes from a warm fire,
Smoke of dogwood.[4]
Goblets of wine joined with a sash,
A new bride in raptures,[5]
Wind by moonlight blowing the dew,
Cold outside the screen,
As crows cry from the city walls,
The girl from Chu sleeps on.

# Walking through the South Mountain Fields

The autumn wilds bright,
Autumn wind white.[1]
Pool-water deep and clear,
Insects whining,
Clouds rise from rocks,
On moss-grown mountains.
Cold reds weeping dew,
Colour of graceful crying.[2]

Wilderness fields in October—
Forks of rice.
Torpid fireflies, flying low,
Start across dike-paths.
Water flows from veins of rocks,
Springs drip on sand.
Ghost-lanterns like lacquer lamps
Lighting up pine-flowers.[3]

## Joys of a Princess Travelling in Battle Array

Bondmaids on horseback in linked chain armour
Of yellow bronze,
Silken banners on perfumed staves
With gold-painted leaves.

In He-yang city, drunk with wine,
The leader lingers,
Her graceful Purple Swallow whinnies,
Pawing the flowers.[1]

The pink-jade general of cavalry riding
Through her vernal camp,
Shaking a whip, mounts the green void
On her galloping steed.

A pale moon over the battlements
As the horns crow out,
Though the pennoned tent is not yet open,
They share the brocades.[2]

## "After A Drinking-Party" Zhang-Che, My Elder, Once Presented Me with a Poem on This Theme. At That Time Zhang Was Serving as Adviser in Lu-Zhou.

Long-bearded Master Zhang
Is thirty-one,
A poet sent down from Heaven
With flowers for bones.
Who of our company could replace
This dragon-headed man,[1]
That a princess sent to hold
The fish-barb tablet?[2]

The green grass of Tai-hang
Has climbed your robe.[3]
Essays, memorials in your casket
Rolled tight as silk-worms:
Golden Portals, Stone Pavilion,
I know you will have,[4]
Horn of unicorn, fragrant cloves,
Dawn and dusk you'll employ.[5]

But Chang-ji of Lung-xi
Is a wreck of a fellow,[6]
Waking from drunken sleep
With unquiet heart.
Coarse, linen clothes all tattered
Though it's autumn in Zhao-cheng,[7]
Chanting poems the whole night long,
Till the east grows white.

# Verses on Being Presented with a Length of Summer Cloth by the Mountaineer of Luo-fu.

Finely-spun and well-woven,
Sky in the rain-drenched river,
An Orchid Terrace breeze that blows
In rainy July.[1]
When the ancient Immortal of Luo-bo[2]
Brings this cloth from his cave,
From thousand-year-old benches of stone,
Demon weavers wail.[3]

Venom of serpents, thick and congealed,
Soaks the caverned halls,
Fish in the river will not eat,
Standing with mouths full of sand.[4]
I want to cut a foot of sky
Out of the river Xiang.[5]
Maidens of Wu, never dare to say
Your scissors are blunt.[6]

# A Few Remarks Addressed to Huang-Fu Shih from the Jen-ho Quarter

From my father's brother I've borrowed a horse,
With a lean and hungry look,
A kinsman has lent me a house of his,
With ruinous walls.
Round its courtyard's bare and trampled earth
The rat-tracks run,
Over the fence grows a big date tree,
Its pendant reds all spoilt.

A gentleman from An-ding
Cut off his yellow ribbon,
Removed his cap-strings, shed his robe,
Drank wine day and night,[1]
He went back to his family
No white brush on his head,[2]
No wonder my reputation fell
Far behind others![3]

In vain you deigned to call me friend
I offended your eyes,
Just when you were going to haul me up,
Your strong rope snapped.
With the Luo-yang wind to escort my horse
I rode the long pass,
But before the palace gates swung wide,
The mad dogs found me.[4]

Who would believe that Jian or Du
Were careless judges?[5]
Lonely on my traveller's pillow
I watched spring grow old.
I came back home, all skin and bones,
A fleshless face,
A murrain lighted on my head.
My hair fell out.[6]

I'm going to play around with words
For the Office of Heaven,[7]
For who would pity a royal scion
Left unemployed?
Tomorrow, midway through the tenth month,
I'm heading west once more.[8]
In the Kong-tong hills I'll be far from you,
Far as the sky.

# Song of a Palace Beauty

꧖

Light of tapers, hung on high,
Shines through the gauzy air.[1]
In flowery chambers at night they pound
Red palace-wardens.[2]

The elephant's mouth puffs incense forth,[3]
My Persian rug feels warm.
When Seven Stars hang over the city-wall,[4]
I hear the clepsydra's gong.

The cold creeps in past the eaves-net[5]
As palace shadows darken.
Coloured simurghs on lintels of blinds
Bear scars from the frost.
Crying mole-crickets mourn for the moon,
Beneath hooked balustrades.
Crook-knee hinges and door-plates of bronze
Lock in this poor Zhen.[6]

In dreams I go through the gates of my home,
And walk sandy isles.
Where the River of Heaven falls to earth
Lies the Long Island road.[7]
I wish that my lord, who is dazzling bright
As the Great Light itself,
Would set me free to ride off on a fish,
Attacking the waves.

## Hall After Hall

Hall after hall, hall after hall again!
Though pink has fled, plum blossom ash is fragrant.[1]
For ten long years wood-worm have bred
In painted beams,
What hungry beetles would not eat
Piles up in broken yellows.
Orchid petals wither,
Peach-leaves grow long.
Hanging blinds of the Palace
Block out imperial light
In Hua-qing hot springs, arsenic stone
Boiling the water,[2]
Where once a white phoenix wandered,
Following her lord.[3]

## Be Sure to Take Care of Yourself
## Two Poems Written When I Escorted
## Young Li on His Way to Mount Lu.

1

No dish and platter in the wilds outside Luo-yang,[1]
Just a shaming old horse from a tumbledown stable.
The little goose will wing past Incense-burner Peak,[2]
Its shadow falling on the waters of Chu.[3]
The long boat will float moored upon clouds,
Below Stone Mirror, in the cold, autumn night.[4]
Even a man who was not sick for home
Would groan for sorrow, gazing at that moon.

2

Willows of parting at your horse's head,[5]
On the highway, ash-tree buds like rabbit eyes.
We are going to endure a thousand-league parting,
All this suffering just for a peck of millet!
Southern clouds, northern clouds,
Block off my view,
My heart-threads ravelled as spring's pendant silk.[6]
Blue eaves and wheeling trees,
Moonlight floods my bed.
In dreams I see a hungry lad off to the provinces.

Your elder brother is now turned twenty,
The mirror tells him how his beard is rowing.
Three years ago he left our home—to come to this!

Begging rice at princes' gates,
An utter failure.

In weed-grown drains, standing water
Bright as a blade,
In old willows south of the courtyard,
Cutworms breed.[7]

I worry about you, young
Traveller to the River,
Over fields of the waste the evening
Horns moan sadly.[8]

# Let Wine Be Brought In!

For a lonely failure—a cup of wine.
The host lifts his goblet, pledging our health.
Zhu-fu was too poor
To return from the west,[1]
Though his family snapped the willows
In front of the gate.[2]

Long ago in Xin-feng,
Ma Zhou was a mere retainer,
Thinking heaven was desolate, earth grown old,
None knew his worth.
Yet a couple of lines
Dashed off in a moment of leisure,
Went straight to the throne
And won him imperial favour.[3]
My wandering soul has strayed away
Long past recall,
Yet at a single cock-crow
The sky will turn white.
A young man's heart should strive to reach
The very clouds,
Who heeds a man who sits and wails
Out in the cold?

## Long Songs After Short Songs

Long songs have split the collar of my robe,
Short songs have cropped my whitening hair.[1]
The king of Qin is nowhere to be seen,[2]
So dawn and dusk fever burns in me.
I drink wine from a pitcher when I'm thirsty,
Cut millet from the dike-top when I'm hungry.
Chill and forlorn, I see May pass me by,
And suddenly a thousand leagues grow green.

Endless, the mountain peaks at night,
The bright moon seems to fall among the crags.
As I wander about, searching along the rocks,
Its light shines out beyond those towering peaks.
Because I cannot roam round with the moon,
My hair's grown white before I end my song.[3]

# Song: Do Not Dance, Sir!

Preface:
The song called *Do Not Dance, Sir!* celebrates the way Xiang Bo protected Liu Pei. The exploits of that warrior at the feast have won such fame that no one has bothered to write of them again. Among the northern and southern ballads, however, there is one song which celebrates his feat. I thought this too crude, so I wrote another song of this title.

Flowers on ancient plinths of stone,
Nine pillars in a row,
Blood of slaughtered leopards dripping
Into silver pots.
Drummers and pipers at the feast,
No zithers or flutes,
Long knives planted in the ground
Split the singing lute.[1]

Lintels hung with coarse brocade
Of scarlet woof,
Sunlight fades the rich brocade,
The king still sober.[2]
Three times Yu saw the precious ring
Flash at Fan's belt,
Xiang Zhuang drew sword from scabbard,
And stood before Liu Pei.

"Ensign! Your rank is far too low
You may not dance.[3]
Our guest is kin to the gods themselves,
A red dragon's seed."[4]
On Mang and Tang auspicious clouds
Coiled in the heavens,[5]
In Xian-yang city, the royal aura
Shone clear as water.

Iron hinges, iron barriers
Fettered the passes,
Mighty banners, five fathoms long,
Battered the double gates,[6]
"Today the King of Han possesses
The Seal of Qin.
Smash my knee-caps, disembowel me,
I shall say no more."

# Four Poems about New Bamboo-Shoots in My North Garden at Chang-gu.

❀

1

Bamboo-skin sloughs from the long stems
Like peeled jade.
You, sir, can see this mother-bamboo
Has the stuff of dragons.[1]
Just let it thrust a thousand feet
In a single night,
Leaving behind it inches of mire
By the garden pool.

2

I scrape off their green lustre,
To inscribe my Songs of Chu.[2]
Over rich fragrance, spring powder,
The black ink coils.
Tranquil or sorrowful—
Who will see my poems?[3]
Weighed down with dew, mourning in mist,
These countless branches.

3

Through gaps in the stones round our family well—
Two or three bamboo-shoots.
At dawn I glimpsed their hidden roots
Growing through a purple path.[4]
This year on the sands of spring

By winding waters,
I'll strip away the jade and green
From new bamboos.[5]

4

Ancient bamboos whose aged tips
Tease emerald clouds.
Like Mao-ling, I've come home to rest and sigh
At my pure poverty.[6]
A gust of wind and a thousand arpents[7]
Whistling greet the rain.[8]
Birds sit so heavy on this one stem
It dips into my flagon.

## She Steals My Heart

꽃

Sung Yu's vain hopes have vanished in melancholy,
What a graceful beauty she is, dusted with rose.[1]
I hear her singing among dewy spring grass,
Her gate is closed, drifted over with apricot blossom.
She rouges her mouth, a little cherry,
Pencils her brows, deep-green as cassia leaves.
At dawn by her vanity-box she makes up her face,
Night-fragrance fades from the tube in the bed.[2]
On her inlaid mirror flies a lonely magpie,[3]
On a river-view screen, waterweed is painted.
Her hair swirls up and down, a blue-black phoenix,
With golden insects quivering up on it.[4]
She is an iris brimming with clear dew,
A cattail with its cluster in purple shoots.
Black eyebrows crescent-moons, unfrowning,
Her dimples red as folded flowers.
Her heavy hair curls round her like a mist,
So slender-waisted, a breeze could break her.
She writes love-letters capped with cardamoms,
Laughing at "lotus," that secret word.[5]
Do not lock up the box of purple brocade,
Nor open the basket quilted with kingfisher feathers.
Playing with her pearls she scares the southern swallows,[6]
Burning honey she entices the northern bees.
She casts red nets dappled with white,
And hangs up gins of thin, green gauze.[7]
She teaches her lovely girls to handle money,[8]

Asks her servant from Ba what medicine to buy.[9]
On her powdered cheeks a slanting line of geese,
Moving the lamp, she broods on dreams of bears.[10]
Her feelings are not tight as tied bamboo,
The flesh of her belly is suddenly taut as a bow.
At dusk new butterflies go astray in the trees,
Fading, a female rainbow longs for a vanished male.
Long ago, a bird tried to fill in the Gulf of Chihli,
Today an old man tunnels the Kong Tong hills.[11]

From an embroidered rope long curtains hang,
Her silken skirt is tied at its short seam.
Like a dancing crane her heart flutters about,
Her bones are sticking out like a fallen dragon's.[12]
From the side of the well green lacquer drops,
The door-rings are bound with white brass.
Hugging the flowers a rabbit-track opens,
Hard by the wall, print of foxes' feet.
The light blinds are studded with tortoise-shell,
The folding screen of glass is warm.
Her ivory bed has sides of white cypress,
Her rolled jade-mat is fragrant as water-shallot.
She plays her small pipes by the curtain sat dawn
On fragrant wine-lees maple-leaves fall at dusk.[13]
"Should-have-a-son" grows in the lanes of Chu,[14]
Gardenias blossom around Golden Wall.

The open screen is rough with tortoise-shell,[15]
Her goose-feather brush soaks up the rich, black ink,
The "Yellow Courtyard" detains this Wei Huan.[16]
In the green trees she feeds the Han Peng birds.[17]

At cockcrow stars hang in the willows,
Crows cry as dew drops from the plane trees.
When this yellow-painted beauty takes her seat,
Her little sisters follow in her train.
When waxen tears have fallen, fragrance vanished,[18]
With a grass broom she sweeps the ornate lattice.
She plays an old tune on her mouth-organ,
While waiting to buy wine from Xin-feng,[19]
Sorrow thick as the grain on her short pendant,[20]
Fingers slender as chives plucking the long-stringed lute.
In the Serpentine, the ducklings are all sleeping,
In the small pavilion, the pretty maid servant dreams.
Her well-stitched mattress is sewn with double thread,
Her buckled belt has five braided tassels.

Mist from Shu flies over the rich brocade,
Rain from the gorge sprinkles her silken night dress.[21]
She rubs the mirror, shy before Wen Qiao,[22]
Flees from Jia Chong in his perfumed dress.[23]
A fish lies under a jade lotus-root,
Someone is held fast by a stone-lotus.[24]
She knits her blue eyebrows, mouth full of water,
From the terrace she sprays his horse's mane.[25]
The Governor lives in a winding street,[26]
The Guardian of the Royal Tombs dwells in Lin-chiung.[27]

A warm ball of fragrance hangs from her cassia curtains,
From brazen incense-burners, wisps of smoke.
These long, spring days, Master Wang's ways are winning,[28]
Orioles sing, so she thinks of Xie's languorous maid.[29]

The jade water-clock says the Three Stars shine bright,
By the Bronze Camels the five-horse carriages meet.[30]
Rhinoceros horn banishes fear from her gall,
Mercury calms the fluttering of her heart.[31]
She uses a bracelet to tell a man's destiny,
Strums her lute and sings of good luck and bad.
"The Royal Hour occurs on the Seventh Night,[32]
Your lover has a post in the Triple Palaces."[33]

Since I had no strength, she fed me powdered mica,[34]
Sought many prescriptions from an old medicine seller.
She sent me a blue-bird bearing an amulet,
The bag was sewn with thin, red silk.
As I passed the bridge the palace bells stopped ringing.
When my middle-aged maid awakes in the moonlight,
She will laugh to see my painted room is empty.[35]

# Five Exhortations

## 1

He-pu has no more shining pearls,
Lung-zhou has no more "wooden slaves"[1]
Enough to show us that the powers of Nature
Can never meet officialdom's demands.
The wives of Yue had not begun their weaving,
Silkworms of Wu had just started wriggling about,
When a district official came riding on his horse,
He'd a wicked face, a curly purple beard.
Now in his robe he carried a square tablet,
And on this tablet several lines were written.[2]
"If it were not for the Magistrate's anger,
Would I have come in person to your house?"

The wife of Yue bowed to the district official,
"The mulberry leaves are as yet very small.
We'll simply have to wait till the end of spring,
Then silk reels will begin to spin and spin."
While the wife of Yue was making excuses,
Her sister-in-law prepared some yellow millet,
The district official ate it, kicked over the dishes,
Then sent his petty clerks into the house.

## 2

Geniuses don't know what it is to be young—
How the sun's chariot limps upon its way![3]
Long years of striving for a double ribbon[4]

Left me with nothing more than whitened hair.
The bluebottles have long since ceased to whine
Round Jia Yi's grave by the gates of the capital.[5]
At the Cold Food Festival, with skies awhirl,
The angry landscape seems as bleak as winter.[6]
Of the twelve emperors of Former Han
Only one deserved to be called wise.[7]
Yet even he one evening listened to fools,
And ended forever his splendid reputation.

3

The melancholy of the Southern Mountain,[8]
Ghostly rain drizzling on desolate grass!
Back in Chang-an, this autumn midnight,
How many men are withering in this wind?[9]
Dim and uncertain these paths in the yellow twilight,
Tossing by the road, dark chestnut-oaks.
Moon on high, trees standing in their shadows,
The entire mountain shrouded in white dawn.[10]
Lacquer torches are out to welcome newcomers,[11]
Over lonely tombs the fireflies are flickering.

4

By now the stars have faded, heaven is high,
All nature knows another day is dawning.
Born into this world, I have to feed myself,[12]
So out of my gate I go, with burdened back.
Jun-ping was long gone and did not return,[13]
Kang-bai ran away on the state highway.
"What a rowdy place this is!" I think at daybreak.
Round the market gates, a thousand chattering men.[14]

5

At the rocks' foot, bright autumn water,
At the rocks' side, thin autumn grass.
Fragrance of wild bamboo pervades my clothes,
Countless leaves drooping luxuriantly.
Over the peaks the moon returns,
Toad-light hanging gracefully in the sky.[15]
The dewy cassia face the fairy maiden[16]
Twinkling droplets fall from the loitering clouds.[17]
Chill and lonely, the gardenia drops its seeds,
A mountain crevice weeps with crystal tears.
Down below Zhang Zhong-wei is living,[18]
Opening his books, he finds his desk mouldering away.

## In the Third Month I Pass by the Imperial Travelling Lodge

Moat water, vexed with red,
Isolates the palace.[1]
Little leaves flirt with the breeze,
Mimicking palace girls.
How many springs have they watched growing old
Hidden by hanging blinds,
Locked up here for a thousand years
Of long, white days?

## Following the Theme of He and Xie: Singing-Girls in the Brazen Bird Tower

A lovely girl pours out a bowl of wine,
Autumn landscape stretches a thousand leagues.
Stone horses slumber in the early mist,[1]
No words to fit such melancholy.
Faint singing wafts upon the wind
Rustling in the trees upon his tomb.
The tower is oppressed by their long skirts,[2]
Tearful eyes gaze at the flower-filled table.[3]

# Seeing Off the Banquet Officer Qin on His Military Expedition to the North

⸙

Melting our bow-glue, we fight northern nomads,[1]
On autumn sands at dawn, the din of drums.
Bearded tribesmen violate our borders,
Arrogant as rainbows arched on heaven.
Warships bear soldiers over Ba river,[2]
At Little Willow, our camp-gates open wide,[3]
The general gallops round on his white horse,
His gallant men display their virile mettle.
Their arrows shoot down threatening comets,[4]
Banners soar higher than the sun or moon.
Where mountains loom through bare-branched elms,[5]
Horses are whinnying, loaded down with armour.
Starlight fades from the far-off sky,
The short grass hugs the level sand.
Wind howls around the cloud-swathed beacons,
Mud fouls the snows that fall upon Jade Gate.[6]
Many a nomad Khan he has beheaded,
And planted fire in many a traitor's belly.[7]
The *Tai-chang* still enjoys his former honours,[8]
Yet has been raised to the rank of Banquet Officer.
On his precious ring a unicorn starts up,
On arrow-jars of silver, baboons howl.
Out he rides, his horse dappled with peach-blossom,[9]
Ornate silks beating against his saddle.
His arm weighed down with a dangling, gold seal,
He moistens his lips from a wine-jar of jade.

He dines on clear cheese and ant-froth wine,[10]
Washes down the purple fat with brimming cups.
His horse caparisoned with tiger-skins,
His Fish-gut sword could cleave a rhino's hide.
His fleet-foot hounds come from the Western Rong,
His slant-eyed slaves, captives from Northern Qi.
Dogs guard his tent where evening incense fumes,
Slaves watch his falcons through the weary night.[11]
Journeying to Yellow Dragon he parted from his mirror,[12]
At Green Grave his thoughts turned to Sunny Terrace.
As Zhou Chu slays the dragon at Long Bridge,
Hou Tiao plays mournful tunes upon her harp,[13]
He took two phoenix-wings from Qian-tang,[14]
His wife presented him with simurgh-hairpins.
His lady plucked a branch from a jewelled tree,
A nomad boy played the tune called "Falling Plum."
Oh, when will he return, the dragon slain?[15]

# Written in Reply

❧

1

Young gentleman with the golden fish[1]
And long lined gown,
Embroidered robe, leather belt
And square-holed jade.
The spring wind follows your horse's tail
All the way,
Willow floss beats against
The palace-lady's perfume.[2]

2

March in Yong-zhou—spring has come[3]
To the plum-blossom pool.
By the royal canal night-herons stand
In warm, white duckweed.[4]
We may well ask: "Who is that man
Plucking flowers this morning,
Singing and beating time
Down by the wine-shop?"

## On a Painting of the Walls of Yong-dong

Wheeling, the River of Heaven, day breaking bleakly,
Crows flying up from lofty battlements.
Distant sails signpost the shores of Yue,
From the cold ramparts hang the swords of Wu.
Mussels are born in the chill sunshine,
Fish-eggs spurt into the white waves.
As water-flowers spray their head-bands,
With drums and flags they welcome the night tide.[1]

# Bachelor Xie Had a Concubine by the Name of Gao-Lian Who Deserted Him for Another Man. Xie Tried to Make Her Stay with Him, but was Unsuccessful. Later She Grew Sentimental about Him. Those of Our Party Wrote Poems Satirizing and Vilifying Her. Later I Added Four Poems of My Own.

꧁❀꧂

1

Who'd ever guess that mud could dream of clouds![1]
Her hopes are dashed, pear-blossom spring is over,
She weaves glossed silk of lotus on her loom,
Cuts out a skirt patterned with lotus leaves.
In the bright moonlight my elder sister is weeping,[2]
Thinking she meets her love by a guttering lamp.
Has a golden fish hanging from his belt.[3]

2

By a bronze mirror stands a blue-green simurgh,[4]
She puts on rouge from Yan with a purple brocade.[5]
Her blossoming cheeks are brushed with dusky powder,
Cold tears invade the corners of her eyes.
Once Emerald Jade had split the melon
Her lute of jade was played by another hand.[6]
Today things aren't the same as in the past,
What man is there dare look her in the face.[7]

3

In sequestered chamber her thoughts unchecked
Do as the bee does in the hearts of flowers.[8]

Ash lies warm by the crumbling incense-stick,[9]
Her hair spreads cool beneath blue insect-pins.[10]
As night wears on, the lamp-flame gutters low,
Soundly she sleeps in the depths of a little screen.
How sweet to dream of coupled mandarin ducks![11]
South of the walls they have stopped pounding the blocks.[12]

4

As a rule, she despised Sung Yu,[13]
Today she is the wife of this Wen-ying.[14]
Halberd-handles top his dragon-stands,[15]
By the cassia window he toys with a ring-handled knife.[16]
He welcomes his guests wearing a short-sleeved gown,
While sitting upright on a folding chair.[17]
Her red silk kerchief is drenched with tears,
She watches a crow perched on the painted beams.[18]

# While Studying in Chang-gu, I Showed This Poem To My Servant-Lad from Ba

Insects were singing and the lamplight was wan,
The cold dark heavy with fumes of medicine.
You pitied the one with drooping pinions,[1]
And through his suffering went on serving him.

## The Servant-Lad from Ba Replies

My great nose goes with my mountain dress,
Your beetling brows suit your bitter songs.
If you didn't chant those ballads of yours,[2]
Who'd know how much you hated autumn?

## I Take Cui's Place in Seeing Off a Traveller

A traveller's awning under misty willows,
Horses' hooves trampling in white.
I'm afraid my friend will suddenly disappear—
How can he bear to use his whip again.[1]

## Leaving the City

Sparse cassia blossom, falling snow,
A crying crow, struck by a bolt, came home.
In a pool by the Pass, a shadow riding a donkey,[1]
His hat and tassel awry in the Qin wind.[2]
It felt so good to be back home again,
Yet he could only grieve he held no seal.[3]
The woman he loved asked him no questions[4]—
Her face in the mirror bore two streams of tears.

## Plant No Trees

❧

Plant no trees in your garden,
Trees fill four seasons with sadness.
Sleeping alone, the moon at my southern window,[1]
This autumn seems all autumns past.

## Setting Out

❧

Mats from my eastern bed are rolled away,
I'm just a misfit off on another journey.
Autumn whitens the infinite heavens,
Moon bathes the high road running past my gates.

## Four Poems Written after Looking at a Painting of the Jiang-tan Park

❧

1

Viridian dawn in the park at Wu,[1]
And palace ladies clad in gosling-yellow,
(Switches of false hair, a touch of rouge and powder)
On horseback with pearls dangling from their belts.
On the road they point to the distant Tai-cheng palace[2]—
Such fragrance from their sendal riding-skirts!
Journeying clouds drench the kingfisher carriage,[3]
Today you'd swear you saw King Xiang himself.[4]

2

Jewelled slips under thin chrysanthemum gowns,
Banana-flowers cold with clustering dew.[5]
Hair shining like water, glossy as orchid leaves.
Heavy belts patterned with knife-money.[6]
Once the horn is warm, it's easy to draw the bow,[7]
Wearing long boots makes riding difficult.
Last night their bed-curtains were wet with tears,[8]
Now powdered faces are mirrored in golden saddles.

3

Young goshawks, in slanting line, with scissored wings,
Jessed to swivels of ornamented jade.[9]
Bridles dangling, filigree-patterned with millet,
Quivers studded with carved ivory.
Baboons screaming deep in the bamboos,
Night-herons standing venerably on wet sand.
As palace servants light the hunting fires,
Flying ashes sully lead-powdered faces.

4

Ten riders clustered together like lotuses,
A red platoon all clad in palace dress.
Their scent has perfumed the magpie hounds,[10]
As they tramp Black Dragon looking for their arrows,[11]
The banners are drenched, their gold bells heavy,
Over dry frost jade stirrups dangle empty.[12]
Today they painted in their brows at dawn,
Not waiting for the bell from Jing-yang tower.[13]

# While Recovering from a Drinking-Bout in the Elder Zhang's House in Lu-zhou, I Sent This Poem to My Fourteenth Elder Male Cousin through the Agency of a River Messenger.

Only when autumn comes to Zhao-guan,
Will you know how cold it is up here in Zhao.[1]
I tied this letter to a short-feathered summons,[2]
Cut out a long screed for a recital of woes.
Through the clear dawn I slumbered in my sickness,
While the sparse plane-trees cast fresh emeralds down.
The city crows cried from white battlements,[3]
Military bugles saddened the mist in the reeds.[4]
With turban askew, I lifted the silken curtains,[5]
In dried-up pools the broken lotus lay.
On the wooden window, traces of silver picture,[6]
On the stone steps water had left its coins.[7]

The traveller's wine caught at my ailing lungs,[8]
While songs of parting rose from languid strings.
I sealed this poem with a double string of tears,
And culled a single orchid wet with dew.
The sedge is growing old, the cricket weeping,
While broken gargoyles peer from withered pines.[9]
Waking, I sit astride a horse from Yan,[10]
Dreaming, I voyage on a boat through Chu.[11]
Pepper and cinnamon poured above long mats!
Perch and bream sliced upon tortoise-shell![12]
Surely you can't forget the roads leading home,
To spend your youth on river-girdled isles?[13]

## Song: Hard to Forget

In the narrow lane, gate faces open gate.
Weeping willows droop over painted halberds.[1]
Shadows of blinds throw bamboo patterns,
Sound of a flute blowing the sunlight.[2]
Bees talk to her, circling her vanity mirror,
She paints her brows, studying spring emerald.
Clove branches, intricately interlaced,
Cover the balustrade, flowers turned to the sunset.[3]

## The Noble Son-in-Law of Jia Gong-lü

In full court-dress (robes none too long),
Flower nodding to flower on his stitched gown,
He rides his tinkling white horse,
Its head bowed down with golden trappings.

This morning perfume sickens him,
His coral pillow feels too rough,[1]
He's longing for a playful girl,
Drunk on warm sand among the reeds.

Chattering swallows tread the curtain-hooks,
A sunny rainbow emeralds the screen.[2]
When Governor Pan is in He-yang,
No girl puts death before dishonour.[3]

# Song: Drinking All Night, Asleep All Morning

Flushed with wine she leaves her seat,
As the east grows light.
The sash at her waist is half-untied,
Under weary stars.

In the willow-garden crows are cawing;
A drunken princess!
Flowers bow down beneath light dew,
Melilote's breath.
Windlass of jade and rope of silk,
Draw the dawn water,
Her powdered face, like rose carnelian,
Hot and fragrant.[1]
Drinking all night, asleep all morning,
Not a care in the world,
Beneath her curtains of southern silk,[2]
Sleeps the Emperor's child.

# Written by the Tomb of Wang Jun

No more little Dongs left in the world today—
Yet still we sing of "Dragons in the Water."[1]
White grasses, dead beneath invading mist,
Red coils of autumn goosefoot on the earth.
Ancient writing effaced from the black stones,
The green bronze spirit-sword is broken.[2]
Ploughlands rising like scales of a fish,
Tomb's slope sharp as a horse's mane.[3]
Petals of chrysanthemum drooping, wet with dew,
Dry wormwood lying on the date-tree path.
Poignant, the harsh fragrance of pine and cypress,
How many nights wind moaned these southern fields![4]

# The Traveller

An aching heart for a thousand leagues,
Sunshine warm on the rocks of South Mountain.[1]
I could not stay in the Cheng-ming Lodge,[2]
Growing old I'll be a guest of Lord Ping-yuan.[3]
Four seasons away from my ancestral temple,
Three years gone by since I left my native place.
Often I sing a traveller's song, beating my sword,[4]
Sometimes, on a strip of silk, I say I'm coming home.[5]

# After Days of Rain in the Chong-yi District

Who can he be, this sad and lonely man,
Who's come to suffer autumn in Chang-an?
Young as I am, brooding on stifled sorrows
Weeping in dreams until my hair turns white.
I feed my skinny nag on mouldy hay,
As gusts of rain splash in the chilly gutters.
The Southern Palace is darkened by ancient blinds,
Its sundials blank beneath a watery sun.[1]
My mountain home's a thousand leagues away,
East of here, at the very foot of the clouds[2]
Sleeping in sorrow, my sword-case as my pillow,
In bed at an inn I dream of a marquisate.[3]

# Feng Hsiao-lien

At a bend in the river I saw Xiao-lian
And asked her to play for me on her lute.
Though she dispels our love-lorn melancholy,
How very little she has earned today.[1]
Her skirt hangs from a belt of bamboo leaves,[2]
Mist-hung apricot-blossom soaks her hair.
The jade feels chill, the red strings heavy,[3]
She has saddled her horses and left the palace of Qi.

# Presented to Chen Shang

In Chang-an city lives a lad of twenty
Whose heart's already so much rotten wood.
The *Lànka* sutra heaped upon his table,[1]
The *Songs of Chu* piled up beside his elbow.
All his life he's bowed beneath his troubles,
When twilight falls he sips a little wine.
He knows by now the way is blocked to him,
No need to wait until his hair turns white.

Chen Shu-sheng!—you too are poor and wretched,
Shabbily clad, toiling at rites and music.[2]
You imitate the style of Yao and Shun,
Despising your fellows for writing decadent prose.[3]
By my brushwood gates, the carriage-ruts ice over,
Elms fling gaunt shadows as the sun goes down.
You come and visit me in the yellow dusk,
Bitter seasons have etched your face with lines.

Mount Tai-hua soars up forty thousand feet,[4]
Sundering the earth, it towers above us all.
Not a foot of flat ground anywhere around it,
It strikes the Ox and Dipper in a single bound.[5]
Though high officials may not sympathize
They cannot put a padlock on my mouth.
For I have taken Tai-hua as my master,
Ensconced myself there to gaze at the white day.
Frost has warped me into a stunted oak,[6]

Whom kinder weather would make a willow in spring.
The Office of Rites has forced me from my true nature,
I look haggard and worn, like a straw dog cast a side.[7]
In wind and snow, I serve at the Altar of Fasting,
My black belt threaded through a brazen seal.[8]
The work I do is fit only for slaves and bond-maids
Who want no more than to wield dustpan and brush.
Whenever will the eyes of Heaven be open
And these antique swords together give a roar?[9]

## Fishing

Fishing in a red canal at the autumn floods,[1]
I hoped to catch the Fairy's white silk letter.[2]
My lone cocoon tangled in water-chestnut thread,[3]
Beneath wild paddy a couple of fish lay low.[4]
Dangling a bamboo rod by a clear pool,
I let my long line trail through its emerald void.
A spring newt swung upon my bait
And pulled the little frog from off my hook.[5]
Fishing filled Master Zhan with boundless joy,[6]
But plunged the Lord of Long-yang into despair.[7]
I thought I saw upon the mist-wreathed shore[8]
A girl from Chu whose tears had soaked her dress.

## Poem Presented to My Second Elder Cousin (Its Rhymes Harmonizing with a Poem of His) When He Stopped Being a Messenger, Sent Back His Horse, and Went Home to Yan-Chou

To no avail you kept your yard-long blade,
They could not use your single ball of mud.[1]
Your horse has gone back to its sandy plains,
You have come home to your native land again.
Once your sad flute played the Long-tou song.[2]
Spring ashes now filter our joyful wine.[3]
Your baldric no longer startles wild-geese,
You spur on fighting-cocks in your silken robes.[4]
Long months have passed since you returned to Wu,
But do not fret, for you'll enter Ying again,[5]
You're a peach-tree in flower, a blossoming plum!
Be sure that they will beat a path to you.[6]

## Presented in Reply

You, sir, are Zhang Gong-zi himself,[1]
This lady long ago was called "Green Flower."[2]
Rich incense fumes in little elephants,
Cawing crows pair off upon the willows.
Dew lies thick on gold-spangled dresses,
A jade tree sprawls among the empty goblets.
The man selling wine in his Lute Hall
Has just bought a flower for his back garden.[3]

## Written on the Wall of Zhao's House

Your elder wife burns bamboo roots,
Your second wife pounds jade to powder.[1]
For winter warmth, you gather sticks of pine,
A thin haze, half-discerned, across the sun.
Plane trees green with moss,
Plash of water from a stony spring.[2]
Sun on your back, you sprawl in the eastern pavilion,
Peach-blossom covering your flesh and bones.[3]

# Spring Melancholy

❧❀❧

The warm sun leaves me lonely and depressed,
Blossoms only sadden this Bei-guo Sao.[1]
Elm-seeds eyed like plough-money,[2]
Willows fragile as a dancing-girl's waist.
Our baldaquins welcome the holy swallows,[3]
With flying silk we see off the shrike.[4]
Today my northern lute grows rancourous,
Quick-tongued its body of red sanders.[5]

# Immortals

❧❀❧

Strumming his lute, high on a crag of stone,
Sits an immortal sylph flapping his wings.
Whitetail-plumes of a simurgh in his hand,
He sweeps the clouds at night from the Southern Hill.
Deer should drink down in the chill ravines,
Fish swim back to the shores of the clear sea.
Yet during the reign of Emperor Wu of Han
He sent a letter about the spring peach-blossoms.[1]

# Song of He-yang

When you dye silk clothes
Autumn blue is a difficult shade to get.[1]
Like that man from Lin-chiong[2]
I am not without a heart.

Blossoms burn in Zhung-dan city,[3]
But Master Yan is old by now.[4]
I'm sorry I let those two young girls
Pluck my heart like a spring flower.

Today, I noticed their silver plaques,[5]
Tonight, they'll beat jade pendants at a feast.
Ox-heads, a foot high.[6]
You could hardly miss them, sitting there apart.
Moon rising east,
Wine circling east.[7]
Greedy mouths red on the flagons.[8]
A thousand beeswax candles shining.

# Song: An Outing among Blossoms

Preface:

On the day of the Cold Food Festival,[1] several princes, accompanied by singing-girls, went on a picnic. I was one of the party. I wrote a song called *An Outing among Blossoms* which harmonized with a poem of Emperor Jian-wen of Liang [*regnet* 549–51] and gave it to the girls to play and sing.

Spring willows on the southern path,[2]
Cold flowers degged with chilly dew.
This morning, drunk outside the city walls,
Rubbing our mirrors, we brush on our rich brows.
In drizzling mist we fret in clumsy carriages,
Red oil-cloth covers up our painted clothes.
These dancing-skirts, though perfumed, are not warm,
Our faces flush but slowly from the wine.[3]

# Spring Morning

In Vermilion City[1] they announce the spring
As the water-clock turns.
A sunny breeze stirs the lotuses
As it blows through the little palace.
Thin grass can just bear a comb,
Willows long as silk threads.
The Emperor of Qin rolls up the clothes,[2]
Swallow of Zhao brushes on her powder.[3]
Sunshine caught in painted drapes,
Bees lighting on silken mats.
Flowers on the Ping-yang rockery,[4]
Flowers in He-yang county.[5]
Wives of Yue propping up their looms,[6]
Wu silkworms spinning cocoons.
Water-chestnuts girdle the shores,
Girls with fans recline by lotus-pools.
South of the Yangzi all is joy,
North of the Passes, boundless lands.

## The Palace of Peace and Joy

By the deep well, crows rise from the plane-trees,
As the Wardrobers draw up the crystal water.[1]
Before the Prince of Shao-ling had washed his face,[2]
Long, azure waves were stirring in the vase.
When the Palace of Peace and Joy was newly built,
Its roofs were like the phoenix's outspread wings—
Circling songs, click of waxed castanets,
Zuo Guan himself to act as cup-bearer.[3]
Now green wormwood saddens these winding waters,
As mountain dogwood parts with its autumn fruits.[4]

## Butterflies Dancing

Willow catkins beat at the curtains,
Under sweltering spring clouds.
Screens of tortoise-shell
And dazzling clothes.

Butterflies from the eastern neighbour
Come fluttering to the west.
Today the young man has returned,
Riding his white steed.[1]

## A Young Nobleman of Liang

He bears the stamp of the Xiao family,
As handsome as that bullrush flower.[1]
In South Pool lotus seeds ripen,[2]
Along the Yangzi sand she waters his horse.
On royal notepaper, cold lines of silver,[3]
Coiled phoenixes across his bamboo mats.
Tao Kan's willows shade the camp[4]
Where he writes his letters to a singing-girl.[5]

## Song: Planting Tree-Peonies

꽃

When lotus stalks are but half-grown,
Thoroughwort and asarum fading,[1]
Riding our horses, laden with gold,[2]
We're off to hoe peonies.
Water drenches fragrant mud
In their crescent pots,
After one night their green chambers
Greet the white dawn.

Lovely girls chatting tipsily,
Mist-hung gardens.
Evening petals scattered by now,
Butterflies fade.
The Prince of Liang grew old and died,
Sendal robes remain,[3]
Waving their sleeves as the breeze plays
"Zithers from Shu."[4]
Wavering mists return in tatters,
Broidered awnings in shadow,[5]
Bewitching reds tumble to dust,
Favoured no more.

Master Tan and the Xie girls[6]—
Where are they sleeping?
Moon shines bright on terrace and tower,
Swallows chatter all night.

# Song: Digging a Well in the Back Gardens

Over the well a windlass turns
Upon its bed.
Slapping of water,
Faint murmur of a lute.
What sort of love am I seeking?
That of Xun Feng-qian.[1]

O sun above the city wall,
Forever stay above the city wall!
Let a single day be as a thousand years,
And never sink to rest.

# Song: Throwing Off My Sadness
## Written under Mount Hua

An autumn wind blows over the earth,
The grasses die,
Mount Hua becomes a sapphire shadow
In the chill of dusk,[1]
Though I have reached my twentieth year,
I've missed my goal.[2]
My whole heart sad and withered
As a dying orchid.

Clothes like the feathers of a flying quail,[3]
Horse like a hound,[4]
Where the road forks I beat my sword
With a brazen roar.
Dismounting at a tavern I shed
My autumn gown,[5]
Wishing to pledge it for a jar
Of Yi-yang wine.[6]

Deep in the jar I called on Heaven—
No clouds rolled back,[7]
The white day stretched a thousand leagues,
Cold and forlorn,
My host urged me to cultivate
Both body and soul,[8]
Nor care at all if the vulgar crowd
Made mock of me.

# Qin Gong

Qin Gong of the Han dynasty was a favourite slave of General Liang Ji. He was also granted the favours of Liang's wife and so gained the reputation of being arrogant and haughty. I looked into this old story and wrote a long poem on this subject comparing Qin Gong with Feng Zi-du. It is also said that long ago another poem on this subject was extant.[1]

Waving sleeves of his Yue sendal gown
Greet the spring wind,
He wears a red belt figured with jade
And patterned with unicorns.
A party on top of a palace tower,
Immortals talking,
Mouth-organs playing under awnings
In thick, scented mist.[2]

Warm wine drunk at leisure,
Spring spreads everywhere,
Flowering branches stray through screens,
The long, white day.
By the high windows of the double gallery
They count the cups they quaff, [3]
At midnight in the brazen bowls
Candles burn yellow.

Wearing a short-sleeved, low-cut robe
He's teaching a parrot to talk,

In purple brocade and flaxen shoes
He treads on a roaring tiger.[4]
Burning cassia in golden braziers
He prepares for a banquet at dawn,
Up till midnight boiling clear cheese
From rare, white deer.[5]

In eternal galleries of flowering paulownia
He tries out a new horse,[6]
Great screens in the inner rooms
Adorned with living pictures,
He opens the gates and squanders the gold
From the emperor's private purse,
He rolls up this Yellow River,
And pours it over himself.[7]


Even high heaven was once unlucky
And split and broke,[8]
But Qin Gong spends his whole life
Under the flowers.
He goes off with her simurgh comb,
Nor will he give it back,[9]
Sleeps drunkenly on the Persian rugs
In the moonlit hall.

# "Ballad on the Boys by the Walls of Ancient Yeh" An Imitation of Wang Can's Satire on Cao Cao

In the city of Ye
Dust rises at dusk.
Those drawing black balls
Behead civil servants.[1]

Brambles for whips,
Tigers for horses,
Running in packs
Under Ye's walls.

Swords to cut jade,
Sun-shooting bows,[2]
Presented to whom?
Why, to the Minister.

Propping his chariot-hubs
Boys from west of the Pass.
Sweep the roads with perfume!
The Minister comes home![3]

## Singing of Yang's Purple Inkstone with a Green Pattern

Stone-masons of Duan-zhou, subtle as spirits,
Trod the sky, hewed purple clouds with polished knives.
How true they trimmed the well of stone
That brims to its lips,
Darkly soaked with cold stains—
Blood of Chang-hong.[1]

Silken curtains warm in daytime,
Ink-flowers in spring,
A floating froth in airy bubbles
Fragrant with pine and musk.[2]
Ink dry or oily, thick or thin,
Its feet stand firm.[3]
Just a few inches of autumn sunshine
That dusk cannot touch.
Often the round brush whispers on
The stone, forever new.
Master Kong's inkstone, broad and stubborn,[4]
Was no match for this.

## Thoughts in Her Chamber

New cassia-crescent like a lady's brow,[1]
The autumn gusts blowing down little emeralds.
Sound of the traveller's wheels leaving our gate,
Jade simurgh-bells tinkling intermittently.[2]

Wind-blown dew drops on the moonlit verandah,
The courtyard bleak and lonely in the dawn.
Who could endure such loneliness?
Lying awake, I listen to the crickets' tears.[3]

# Dawn in Shih-cheng

The moon is setting over Great Dike,[1]
Up from the battlements fly the roosting crows.
A fine dew soaks the crimson spheres,[2]
Their cold scent clears the drunken fumes of night.

Lady and Herd-boy cross the River of Heaven,[3]
Misty willows cover the coigns of the walls.
A noble guest leaves her a torn-off sachet[4]—
She knits the emerald smudges of her brows.

Spring curtains of cicada-wing gauze,[5]
Half-seen,
Her bed awaits, vaguely patterned,
With golden flowers.
Catkins flying in front of the curtains,
Feathers of geese—
Images of her heart in spring,
What else?

# Lament That the Days Are So Short

Flying lights, flying lights,[1]
I pledge you a cup of wine.
I do not know if the blue heavens are high,
The yellow earth is rich,
I only see cold moon, hot sun,
Both come to plague us.
Eat bears and you'll grow fat,
Eat frogs and you'll grow thin.[2]
Where is the Spirit Lady?
Where the Great Unity?[3]

East of the sky stands the Jo tree,[4]
Under it a dragon with a torch in its mouth.[5]
I'll cut off the dragon's feet,
And eat the dragon's flesh.[6]
The morning will not come back again,
Night will not stay.
So old men will not die,
Nor young men weep.
Why should we swallow yellow gold,
Or eat white jade?[7]

Who is Ren Gong-zi
Riding a white donkey through the clouds?[8]
Liu Che lies in the Mao-ling tomb,
Just a pile of bones.[9]
Ying Zheng lies in his catalpa coffin—
What a waste of abalone.[10]

# Second Year of Chang-ho

Coiled clouds above our fields,[1]
A soughing wind.
Ears of wheat like brushes,
Millet like corn.[2]

For every man in the Pass
A hundred jackets,
Officials east of the Pass
Never shout for taxes.

Strong, young oxen plough in spring
The rich, black earth.
Bullrushes grow in thick clusters
By veins of water.
Since they have courteously
Returned our land-tax,
We can spend a hundred cash
On strolling lute-players.
We roam in springs' radiance,
White flowers on the hillsides,
Burn incense in the wild woods,
Call spirits down to the mats.

We worship the spirits to win long life
For the Emperor,
Till the thread of the Seven Stars snaps
And the Moon Goddess dies.[3]

# Returning to Chang-gu in Spring

I started studying when I reached my teens,[1]
Regretting I had left my plans too late.
Before Zhang Jun earned his official carriage
This Yan-zi's hair turned prematurely white.[2]
The net of Heaven, though truly wide and high,[3]
Trammelled this stubborn man in endless trouble.
My eyes had feasted upon sweet delights
My homeless heart found bitter as the smartweed.
Then came the fiery clouds of March and April,
Their peaks and crags whelming and toppling.
Who hung on high that bowl of crimson jade,
Flooding the eastern sky with reddest fire?
In that hot spring I raised my parasol,
Buds on the roadside elms still rabbit-eyes,
My brain on fire, my sickness on my face,
Gall filled my mouth, cramp twisted my guts.
There in the capital my heart was shattered,
Even in dreams I rarely saw my home.[4]
My brakes released outside the Eastern Gate,
Sky and earth stretched infinite before me.
Green trees were burgeoning atop Mount Li,[5]
A flowery wind invaded the Qin roads.
The palace towers, in dazzling disarray,[6]
Unfurled in painted scrolls on peaks and crags.
Tender, green leaves, rondures of scarlet blossom,
Weeping and smiling, strewn along my way.
Down to that plateau perfumed breezes wafted,[7]
Saddle and horse glittered in ornate splendour.

But I rode alone, in a hencoop of a cart,
Aware that I was clean out of the fashion.
Deep in my heart Substance held talk with Shadow.
Could I be happy journeying all alone?
Surely I could not lay aside my burden,
I'd tried to be a swan, but lost my luck.
Under the gloomy shades of Mount Tai-hua,[8]
Where ancient cypresses plant soldiers' banners,
I rode past dragons' hides strung out in lines,
And ever-fluttering wings of kingfisher-blue.[9]
Though faint and weary from my wayfaring,
The scenery still wrung a smile from me.
Flowering vines caught at my curving yoke,
Thin, silken mist shrouded the sunken trail.[10]
A fine, young man—a fine, young failure too—
I'm home to bring my aged mother shame.
Listening to a sutra, I pace beneath great trees,
Reading a book, I walk by a winding pool.
I realize I'm no tiger loosed from cage,
Rejoice to be a panther veiled in cloud.[11]
Stringed arrows bring the birds of Han to earth,
Fish-baskets catch the dace of the River Xiang.[12]
This narrow path leads to no broad highway,
Why must a man fret over petty things?

# Chang-gu (A Poem Written on the Twenty-Seventh Day of the Fifth Month)

❧❧❧

Paddy fields at Chang-gu, in the fifth month,
A shimmer of green covers the level water.
Distant hills rise towering, crag on crag,
Precarious greenery, fearful of falling.[1]
Dazzling and pure, no thoughts of autumn yet,
A cool wind from afar ruffles this beauty.
The bamboos' fragrance fills this lonely place,
Each powdered node is streaked with emerald.
The long-haired grass lets fall its mournful tresses,
A bright dew weeps, shedding its secret tears.
Tall trees form a bright and winding tunnel,[2]
A scented track where fading reds sway drunkenly.
Swarms of insects etch the ancient willows,
Cicadas cry from high sequestered spots.
Long sashes of yellow arrowroot trail the ground,[3]
Purple rushes criss-cross narrow shores.
Stones coined with moss lie strewn about in heaps,
Plump leaves are growing in glossy clusters.
Level and white are the wave-washed sands,
Where horses stand, printing dark characters.[4]
At evening, fishes dart around joyfully,
A lone, lean crane stands stock-still in the dusk.
Down in their damp, mole-crickets chirp away.
A muted spring wells up with startled splash.
Crooked and winding, Jade Purity Road,
Where the Divine Maiden dwells among orchid blossoms.[5]

Cotton-moss winds around the stones in the stream,
Crimson and purple, mountain fruits hang down.
Small cypresses with leaves like layers of fans,
Plump pines oozing essence of cinnabar.
A singing stream runs on melodiously,
Ripe wheat on the dike trails its glowing head.
Orioles trill songs of a girl from Min,[6]
A waterfall unfurls satin robes from Chu.
Windblown dew fills laughing eyes
That blossom or wither in crannies and clefts.
Tangled branches jut from stony heights,
Tiny throats chatter by an island spring,
The sun's rays sweep aside the shadow of dusk
New-risen clouds open their ornate deeps.
Pure and still, these oppressive summer days,
Yet a west wind whispers of a cooling air.
Luminous, on high her jade-white face
As I burn cinnamon on the Heavenly Altar.
Her robes of mist are fluttering in the night,
She drowses by Her altar, pure of dreams.
The simurghs have aged, awaiting the Emperor's carriage,
The pepper-walls of the ancient palace are ruined.[7]
Yet several of the bells still tinkle faintly,
Arousing this wandering courtier to desolate thoughts.
Dark creepers twine about the scarlet bolts,
In dragon-curtains lurk the mountain trolls.
Flowering tamarisk clings to emerald brocades,
These scented quilts served nobles long since dead.
No songs now stir the dust on worm-eaten beams,
Where dancers' coloured robes hang like long clouds.

This precious land is cut from fissured silk,
Our villagers prize truth and righteousness.
No sound of pestles is heard when a neighbour mourns,
No evil rites are used to drive off plagues.
The fish-skinned oldsters, virtuous and kind,
The horn-haired children, modest, quick to shame.[8]
The county justices have nothing to do,
No dunning tax collectors call on us.
In bamboo groves we repair our tattered books,[9]
From stony jetties drop in the hook and bait.
Winding rivers girdle us with water,
Banana leaves are slanting paper from Shu.
Light on the peaks, a dazzling silk collar,
The setting sun brushes away my cares.
Our springs are beakers of Governor Tao's wine,[10]
Our moon, the brow of Xie's singing-girl.[11]
Clang of a hidden bell far away
On high, a solitary bird wings home.
Rose-mist pinnacles, red and black peaks,
High cataracts roaring as they contend.
Pale moths floating in calm emerald,[12]
A veiled moon, distant, faint and sad.
Its cold light penetrates the river gorge,
Infinite my thoughts among these mountains.
The fisherman's boy lowers his midnight nets,
Frost-white birds soar up on misty wings.
On the pool's mirror, slippery spume of dragons,
And floating pearls exhaled by fishes at play.
Windy *tong* trees, lutes in jasper cases,
Fire-flies' stars, envoys to Brocade City.[13]

Willows join their long green sashes,
Bamboos quiver, short flutes playing.
The base of the crag emerges from green moss,
Reed-shoots are peering from the cinnabar pond.
Ripples and eddies sport with sky's reflection,
The hands of ancient junipers grasp the clouds.
The mournful moon is curtained with red roses,
Thorns of fragrant creeper catch the clouds.
The bearded wheat lies level for hundreds of leagues,
On the untilled acres stand a thousand shops.
This man from Cheng-ji, restless and fretful,[14]
Would like to emulate Master Wine-sack's ways.[15]

## Lament of the Brazen Camels

꧁꧂

At the end of the third month, out of office and poor,
I went to the eastern suburbs in search of flowers.[1]
Who was it wrote a farewell song to spring?
The brazen camels lament on the banks of the Luo.

South of the bridge are many riders on horseback,[2]
The northern mountain is girdled with ancient graves.[3]
While men are quaffing cups of wine,
The camels sit and mourn ten million springs.

Useless to toil away in this life of ours,
It's only a wind-blown candle in a bowl.[4]
Tired of seeing peach-trees smile again,
The brazen camels weep as night comes on.

# I Journey from Chang-gu and Arrive at Luo-yang through the Rear Gate

꧁ꕥ꧂

In the ninth month, the great wilderness is white,
And azure peaks rear up their autumn portals.
In the bitter cold of the tenth month's ending,
Snow and sleet confound both dawn and dusk.
The sky stays steely-grey throughout the day,
My heart feels like the clouds that clog the air.
Along the road, wind blows a thousand leagues,
The wild bamboos are scarred with snaky venom.[1]
From stony ravines, the sound of freezing waves,
A cock crows out in the cold of a clear dawn.
I keep pushing on till I reach my house in the east,
Turn loose my horse, then rejoin my old neighbours.
My eastern neighbour's personal name is Liao,
In our district he carries on the line of Xin.[2]
The money on my staff is not for wine,[3]
I need it for a visit to this fellow.
At first I wanted to go south to Chu,
Now once again I am heading west to Qin.
As for the king called Xiang and Emperor Wu,[4]
Both of them wanted to stay young forever.
I have heard tell that to the Orchid Terrace,
Song Yu's soul will never return again.
Among twin rows of characters in blue and light-yellow,
Torpid insects have eaten the autumn rue.
What of my future among the towers of Qin?
Will it be my fate to carry firewood there?[5]

## On the First Day of the Seventh Month at Dawn I Enter the Tai-Hang Mountains

꿈꿈

In just one night autumn invests the hills
Fragrant dew bathes dodder and royal-grass.[1]
New bridges cling to cloud-hung slopes,[2]
Seasonal insects cry in dewy groves.
By now I'm far from the south of Luo-yang,[3]
How can I lie snug in my Yue quilt?
The rock's breath chills me to the bones,[4]
The aging sedge looks like short arrow-heads.

## Autumn Cold: A Poem Sent to
## My Twelfth Elder Cousin, the Collator

Shutting the gates, I feel the autumn wind—
My loneliness is due to our long parting.
Beneath a white sky the great wilderness stretches,
A killing blast sweeps the wide heaven and earth
Shining dew weeps over withered orchids,
Cry of insects sounds out night and day.
In my cold room the candle-stump burns dim,
My red silk curtains tattered by the wind.
I open my books to the old scent of rue,
Sing resentfully now your handsome face has gone.
For a hundred days we have not seen each other,
Bright flowers fade in this bitter season.
Of all my brothers, who worries most about me?
I already have the letter you sent to me.
Clad in blue jacket, riding a white horse,[1]
You send your drafts up to the Eastern Gate-towers.
In my dream we are laughing together—
Then I wake to a half-moon over my bed.
Endless my thoughts, like a bracelet on my wrist,
My sorrows run wild like spreading arrowroot.

## Mowing Grass and Setting Our Nets

In cloak of brocade,
And broidered suit,
How busily you drink and peck,
Feeding your fledglings!

East of the dike, ripe grain lies flattened
By wind and rain,
Don't listen to the decoy bird
West of the dike!

Men of Qi have woven nets
Limpid as air,[1]
Strung them out in the wild fields'
Level emerald.
Silken nets spread far and wide,
Without shape or shadow,
Run foul of them, your head will wear
A scarlet wound.

Who gathered this gay greenery
Of moxa leaves?[2]
You cannot guess at the cunning trap
Hidden within.

## Music Rising to the Clouds

Flying fragrance, running reds—
It seems spring fills the sky.
Flowery dragons coil and writhe,
Up to the purple clouds.[1]
Some three thousand palace girls,
Living in golden rooms,
Fifty-string zithers sounding out
To the shores of the sea.[2]

The Heavenly River is shattered—
A road of silver sand.
The Ying girls at their loom
Cut misty, white silk,[3]
Then sew their dancing gowns.
On the first day of the eighth month
They dance before their lord.

# Mo To Lou Tzu

From Jade Pass to the Golden Man[1]
Is twenty-four thousand leagues.
Wind swirls sudden clouds of sand
Over the waters of Liao.[2]

A white sky, water like raw silk,
Our armour's double thread broken.
"May no hardship mar your journey!"
A fading crescent over the Wall.

Northern mists rising in chill of dawn,
Nomad horses mincing on little hooves.
The travellers come to the sundering stream,
The river Long parts them, stretching east and west.[3]

# Ballad of the Savage Tiger

No one attacks it with a long lance,
No one plies a strong cross-bow.
Suckling its grandsons, rearing its cubs,
It trains them into savagery.
Its reared head becomes a wall
Its waving tail becomes a banner.
Even Huang from the Eastern Sea,[1]
Dreaded to see it after dark,
A righteous tiger, met on the road,[2]
Was quite enough to upset Niu Ai.
What good is it for that short sword
To hang on the wall, growling like thunder?
When from the foot of Tai mountain
Comes the sound of a woman weeping,
Government regulations forbid
Any official to dare to listen.[3]

# Ballad of the Rising Sun

The white sun sets below the Kun-lun range,[1]
Its rays so many silken threads unravelled.
It merely shines on the sunflower's heart,[2]
It never lightens up a traveller's sorrow.

The Yellow River curves and winds about,
The sun wheels straight across the sky.
I've heard the sun comes out of Sunny Valley,[3]
I've never seen the Ruo-tree, where it sets.[4]

No stopping you from smelting rocks,
But why melt men away?
If Yi could bend his bow and shoot an arrow?[5]
Then why could he not hit the sun-crow's foot,
So that the crow would never fly again,
So that the fire would never move at all?[6]
Why must it glare at dawn, grow dim at dusk?

# Bitter Bamboos: A Diao-xiao Ballad

A word or two about the days
When Xuan-yuan reigned.[1]
Ling Lun cut bamboos
Four-and-twenty of them.
Ling Lun gathered them
Upon the hill of Kun.
Xuan-yuan ordered him
To halve them, making twelve.
Thus Ling Lun regulated
Musical pitch,
And with this Xuan-yuan
Ordered the Primal Breaths.[2]

When the Yellow Emperor
Ascended into heaven,
Three-and-twenty pitch-pipes
Followed in his train.
Only a single pipe remained
For men to play,
Yet since they lacked virtue
This pipe was not for them,
So it was buried deep
Within the shrine of Shun.[3]

## Lyric for the Duster Dance

Songs of Wu maidens rise to the heavens,
Across the sky unhurried clouds go drifting.
And yet one day the emerald moss must grow
Outside these gates where horse and carriage throng.

This goblet brimmed with Wu-cheng wine,[1]
Will spur you on to live a million years.
Better than Emperor Wu in his ornate tower,[2]
Gazing at dawn on a clear, cold sky
And sipping dew from flowers.

Suppose the sun stood always in the east,
In heavenly radiance never in decline?
By eating cinnabar you may become
A serpent riding a white mist,
A thousand-year-old turtle in a well of jade.[3]

Can't you see yourself transformed to snake or turtle
For twenty centuries,
Dragging your life out, year after year,
On the grass-green dikes of Wu?

Eight trigrams on your back,[4]
Blazoned "Immortal."
Your cunning scales,
Your stubborn armour,
Slimed with a fishy spittle!

# Song: Sitting through the Night

Clatter and clatter of horses' hooves—
But who will visit me?
My eyes watch the Northern Dipper stand
In the River of Heaven.
The west wind ripples my awning of gauze,
Kingfisher-green.
As leaden flowers bloom on my face,
I knit blue brows.[1]

For you I rose and sang my song,
Long thoughts of love.
Outside the screens, in bitter frost,
All falls and flies.
The shining stars are glittering
On the eastern bounds.
Red mists of dawn come creeping forth
From the southeast shores.
Now Master Lu has ridden away
On his dappled horse.[2]

## Song for Vertical Harp

Oh, where are you off to, sir, with your wine-jug?
Qu Ping drowned in the Hsiang,
Don't be like him!¹
Xu Yan plunged into the sea—
He was really a fool!²
There are mats of sedge upon your beds,
Fish in the bowls.
Your elder brother lives in North Village,
Your eastern neighbour has a young sister-in-law,
Millet and Indian rice grow thick
In the fields round the dike,
Flecked with light foam, the cloudy wine
Fills all your wine-jars.
Come eat the millet,
Drink the wine—
Oh, what are you trying to do!
Why are you rushing wild-haired into the water?
Your brother and the girl are weeping bitter tears.

# Mount Wu Is High

A cluster of emeralds
Piercing high heaven!
Over the Great River's swelling waves
Spirits trail their mist.
The King of Chu's soul sought a dream
In a bitter wind.
In dawn wind and flying rain,
Grow coins of moss.
The Jade Princess has been gone
A thousand years,
Amid lilac and Sichuan bamboos
Old gibbons wail,
Her ancient shrine is close to the moon's
Chill toad and cassia,
Pepper flowers shed scarlet petals
Among drenching clouds.

## Under the Walls of Ping City

Hungry and cold, under Ping City's walls,
Night after night we guard the shining moon.
Our farewell swords have lost their sheen,[1]
The Gobi wind cuts through our temple-hair.[2]

Endless desert merges with white void,
But see—far off—the red of Chinese banners,
In their black tents they're blowing short flutes,
Mist and haze soaking their painted dragons.

At twilight, up there on the city walls,
We stare into the shadows of those walls,
The wind is blowing, stirring dead tumbleweed,
Our starving horses whinny within the walls.

"Just ask the builders of these walls
How many thousand leagues from the Pass we are?[3]
Rather than go home as bundled corpses
We'll turn our lances on ourselves and die."[4]

# Pleasures South of the Yangzi

Green mist over the River,
Cold waves rising
Skywards, crag is heaped on crag,
Jagged red rocks.[1]

Wind on water, clouds on shore,
Ancient bamboos.
From the darkening beach a rush-sail seems
Just a strip of cloth.
We have a thousand gobies,
A hundred kegs of wine.
Sprawled flat among the wine, we see
Green southern hills.
Catches of Wu, ballads of Yue—
Our songs never stop.
Over the River a cold jade is pasted,
Round as a ball.[2]

## Joys of the Rich

A young, owl-shouldered nobleman
Just turned twenty,[1]
Teeth like cowries,
Scarlet lips.

Rainbow-spirited,
Could drink like a rain-jar!
Galloping homewards at night
Past watchmen calling the hours.

He'd go straight to the Palace galleries,
Wander through the Pepper Apartments. [2]
Motley furs and golden rings
Gleaming with ornate patterns.[3]
Laughing and flirting in jade halls
With girls from gold houses,
Playing, mimicking under the stage
The Han-dan singing-girls,[4]
Singing and telling stories,
The perfect ladies' man.
All brocade sleeves and embroidered face
He came to the emperor
Who presented him with ten bushels of pearls
And a pair of white jade rings,
Bestowing on him a new, gold seal
Dangling from a purple sash.
Resplendent!

Horses flying past!
Rivers of people!
Nine Ministers, six Officers,
Eyes fixed on his shoes.
Did he want the sun and moon to spin?
He turned his palm around.
Or did he want a river?
He drew a line on the ground.

His towering, high-cornered hat
Seemed to cut the clouds,
As he hurried along at dawn,
Rattling his sword,
Cleaving the purple mist.
He would give mere lictors a thousand yards
Of embroidered silk,
And present a thousand pounds of gold
To household servants.

Around the twelve gates of Luo-yang
His mansions sprawled,
Through warm, spring air to the sapphire sky
The slow smoke crawled.
Golden door-rings threw back the sun's
Dazzling red light.
Brazen dragons, mouthing rings,
Writhed locked in fight.
On perfumed mats his jewelled girls
Lounged drunkenly,
Merman-pongee netted his casements

Invisibly.
He'd dine on a phoenix from Cinnabar Hill
When he wished to "rough it,"[5]
As for *potage aux petits macaques*,
He'd never touch it.[6]

Golden toads with gaping mouths
Burnt fragrant,
orchid candles,
Singing-girls in battle-array,
With jangling armour.
Nobody knew if the blossom-rain
Had fallen at night,[7]
Only that spring grass grew more lush
By the terrace pools.

Clamour of strings and pipes encircled
The gaping heavens,
The sound of Hong Yai's flute came stealing
From the azure void,[8]
A single arrow shot at the welkin
Pierced two tigers,
They held the reins, let their steeds gallop on
Among the clouds,
Thunder from a rainless sky!

Wild sleeves criss-cross like bamboos,
Flute-girls were dancing,
Singers from Wu, like green parakeets
Just learning to talk.

He was wealthy enough to fill a cave
With purple gold,
Yet asked for presents of rare costly rabbits
Burnt with his brand.[9]

Three empresses,
Fifty colonels,
Seven noblemen,
A pair of generals—
All from his family.
Though these once gorgeous clouds dislimned
And flew away,
Translated to our capital
They brought us spring today.[10]

# Let's Drink Wine

Xi and He gallop their six steeds[1]
Days and nights leave us no leisure,
Chasing the crow to Mount Yan-zi's bamboos,[2]
They flog their horses with a Coiling Peach whip.[3]
Ru Shou no sooner breaks the kingfisher willows
Than the Green Emperor creates red orchids again.[4]
Millions of years have rolled by
Since Yao and Shun,
And no king halted his chariot more than a moment.
Green coins, white jade-rings cannot buy time.
We should be merry, make the most of the present.
Turtle-soup and bears' paws—why bother with them?
Let's drink the North Sea out of flagons,
Cross-legged on South Mountain,
Sing loud and long
To the low lilt of flutes,
Bestowing gifts of tattoo gold[5]
For the amorous glances of singing-girls.
This is life at its best!
Why struggle to fathom the mind
Of the Creating Power?[6]

Let's urge each other to drink,
Drink without stopping.
May the Emperor's great name
Endure without end!
His sons and grandsons spread abroad
Like arrowroot on rocks!

From Luo-yang to Chang-an
Stretch lines of carriages.[7]
Liang Chi's ancient mansion![8]
The old gardens of Shih Chong![9]

## Delights of the Jasper Flower

High-King Mu
Urged on his dragon-steeds,[1]
Eight bridles jingling
As they drove round the heavens,[2]
Five planets swept the earth for him,[3]
Thick clouds rolled back.

Upon the high gates left and right
Sun and moon were door-rings,
On all four sides rich filigree
Rose in blood-red tiers,
Rosy mists with drooping tails,
Coiling around.
Limpid as a river, chaste as the sea,
The face of the Spirit Mother.
Painted with rouge and brushed with green—
Mirrored in the Sunset Pool![4]
Clothed in clouds, and trailing jade,
She descended Kun-lun mountains,
Pennons arrayed like pine trees,
Awnings spread like wheels.
The metal wind ends autumn,[5]

The Pure Brilliance starts spring.
Eight horse-bells for each of ten carriages,
Fabled horses like gathering clouds.
Jade cups on jewelled mats,
Degged with sweet dew,[6]
Black Frost and Scarlet Snow
Not worth a mention.[7]
I shall present to you,
"Perfumed Plum, Dyed Willow,
And Lead-flower Water
To wash your very bones.
Here I shall sit with you
While you grow immortal."

## Cold up North

One quarter lowers black while three turn purple,
Ice vaults the Yellow River, fish and dragons die.
Tree-bark three feet thick splits against the grain,
Chariots of a ton or more travel on the river.

Frost-flowers on the grass, big as silver coins,
No brandished blade could penetrate this sombre sky.
Swirling in a raging sea the flying ice-floes roar,
Soundless hang mountain waterfalls, rainbows of jade.

# Reflections on the Ancient Terrace of Liang

Terrace and pool of the Prince of Liang
Rear out of empty air.
The waters of the River of Heaven
Fly down to them at night.[1]
In front of the terrace, mortised jades
Form scaly dragons.
Green-powdered bamboos sweep the sky,
Grieving, damp with dew.

To the chime of bells he drank his wine,
Shot arrows at heaven.[2]
Golden tigers crowded his furs,
Dappled with spurted blood,[3]
Dawn after dawn, dusk after dusk,
He mourned that the seas spun round.
To a long rope he tethered the sun,
To fill his years with joy.

Lotus flowers' clotted crimson
Faded with fall.
Orchids' faces wept endless tears,
Parting from spring.
On reedy isles the migrant geese
Announced spring's return.
By the wild lands' desolate waters
Vast autumn gleamed white.

# Do Not Go out of Your Gate, Sir!

Heaven overcast,
Earth in shadow.
Nine-headed serpents devouring men's souls,[1]
Snow and frost snapping men's bones
Snarling dogs, barking
Hunt us down,[2]
Licking their paws, greedy for the flesh
Of the man with an orchid girdle.[3]
Once God sends a chariot to bear you away,
Your misfortunes will end.
His sword adorned with stars of jade,
His yoke of yellow gold.

Though I have a horse to ride,
I cannot go home,
For the waves that drowned Li-yang
Loom large as mountains.[4]
Poisonous, horned dragons glaring,
Rattling their brazen rings.[5]
Lions and griffons drooling[6]
From slavering jaws.
Bao Jiao spent his whole life
Sleeping under straw.[7]
Yan Hui's hair was mottled white
When he was twenty-nine.[8]
Yet Yan Hui's blood was not corrupt,
Nor had Bao Jiao offended Heaven.
Heaven was afraid the jaws would close on them,

So it treated them thus.
If you still doubt my discernment, sir,
Think of the man raving wildly by the wall,
As he wrote his "Heavenly Questions."[9]


## Song of the Magic Strings

As the sun sets in the western hills
The eastern hills grow dark,
A whirlwind blows the horses along,
Steeds trampling the clouds.[1]
Painted zithers and plain flutes
Play soft, weird tunes,
To the rustle of embroidered skirts
She treads the autumn dust.[2]

Cassia leaves stripped by the wind,[3]
Cassia seeds fall,
Blue racoons are weeping blood
As shivering foxes die.[4]
On the ancient wall, a painted dragon,[5]
Tail inlaid with gold,
The Rain God is riding it away
To an autumn tarn.
Owls that have lived a hundred years,
Turned forest demons,[6]
Laugh wildly as an emerald fire
Leaps from their nests.

# Magic Strings

The witch pours out a libation of wine,
And clouds cover the sky,
In a jade brazier charcoal burns—
The incense booms.[1]
Gods of the sea and mountain demons
Flock to her seat,
Crackle of burning paper money[2]
As a whirlwind moans.

She plays a love-wood lute[3] adorned
With golden, dancing simurghs,
Knitting her brows, she plucks a note
For each word uttered.
She calls down stars and summons demons
To savour meat and drink,
When mountain-goblins come to eat,
Men are breathless and hushed.
Colours of sunset low in a coign
Of Zhong-nan range,[4]
Long lingers the Spirit. Something or Nothing?
We cannot tell.[5]
The Spirit's anger, the Spirit's delight
Shows in her face,
Ten thousand riders escort him back
To the emerald hills.

# Farewell Song of Magic Strings

The Maiden of Witch Mountain now departs
Behind a screen of clouds,[1]
In spring a breeze blows flowers of pine
Down from the mountain-side.
Alone beneath her emerald canopy she returns
Through fragrant paths,[2]
White horses and flower-decked poles
Dazzle before her.

On the River of Shu blows a limpid wind,
Water like gauze,[3]
Who will float on a fallen orchid
To come to see her?[4]
A cassia tree on a southern hill
Is dying for her,[5]
Her robes of cloud are slightly stained
By its rouged petals.[6]

# Song of Green Water

Tonight a pleasant wind and moon,
But where is poor Hou?
Because her beauty breaks men's hearts
She has her share of pain and sadness.

Is she gathering lotus by east lake?
Or plucking cattails by south lake?
She has no little sister-in-law in mind,
They're but the tokens of her sorrow.[1]

## Song: Sandy Road

❧

Tamarisk-faces, half-asleep,
The Premier's trees.[1]
Jingle of bridle-bells, as horses
Tread the sandy road.
Lingering scent of burnt-out fires,
Emerald smoke swirling.[2]
Horseman with torches, on clattering hooves,
Riding to Heaven.[3]

Jade dragons in the emperor's home
Open nine gates,[4]
He writes on his tablet in the emperor's presence,
And Mount South trembles.
Alone, his weighty seal controls
A thousand officials,
On its golden face, red characters
Twirl and swirl.

Going home along the sandy road,
He hears nothing but praise,
No drought fires are blazing,
Rain falls everywhere.[5]

## The Emperor Returns

The Emperor returns!
Great banners rejoice,
Hanging red clouds,
Fluttering phoenix tails.

Breaking from its case
His sword leaps like a dragon.[1]
Chi You is dead![2]
The drums are rolling.

Heaven blesses us all,
Thunder falls to the earth.
Over ocean's thousand leagues
No wild waves fly.[3]

# The Grand Official Carriage Comes on a Visit. Written at the Command of Assistant Secretary Han Yu and Censor Huang-fu Shi When They Visited Me.

Ornate robes woven with kingfisher feathers,
Green as shallots,
Bridles hung with rings of gold
Shaking and jingling.
Drumming of hoofbeats in my ear,
Clopping and clattering,
In through my gates they come, alighting,
Auras like rainbows.

"Behold the genius from Lo-yang,
And the Lord of Letters!"
Eight-and-twenty constellations
Ranged within your hearts.
The Primal Essence, burning bright,
Pervades your inmost being.
You write rhymed-prose by the Palace,
Renown reaching the sky.
Your brushes perfect creation,
Humiliating Heaven.

This scholar with bushy eyebrows,
Grieves at autumn tumbleweed,
Yet perhaps even withered grass
May wake in a flowering wind.
With flagging pinions I now cling to

Soaring wild-geese,
Yet some day, shamed no longer,
This snake shall rise a dragon.

## Lady of the Cowrie Palace

Mermaids play with her gold rings,
Jingling softly.[1]
Her sparrow-hairpin cocks its tail,
Both wings furled.
Not for her the Six Palaces,
She is tranquil forever,[2]
Hung on high a silver sign
Reflecting green hills.
Long eyebrows of frozen green—
Unchanging for centuries.
Cold purity, defying time,
This mirrored simurgh.[3]
Her autumn flesh feels faintly
The chill of her jade robes.
Under the heaven's calm, peaceful light
Water confounds with sky.

# The Temple of the Goddess of Orchid Fragrance

Year after year the ancient spring endures,
An idle green caressed by the warm clouds.
Scent of pines and evening blossoms flying,
As willow islands cherish the darkling sun.
The sandy steps are filled with fallen reds,
Round stony springs wild celery is growing.
Lonely bamboos are adorned with new powder,
Moth-green mountains bar her gates at dawn.
Fragile orchids cannot bear the dew,
Mountain flowers, grieving in desolate spring.
Her dancing pendants clipped from simurghs' wings,
Trailing sashes lightly streaked with silver.
Orchid and cinnamon breathe their heady perfume,
Water-chestnut, lotus-root heaped as offering.
Gazing at the rain, she meets Jade Lady,[1]
Borne in her boat, encounters the River Lord.[2]
Playing her flute and drunk with wine,
She knots a girdle round her gold-thread skirt.
Roaming the heavens, she chides at her white deer,
Wandering the waters, whips her bright-scaled steed.
Thick hair flies from her empty headdress,
Flower-tints blended on her glistening cheeks.
Caves of pearl beside her coiling tresses,[3]
Delicate lips framed by her dark brows.
A fluttering butterfly her graceful beauty,
Wind and sun shrink from her slender body.
In secluded curtains, golden ducks grow cold,[4]

On her vanity-mirror, a lonely simurgh gathers dust.
Treading the mist, she's borne home on the breeze,
Her tinkling jades heard on the mountain-top.


# I Escort Wei Ren-shi and His Brother to the Pass

Seeing off my friends, I drink the wine of parting,
After a thousand goblets, no flushed faces.[1]
The most heart-rending sound I know?
Jingle of golden rings on horses' heads.
The coloured wilderness is vast, untamed,
Autumn bright under the boundless sky.
My courage ebbs from me all unawares,
My straining eyes follow my friends in vain.
Roadside pagoda-trees stretch away westwards,
Long, green branches thickly bunched together.
I've escorted these gentlemen to the waters of Qin,
I must return to Luo-yang's mists again.
The brothers Wei are both fine fellows,
Their brushes pour forth characters like jade.[2]
I live in a little hut on top of a hill,
Around it, a weed-grown patch of stony ground.
On rainy nights, the tax collector's shouts
Darkly mingle with thump of pestle on mortar.
Who can understand my weary heart?
Only Mount South rears its green before me.[3]

# Outside the Walls of Luo-yang, I Take Leave of Huang-fu Shi

Through Luo-yang city blows a parting wind,
At Dragon Gate rises estranging mist.[1]
Winter trees—bundles of bare, harsh branches,
Twilight purple congeals in the dappled sky.
Alone in the frosty wilderness I go,
On a jaded horse, through flying tumbleweed.
I lean on your carriage, shedding a tear or two
Falling as tribute before your green robe.[2]

# A Cold Gorge at Twilight

A white fox barking at the moon,
The mountain wind.[1]
Autumn chill sweeps off the clouds
Leaving an emerald void.
Jade mists on green water,
Like pennants of white.
The Silver Torrent winds at dawn
To the eastern sky.
Beside the stream an egret sleeps,
Dreaming of migrant geese.[2]
Delicate ripples, unmurmuring,
Stir scarcely at all.
Storied crags and twisted peaks
Coil on coil of dragons.
Bitter bamboos for a traveller
Play singing flutes.[3]

## The Official Has Not Come
## A Poem Written in the Office of My Senior,
## Huang-Fu Shi

The official has not come!
Autumn in his office courtyard.
Twisted trunks of kolanut trees—
Green dragons grieving.
Clerks and deputies
Milling like cattle.
I keep asking his assistants:
"Is he coming or not?"
The official is not coming,
His gateway darkens.[1]

# Song of an Arrowhead from Chang-ping

Flakes of lacquer, dust of bones,
Red cinnabar,
The ancient blood once spurted forth
And bore bronze flowers.
White feathers and its metal stem
Have rotted in the rain.
Only the three spines still remain,[1]
Broken teeth of a wolf.

I searched this plain of battle
With a pair of nags,
In stony fields east of the post-station,
On a weed-grown hill.
An endless wind, the day short,
Desolate stars,
Black banners of damp clouds
Hung in void-night.
Souls to the left, spirits to the right,
Gaunt with hunger, wailing.[2]

I poured curds from my tilted flask,
Offered roast mutton.[3]
Insects silent, the wild geese sick,
Reed shoots reddening,
A whirlwind came to see me off,
Blowing the ghost-fires.[4]

In tears I sought this ancient field,
Picked up a broken arrow,
Its shattered point, scarlet and cracked,
Once drove through flesh.
In South Street, by the eastern wall,
A lad on horseback
Urged me to exchange the metal
For a votive-basket.[5]

## Song: The Mansion by the River

Before her house the water flows,
Road to Jiang-ling.
The carp-fish wind has risen,[1]
The lotus grown old.

At dawn she hastily pins her hair,
Talks to the south wind.
"To hoist his sail and come back home,
Is but one day's work.

Since the crocodile cried by the harbour
And the plum-rain flew,[2]
The wine-flags on their poles have changed
To green ramie.[3]
When white waves roared and blustered,
Clouds scudding wildly,
I sent a powder-yellow raincoat
To my husband.

Drip of new wine into vats
Sad and faint,
Acres of South Lake turned white
With water-chestnut.
Suddenly my eyes perceive
A thousand leagues of sorrow
When Little Jade draws back the screen[4]
And I see the coloured hills."

# Song: Beyond the Frontiers

꧁꧂

Barbarian horns have summoned the north wind,
Thistle Gate is whiter than a stream![1]
The road to Green Sea vanishes into the sky,[2]
Along the Wall, a thousand moonlit miles.

While dew falls drizzling on our flags,
Cold metal clangs the watches of the night,[3]
Barbarian armour meshes serpents' scales,
Horses whinny where Green Grave gleams white.[4]

In autumn stillness see the Banner Head,[5]
On the vast sands the mournful furze.
North of our tents the sky itself must end,
Across the frontier comes the River's roar.[6]

## Dyed Silk on the Loom in Spring

She draws water in jade jars
From the empress-tree petal well.
Silk dyed with madder, water-steeped,
Like a cloud's shadow.

This lively girl is tired,
Her rouged face looks sad.
In spring her shuttle clicks away,
Humming in the tall tower.

Bright-hued silk, knotted in
Double folds on the back—
A handsome man in a white-collared coat
Sent Peach-leaves this present.[1]

"Embroidered with simurghs
Is the belt I have made you.
I want you to roam round
Drinking spring wine."

# Song of the Young Five-Grain Pine

Bachelor Xie and Du Yun-qing once asked me to write a song for a young five-grain pine. I was very busy with my books at the time and could not write this lyric for them. Ten days later I composed these eight lines to fulfill their request.

Snake's son, snake's grandson,
Scales coiled like a dragon's.
My grains, new and fragrant,
Were food for Hong Yai.[1]
Leaves lapped in green wavelets,
Glossy and rich.
Neat bundles of dragons' whiskers,
Trimmed off with scissors.[2]

On my owner's wall
Maps of the district.
Round my owner's hall
Mobs of uncouth scholars.[3]
Bright moonlight, white dew,
Autumn tears falling.
Pointed stones, stream clouds,
May I send you this letter?[4]

## Song: By the Pool

Lotus flower degged with chill dew,
The petals ragged, the root grown harsh.
A lonely mandarin-duck comes winging down,[1]
With gentle splash in the waters of the pool.

## Song: General Lü

General Lü,
The valiant-hearted,
Riding alone on Scarlet Hare[1]
Out of the gates of Qin,[2]
To weep at Gold Grain Mound[3]
By funereal trees.

Rebellion in the north
Stains in the blue sky.
His dragon-sword cries out at night—
But the general's left idle,

To shake his sleeves,
And stroke his cross-guard.
"Round the jade towers of Vermilion City,
A maze of gates and pavilions."[4]

Slowly, the silver tortoise swings
To the gait of the white horse.[5]
A powdered lady-general rides
Under a fiery banner.[6]

The iron horsemen of Mount Heng
Call for their metal lances.[7]
They can smell from afar the ornate arrows
In her perfumed quiver.

Cold weeds grow in the western suburbs,
With leaves like thorns,
High heaven has just now planted them,
To feed our thoroughbreds.
In tall-beamed stables, row on row
Of useless nags.
Stuffing themselves on green grass,
Drinking white water.[8]

Inscrutable that vaulted azure,
Arching over earth,
This is the way the world wags
In our Nine Provinces.
Gleaming ore from Scarlet Hill![9]
Hero of our time!
Green-eyed general, you well know
The will of Heaven![10]

# Don't Wash Red Cloth!

Don't wash red cloth!
For washed too often it will fade.
You are so full of youthful pride!
Yesterday we met at the bridge of Yin.[1]
Come home soon with a marquisate!
Don't be just another arrow from a bow!

# Song in the Wilds

Arrow plumed with duck-feathers,
Mountain-mulberry bow,[1]
Pointed skywards may bring down
A reed-bearing goose.[2]
In linen clothes, all black and greasy,
I brave the north wind.[3]
Drunk at twilight, I'm still singing
Down in the fields.

Though a man may suffer poverty,
His heart's not poor.
"Some men wither, others flourish—
Why rail at God?
This bitter wind will bring to life
The willows of spring,
These bare branches suddenly wear
A new, green mist."[4]

# Let Wine Be Brought In!

In opaque, glass goblets
A viscous amber.[1]
From a little vat the wine drips down
On pearls of red.
From boiling dragons and roasting phoenix
Jade fat is weeping,
Gauzy screens, embroidered curtains
Enclose these perfumed airs.[2]

Blow dragon flutes!
Beat alligator drums!
Dazzling teeth in song,
Slender waists in dance.
Especially now when green, spring days
Are turning to dusk,[3]
With peach-petals falling wildly
Like pink showers.
I beg you now to stay quite drunk
To the end of your days,
For on the earth of Liu Ling's grave
No one pours wine.[4]

## Song: A Lovely Girl Combing Her Hair

Xi-shih dreaming at dawn,
In the cool of silken curtains,[1]
Scented coils of her falling chignon,
Half aloes and sandalwood.[2]

The turning windlass of the well,
Creaking like singing jade,
Wakes with a start this lotus-blossom,
That has newly slept its fill.

Twin simurghs open her mirror,
An autumn pool of light.[3]
She loosens her tresses before the mirror,
Stands by her ivory bed.

A single skein of perfumed silk,
Clouds cast on the floor,
Noiseless, the jade comb lights upon
Her lustrous hair.

Delicate fingers push up the coils—
Colour of an old rook's plumes,
Blue-black, so sleek the jewelled pins
Cannot hold it up.
Light-heartedly the spring breeze vexes
Her youthful languor,

Just eighteen, with hair so rich,
Her strength has fled.

Her coiffure over, the well-dressed chignon
Sits firm and does not slip.
In cloudy skirts, she takes a few steps,
A wild goose treading sand,
She turns away in silence—
Where is she off to now?
Just down the steps to pick herself
A spray of cherry blossom.

## A Shining Wet Moon

A shining wet moon,
Jade in misty waves,
Green sedge, a host of cassia flowers,
Lotuses drifting from riverside trees.

Powdered beauties cold in sendal robes,[1]
Goose-wings, brushing wet mist.[2]
Who can descry Stone Sail or ride
A boat upon the Mirror?[3]

White autumn, new reds dying,[4]
Sweet-scented water, lotus-seeds ripening,
Girls plucking water-chestnut part their dancer's sleeves,
Green thorns clinging to slime-silver gowns.[5]

## The Capital

Out of my gate I galloped, full of hope—
But now my heart is lonely in Chang-an.
Since I have no one to confide in
I chant a poem, alone with the autumn wind.

# Drums in the Street of the Officials

Thunder of drums at dawn,
Hastening the sun,
Thunder of drums at dusk,
Calling out the moon.
In the city of Han, yellow willows
Dazzle on new blinds,[1]
In a cypress mound lie the fragrant bones
Of flying Swallow.[2]
Drums pounding away a thousand years
The sun forever white,
Yet Emperor Wu and the Emperor of Qin
Are deaf to their call.
Your blue-black hair must turn to the hue
Of a flowering rush,[3]
Only the drums with the Southern Hill
Will guard the Middle Kingdom.
How many times have Ethereal Immortals
Been buried in Heaven?
The drip of the water-clock, day after day,
Goes on without pause.

# A Song for Xu's Lady, Zheng
## (She Having Asked Me to Write This When I Was in Her Garden)

Imperial relatives on the distaff side,
Generations of Xus and Shis.
With a thousand yards of palace brocade
He bought his drinking-bouts.
By the Brazen Camels he mulled his wine,
Clear as warm glue,
On ancient banks, where emerald mist
Drapes the great willows.

A stranger came, a cassia-flower,
The renowned Zheng Xiu.[1]
When she reached Luo, her fragrance wafted
From Tripod Gate.[2]
First he gave her a peony,[3]
Then a vanity-mirror,
And after this a nugget of gold,
Big as a bushel.

As Never Sorrow let him dally,
Behind the screen,[4]
She played her lute for his delight,
Fifty melodious strings.
Music sobbed on the wind of spring,
Stirring his soul,
Enraptured, he was moved to saddle
Both their horses.

Twin steeds pacing on twice four hooves
Through an orchid park!
Love clasped tight as knit bamboo—
No prying eyes.

Jade pillows gleaming in the dark,
Phoenix at rest,[5]
Heavy curtains shrouding the portals,
Silk passementerie.

On a long scroll of costly paper,
The ballad of Ming-jun.[6]
Gliding from note to note, her song
Pierced the sapphire clouds
Vanity-patches on her cheeks,
She trod the eastern road—
Now the long-browed girls of the gay quarters
See very few guests.

"On Xiang-ru's tomb the autumn cypress
Flourishes still.
But who are the poets who sing of love
In the capital today?"
Hair piled high, eyes wild with wine,
She asked her friends,
Then came to this scion of a royal house,
To entreat Cao Zhi.[7]

## Song: A New Summer

At dawn a thousand clumps of trees,
Glossy as wax,
Fading scent of fallen stamens
Lingering a little.

On shadowed branches, pale-green down
Of buds still furled,
Summer breezes blow from afar,
Coaxing their verdure.

Villagers grow wheat on ridges,
High on new dikes,
Thick over long balks where I stroll,
Mulberry and silkworm-thorn,[1]

A piercing fragrance fills the earth
From the sweet-flag.
Swallows are chattering on rain-drenched beams,
Sad that I'm growing old,
Whirling petals of the third month,
Fly to River walks.
Enriching heaven, enriching earth,
Willows sweep the ground.

# On the Theme of "Dreaming I Was Back at Home"

Back in Chang-an, on a night of wind and rain,
A student who is dreaming of Chang-gu,
Laughing and carefree in the sitting room,
Cutting king-grass in the gorge with my young brother,
My whole family welcomes me with joy,
Counting on me to fill their empty bellies.
My inmost heart is faint and weary now.
A guttering lamp glimmers on a fish's eyes![1]

## Passing through Sandy Park

Where wild floods sail their watery waves,
Over the yamen the young madder grows.[1]
No one to see the willows turn to spring,
On grassy islands mandarin ducks are basking.[2]
Horses lie on the sands, whinnying in the sun,
The old ones walk off, neighing piteously.
Though spring has come, once again I have not gone home.
On the frontier cries a goose with broken wings.[3]

# On Leaving the City and Parting from Chang You-xin I Pledge Li Han with Wine

Out of the capital I go as spring
Burgeons upon the peaks of the Southern Hill,
Tonight I cannot hear the drums[1]—
Some consolation to my aching heart.
Zhao Yi wrote poems on his unhappy fate,[2]
And Ma-qing's family lived in poverty.[3]
What news comes to me in letters from home?
"Clouds of purple bracken cover the rocks."[4]

Chang-an is a kingdom of jade and cassia,[5]
Halberd-pennants wave at noble gates.[6]
Even in winter's gloom the ground is shining,
Precious steeds prance by from dawn till dusk.
Winter and spring, they hunt in grassy parks,
Their fashionable carriages rumbling and clattering by.
Golden bells dangle from their green nets,
Coiling like mist round the clear pool's brink.
From loosened purses money flows like water,[7]
Just to buy ice to drive off summer flies.
At times the great quilts are split up,[8]
Among guests with swords, in cushioned carriages.

I'm just a nobody, heart like dead ashes,
Where only autumn thorn-bush grows.
The imperial sway governs the four seas,
And all our citizens are gentlemen.

Yet shrouding mists obscure the emperor's radiance,
Tortoise-seals remain mere lumps of silver.[9]
I wanted to play ritual music,
Making sure my cadences were fresh and new,
So ordering things that for ten thousand years
The Imperial Way would be like a god on wing.

Flower and fruit would bloom and ripen,[10]
Glory pour out as from a tilted ewer.
But whelmed in darkness I bite my tongue,
Shed tears of blood and dare not say a word.

Now I am setting off down the eastern road,
With libations of wine I say farewell to Qin,
No brave men now in the six provinces,[11]
So who will wipe the dust from their long swords?
Yang and Wu-cheng are huddled deep in earth,[12]
And racehorses are yoked to carts of salt.

Since both of you are gallant gentlemen,
When it comes to Truth, you can tell black from white,
After tonight, we shall laugh together no more,
Bamboos are sprouting back in my garden at home.
At dawn a wind starts blowing from the west,
A glimmering moon is hanging in the east,
A man who finds the times are out of joint
Has written this poem he now presents to you.
Since partings always soak my breast with tears
I've brought my Yue handkerchief along.[13]

## My Southern Garden

❦

I'm wearing straight collar, orchid belt,
And a bent-cornered hat,[1]
Pallia is withering,
Orchids flower in spring.
Southern hills rear up sharply[2]—
Blue jade fused,
A sudden shower dies away,
Cool clouds wing past.
Apricots ripen in fragrant warmth,
Pear leaves grow old,
Grasses, twigs, and a bamboo fence
Lock in the pond.
Growing old in Cheng Gong's village
I open a flagon of wine,[3]
Sit drinking to strains of Chu music,
Humming "Summoning the Soul."[4]

# 1
# Song: Imitating the Singing of Dragons

Stone grating on a copper bowl,
The song is faint and forced.
Blood spattered from blue eagles!
Lungs ripped from a white phoenix![1]
Cassia seeds fall as clouds
Sway their carriage-awnings.[2]

Dead trees and crumbling sand,
A baleful valley-isle,
There the Western Mother, ageless now,
Once grew immortal.[3]
Grottoes washed clear of dragon's pure spittle,
Gold claws buried in water-lapped coves.

Green shrouds the hillside steps
Mourning in moss,
The River Ladies, drying their tears,
Snapped off these giant bamboos.[4]
The Lotus Dragons left this land
A thousand years ago,[5]
Smell of fish lingers after rain—
And that of iron.[6]

## 2
# Song: A Modest Maiden in the Spring Sunshine

Young butterflies in love with fragrance
Cling to new petals,
Branch after branch is weeping dew,
Shedding heaven-born tears.
Powdered windows choked with perfume,
Tumbling clouds of dawn.[7]
Hills of brocade, strewn with petals,[8]
Hide her spring dreams.
Peacocks shaking their golden tails
Embrace the screen,
Her oriole's silver tongue is calling
Her serving-maids.
Cold dragons in an icy cave[9]—
Ewers of water,
This white simurgh, rising, drives away
The mists of sleep.

## 3
# Joys of Youth

Scented flowers, falling petals,
Earth like brocade,
A youth of twenty roaming
In the Land of Drunkenness.[10]
Red ribbons never stirring
On his proud, white horse,
Weeping willows golden silk
Brush the perfumed water.
The girl from Wu unsmiling,
Flowers folded still,[11]
Green tresses tower and topple,
Orchid clouds arise.
Master Lu, drunk and reeling,[12]
Tugs her gauze sleeve.
Pulls out a jewelled hairpin,
A kingfisher of gold.

# Six Satires

1

Spring's rampant in the world!
Its fragrance wafts through sunlit curtains.
Darting sunbeams redden lonely flowers,
Enter her grottoed room to boast their beauty.
Pattern of golden snakes on her dancing-rug,
Zither and flute set out on ornate stands.
Her eyes are drunken with spring dusk,
Her tears yellow from her powder.
A prince arrives, gets off his horse,
On a winding pool, mandarin-ducks start singing.
How can he guess the carriage of her heart
Roaming the whole earth in a single night?[1]

2

A bitter wind whistles up boreal cold,
Trees of Qin are snapped by bolting sand.
Dancing shadows reel through an empty sky,
Sharp beat of painted drums throbs in my ears.
No autumn letter comes to me from Shu,[2]
Only Black Waters' waves sobbing at dawn.[3]
A whirlwind will bear off my graceful ghost,
The moon of home hang over my lost grave.

3

Fog of dust from barbarian horses,
Forested halberds of frontier troops.
Heaven taught the nomad horseman how to fight,
At dawn the clouds are lowering blood-red.
A lady-general leads our Chinese soldiers,
A dainty kerchief tucked into her quiver.
She's not ashamed of her heavy, gold seal,
Mincing along with bow-case at her waist.
Simple old men, just honest villagers,
Tested the teeth of arrow-barbs last night,
But she sent her courier to cry victory—
Must powder and mascara blind us all![4]

4

When he hunts with crossbow at Green Gate,
His horses throng the empty suburbs.[5]
When did he get those presents from the palace?
Decked out with jade he swaggers in the saddle.
Off he goes, his hounds heading for home,
Back he comes to a banquet of boiled lamb.
A sack of gold couldn't buy such dishes,
He turns his nose up even at badgers' paws.
Dare we ask where this fellow springs from?
His father wears a sword hung at his belt.
Yet in a white-thatched cottage on West Hill
A wise man lives in lonely poverty.

5

Dawn chrysanthemums wet with cold dew,
Seem sad as the wind from her round fan.[6]
Chill of autumn creeps through the Han palace,
Ban-zi wept for her fading beauty.
I would never refuse to ride in the royal sedan-chair,[7]
Nor think of entering an empty palace.
The pearl belt at her waist is broken now,
Ash butterflies flutter by gloomy pines.[8]

6

Pretty girls on a terrace where butterflies flit,
A willow-swept road where harmonicas play.[9]
Ten suns are hanging in the entrance court,[10]
Through ninety days of fall no flowers fade.
Sound of singing borne afar on the breeze,
Cup-like ponds where little white fishes play.[11]
Feasting by the pool, they sup on fragrant meats,
Water-chestnut gleams in green fish-baskets.
Pear-blossom covers luxuriant grass,
Long whistles sound through vernal dark,[12]
They only grieve that fragrant blossoms fall,
Not realizing their whole world must decay.
Brooding on the past has fettered my spirit,
Mount South's unchanging peaks have made me sad.[13]

# Song: Never Sorrow

꿍ꗬꕤ

Below the Pool of Dragons grasses grow,[1]
Up on the city battlements crows are cawing.
Who is it dwells within the city walls,
By pomegranates planted in their corner?
With emerald silk her horses five are bound,
With yellow gold her oxen two are haltered.
White fishes harnessed to her lotus boats[2]
Carry her full ten leagues in a single night.

Then she returns, unknown to everyone,
Unheeded climbs her aloes-scented tower.[3]
She sings to a jewelled lute on her silk-hung couch,[4]
A sliver of moon wanes on the curtain-hooks.[5]
Today the hibiscus must cast down its petals,
Next dawn, the plane-trees feel the autumn come.
It seems her life is one of thwarted love.
Why ever was she known as "Never Sorrow"?

## Pleasure Comes at Night

Curtains lined with red sendal,
Gold-fringed tassels,
Ornate nine-branched candelabra,
Hung with carp.[1]
This lovely girl, a brilliant moon,
Opens her brazen-ringed door,
Pours out wine in spring freshets
From a gibbon jar.[2]
Her price is high: ten incense-sticks
In a costly casket,
Ingots of "red-melon" gold
And "bran-cake" flakes,
A green jade duck in wrappings
Of five-coloured silk—
A smile from this accomplished beauty[3]
Costs a small fortune.

The Milky Way wheels past southern eaves,
Shadows fade from blinds,
In kolanut woods, crows are crying,
Nestling their young.
On sword-pommel, whip-handle,
Green stones and pearls,
His white steed blows out foam,
Frost stiffens its mane.[4]

She speeds her guest to Cheng-ming lodge,[5]
Water-dock dawn,
Then back to her tall mansion,
A bright, lonely moon.
Another guest dismounting
As the first one leaves,
Once more she brushes on green brows,
Combs her elegant black coiffure.


## Deriding the Snow

Yesterday it left the Cong-ling ranges,[1]
Today it's fluttering down on our orchid isles.[2]
Delighted to have come a thousand miles,
It's laughing wildly, promising the spring.
On the Dragon Sands it drenches our Han banners,
Phoenix-wing fans welcome its Chinese white.[3]
"My Liao-dong crane left me so long ago,
By now his feather-robe must have grown sere."[4]

# Ballad: Spring Longings

꙳

Deep in shadows, this fragrant path
Is a flower-hung cave,
Tangled willows wreathed in mist,
Fragrant sashes heavy.
The moon-toad rolls its jade along,
Hangs out a bright bow.
A girl is striking fairies and phoenix
With a golden plectrum.[1]
Clouds tumbling over her jewelled pillow[2]
She seeks a spring dream,
In caskets cold with inlaid sapphires,
The dragon-brain grows chill.[3]
A-hou ties her brocade girdle[4]
And looks for Zhou Yu,[5]
She has to rely on the east wind
To waft her to him.

# Ballad of the White Tiger

❧

The fire-bird's sun sank into shadow,[1]
Surging clouds dislimned.
The King of Qin glared like a tiger
On all the people.
He burnt the books, wiped out the states,
Not wasting a day,[2]
Forging swords, he bawled to his generals,
Rings on his belt.[3]

Libations poured on a jade altar—
Thoughts soared to heaven,
One generation, two generations—
Surely ten thousand years!
Burning cinnabar could not bring him
The immortal drug,
So he sent a fleet to scour the ocean,
Searching for fairies.[4]

Leviathans whipped sea-waves to foam
With flailing flukes,
Half our peasants vanished, turned to
Soldiers' ghosts.
Fierce and cruel as savage fire
He flamed to the heavens,
Never a man who could unlock
The Sky River's waves.[5]

Some who suffered would not suffer
Such suffering,[6]
Righteous men vowed to each other
To help their fellows.
Jian-li sat and strummed his lute
While Jing Ke sang.
Jing Qing held his wine,
Prince Dan of Yan spoke out.[7]

Sword like frost!
Gall like iron!
Out of the walls of Yan he went,
Gazed at the moon of Qin,
Heaven had given Qin its seal,
Its sway was not yet over,
So the dragon robes were drenched
With Jing Qing's blood.

When scarlet banners were planted in earth,
The white tiger died.
Then we knew the true Son of Heaven—
The king of Han![8]

# Someone I Love

Last year, by the wayside we sang
A song of parting.
Today you have sent me a letter
From far-off Shu.[1]
Outside my screens, the flowers are opening
In the April wind.[2]
In front of the terrace, a thousand tears
Bathe the bamboos.[3]
My heart and the lute's are breaking tonight,
Yet will mend again.

My thoughts are with you, astride a white horse,
Carved bow at your side.
No place on earth where the winds of spring
Are not blowing now.
You were not willing to make your heart
As firm as stone.
The beauty of my face will fade
Like the pink of petals.

High in its sapphire, as night wears on,
The Long River glides.[4]
Across that River there is no bridge,
Lonely white waves.
Sadly, before the west wind stirs,
She plies her Dragon-shuttle.[5]
Year after year, she spins her plain silk
Knitting her brows.[6]

Mountains and rivers stretch into the distance,
Endless, unbroken.
My tear-filled eyes gaze at the taper,
Flaring, then dying.
Since I hid myself in my lonely mansion,
Windows firmly barred,
How many times has the Cassia Flower[7]
Waxed and then waned?

Crow after crow, as dawn draws near,
Cries in the grove,
A wind blows from the banks of the pool,
Tinkling musical-jades,[8]
Bleak and lonely breaks the white day
Ending my dreams.
South of the bridge, I ask the Immortal
To tell me our fortunes.[9]

# Ridiculing a Young Man

Saddles of his well-fed greys
Gleaming with gold,
Silken jacket really reeking
Of dragon-brain,
Lovely girls all over him,
Jade goblets flying—
"He's a real swell, isn't he!"
The poor exclaim.

In a tall tower that he's built
By green bamboo-grass,
He hauls red fish from a deep pool
On silken lines.
Sometimes he sprawls—
half drunk of course—
Among his flowers,
Or brings the birds down on the wing
With golden bolts.[1]

"I've never been any man's guest!" he brags,
"In my born days.[2]
Three hundred gorgeous girls I've got,
Or maybe more."
How can *he* know that among the farmers
Tilling our fields,
No girls are left to weave the cloth
For dunning tax-collectors!

Piling up gold, heaping up jade,
He boasts his noble blood,
Bowing to strangers as he goes,
Puffed up with pride.
He hasn't read more than half a line,
Since he was born.
But bought high office for himself
With gleaming gold.

How can a young man hope to stay
Forever young,
When even ocean waves must change
To mulberry fields?
Quick as an arrow, fortune turns
To misery,
Will the Creator shower his favours
Only on you?

Don't think the sunny days of spring
Will last till late—
For white hair and a haggard face
Are lying in wait![3]

# A Private Road in Eastern Kao-ping County

Fragrant and thick the leaves of the scarlet-seed,[1]
Trees and flowers dripping with cold rain.
This evening—autumn on the mountains—
Forgotten forever they blossom in lonely places.
Long, stony path overgrown with rank grass,
Bitter fruit of the wild pear dangles down.
Surely long ago a hermit sought this spot
And asked you to construct this private road.

# Ballad of the Immortals

Where sapphire peaks rise from the sea
Magic books are stored.[1]
The Creating Power chose this place
As a dwelling for Immortals.
On clear, bright days their laughter echoes
Round the empty sky,
As they strive to ride enormous waves,
On the backs of whales.

With words of welcome on spring silk
To greet the Western Mother,
They will feast together in the Red Tower's
Deepest recess.
Wings of a crane, beating the wind,
Too slow to cross the sea,
Far better despatch a messenger
Riding a blue dragon.
Still doubtful whether the Western Mother
Will accept the invitation,
They send a mist-haired beauty
Off with the message.

# Song: Dragons at Midnight

A curly-haired nomad boy
With eyes of green,
By a tall mansion, in the still of the night
Is playing his flute.
Every note seems to have come
Down from heaven.
Under the moon a lovely girl weeping,
Sick for home.

Deftly he fingers the seven holes,
Hiding their stars,
Gong and zhi secretly harmonize
With the pure breeze.[1]
Deep autumn on the roads of Shu,
A cloud-filled forest.
From the Xiang river at midnight
Startled dragons rise.[2]

A lovely girl in her jade room
Broods on the frontier.
Bright moonshine on her sapphire window—
Sadly she hears the flute.

A hundred feet of glossed silk beaten
On the cold fulling-block[3]
Tears congeal as pearls in her powder,
Soak her red gown.

Play no more the Long-tou tune,
Nomad boy!
No one knows a girl's heart is breaking
Beyond that casement.


## The Kun-lun Envoy

Of the Kun-lun envoy
No news at all,
The mist-hung trees of Mao-ling tomb
Wear mournful hues.[1]
Drop after drop of jade dew trickled
Into the golden bowl,
But Primal Humours proved too vast
For men to gather.[2]


Backs of stone unicorns by his grave
Crack into patterns,
Red limbs of little dragons break
Beneath their scales.[3]
Where is the aching heart that yearned
For ten thousand kingdoms?
High in the heavens, a brilliant moon
Lights the long night.

# Tang-ji of Han Sings as the Wine Is Drunk

The emperor's clothes were drenched with frosty dew,
The palace roads all overgrown with thorns.
When gold is sullied over with autumn dust,
No one will wear it as an ornate belt.
All songs were stilled within those halls of jade,
Mist cloaked the fragrant forest trees.
A song came from the tower of Yun-yang.
Wail of a ghost, and all to no avail.[1]
Swords of iron, gleaming and glittering,
Threatened the emperor with their vile intent.[2]
Savage owls gnawing their mother's skulls!
Evil demons slavering for souls of the dead!
Emperor and lady wept as they gazed at each other,
Their tears falling in an endless stream.
Why do you have to drink this crystal wine
Must plunge you deep within the Yellow Spring?
No question of a toppling hill of jade,[3]
But swallow this, death's pallor stamps your face.
Only the Lord of Heaven will hear your plaint,
At least in Heaven you will be safe from harm.
No ornate curtain will be hung for you,
And neither pine nor cypress mark your grave.[4]
I shall drag out my life through weary days,
Your spirit must roam lonely in its night,
No longer will I tend my moth-like eyebrows,
Who'll gaze with love on my white-powdered neck?
Proudly I'll treasure memories of Zhao-yang,[5]
Nor turn my eyes towards the southern road.[6]

# Song: Listening to Master Ying Playing the Lute

Clouds of the Shores of Parting home
From the isle of cassia flowers,[1]
Through strings of a lute from Shu
Two phoenixes talk.[2]
Lotus leaves falling in autumn
As simurghs part,
A king of Yue wandering at night
On Mount Tian-mu.[3]

Hidden girdle-gems of an honest minister,
Tinkling crystals,[4]
Fairy maidens crossing the sea,
Leading white deer.
What vision is going to Long Bridge,
Sword in hand?[5]
What vision is writing on spring bamboo
With ink-soaked hair?[6]

An Indian monk is standing here,
Right at my gate,
An arhat with venerable eyebrows
In a Buddhist temple.[7]
His antique lute, full eight feet long,
Has massive stops,[8]
An ancient tree-trunk from Yi-yang.
Not a puny branch.[9]

Sound of strings through the cold room
Rouses me from my sick-bed,
Leaving my potions for a while
I sit on the dragon's beard.[10]
If you want a song, you ought to ask
A cabinet-maker,
Maestro, do not demean yourself
With a mere clerk.

## Ballad of the World

A little butterfly in Shang-lin park
Trying to accompany the Emperor of Han.[1]
It flew away towards South Wall,
Alighting, by mistake, on a pomegranate skirt.[2]
Purposeful blossom masses on the trees,
Darting swallows wheel around the clouds.
"Outside the gates, I did not know the way,
Yet felt ashamed to ask the passers-by."

# NOTES TO POEMS

### Song: Li Ping at the Vertical Harp
*7-character: 5 rhymes*

Li Ping was one of the emperor's musicians, from the famous Pear-garden School.

1. Shu (Sichuan) was famous for its *tong* trees (paulownia), from which these harps were made. Similarly, the best silk came from Wu, in southeast China.
2. The Ladies of the River Xiang are the two daughters of the legendary Emperor Yao, consorts of the Emperor Shun. Their teardrops, falling on the bamboos growing by the latter's grave, left speckled marks on them. The White Girl played a zither with fifty strings (*se*) for the Yellow Emperor. The tune she played was so sad that he was forced to break her *se*, leaving her with only a twenty-five stringed instrument.
3. Mount Kun-lun was a mythical mountain in the west, said to produce the finest jade. Here the Peaches of Immortality were to be found.
4. Both Chang-an and Luo-yang had twelve gates. The light melts because music had power over the elements.
5. One of the three foremost rulers of Heaven.
6. Nü Gua (or Wa) was a goddess with a snake's body, consort of Fu Xi. When the demon Gong Gong butted his head against the northwest pillar of heaven, tilting the earth downwards to the southeast and making a hole in the sky, Nü Gua repaired the hole by fusing minerals of five colours.
7. The Weird Crone was said to have been an expert performer on the vertical harp.
8. Lie-zi mentions a certain Hu Ba, who was such a performer on the classical zither (*qin*) that fishes danced and dragons leapt whenever he played.
9. All texts read "Wu Zhi," a reference to a man of the Wei dynasty said to have been a fine performer on the vertical harp, but the line appears to allude to Wu Gang, banished to the moon for being too assiduous in his pursuit of immortality, where he must forever unavailingly try to cut down the cassia tree growing there. The music makes him pause from his endless toil.
10. The moon was believed to contain a hare, a toad, and a cassia tree; "shivering hare" is a kenning for "cold moon."

## Song: Gossamer
*7-character: 3 rhymes*

This poem is probably the lament of an aging courtesan. Like the spring, her gossamer youth has vanished, squandered in the pursuit of pleasure and money.

1. Elm seeds look like strings of copper cash. During the Jin dynasty Shen Chung coined his own cash, which became known as "Shen's money." The fallen seeds suggest the reckless squandering of wealth in pursuit of ephemeral pleasures.

## Song: Returning from Guei-ji
*5-character: 1 rhyme*

This poem is an imitation of the style of Yu Jian-wu (487–551). After a rebellion Yu returned to find the capital in ruins, while he himself was too old for high office.

1. The apartments of the Empress were traditionally said to have walls painted with a substance containing pepper and fagara to give them fragrance and warmth.
2. Fireflies were supposed to be born spontaneously from damp.
3. He is referring to the Crown Prince, Xiao Tong (501–31), compiler of the famous anthology, *Wen-xuan*. The Tai-cheng palace stood in Nanjing.
4. Wu (Jiangsu) was the site of the capital.
5. "Golden Fish"—a type of purse worn at the belt by officials of the third degree and upwards during Tang. Our line is an anachronism, since during the Liang dynasty Golden Tortoises, not Fish, were worn.

## Sent to Quan Qu and Yang Jing-zhi When I Left the City
*7-character: 1 rhyme*

This poem was perhaps written in 814 when He left Chang-an after resigning from his post in the Court of Imperial Sacrifices.

1. Old swords were supposed to have magical properties, among them the power to rise in the air. He is saying that if he had really been an exceptional person he would not be leaving the capital in this way.

### To Be Shown to My Younger Brother
*5-character: 1 rhyme*

1. A famous wine made from the water of Lake Ling, in Heng-yang, Henan.
2. "Ox" and "horse" were the names of two of the symbolical animals in the Chinese system of "branches." These branches were used in divination. Note that "ox" and "horse" were also terms used in the *Shu-pu* game described below. The couplet is rich in meanings. Success and failure in life depend mainly on chance. (a) Why then be concerned about one's fate? (b) Why bother consulting fortune-tellers? Why care about who holds what official rank?
3. In the game known as *Shu-pu wu-mu*, played with five wooden black and white counters, five blacks was the best throw. The owl—an unlucky bird—was the name given to the worst throw, namely two whites and three blacks.

### Bamboo
*5-character: 1 rhyme*

1. Beautiful women will sleep on these mats.
2. In ancient times, princes had worn caps lined with three layers of bamboo. He is offering his services to some prince or other.

### Harmonizing with a Poem Written by Shen, the Imperial Son-in-Law, Entitled: "The Waters of the Royal Canal"
*5-character: 1 rhyme*

Shen Zi-ming (the friend who wrote the letter mentioned in Du Mu's Preface) had married the Princess An-luo, a daughter of Emperor Xian-zong.

1. "Yellow-star beauty-spots" were all the rage at this time. The ladies are using the clear water as their mirror.
2. A reference to the stone slabs lining the sides of the canal.
3. "Duck-head" was the name of a green dye.
4. It was an old custom for guests to float wine-cups on a stream during parties.
5. Ho Yan, styled Ping-shu (190–249), was a man of exceptional good looks and talent who, like Shen, had married a princess.

### On First Taking up My Post as Supervisor of Ceremonies My Thoughts Turn to My House in the Mountains of Chang-gu.
*5-character: 1 rhyme*

This poem was written in 811, when Li He first assumed office.

1. He has few visitors and no servants, because he is so poor.
2. *Ru-yi* ("as-you-like-it") was a double-curved sceptre, often used as a back-scratcher, in the form of lotus-flower and stalk.
3. A kind of turban with peaked corners worn at home.
4. The poet Lu Ji (261–303) was supposed to have owned a dog named Yellow Ears, said to have carried a letter all the way from Luo-yang to Lu's family in far-off Wu and then to have come back with an answer.
5. With his body as wasted as that of a sick crane, he regrets he ever came to the capital.

### Seventh Night
*5-character: 1 rhyme*

On the seventh night of the seventh lunar month the festival of the Herd-boy and the Weaving Lady was celebrated. These two lovers, exiled to heaven as stars and parted by the river of the Milky Way, were allowed to meet on this night. They crossed the river on a bridge formed by magpies (see line 3), but had to part at dawn.

1. "Shores of Parting"—the Milky Way.
2. Probably a reference to the Weaving Lady, now left desolate again. It might, however, refer to He himself.
3. It was the custom on this night for women to leave seven needles threaded with silk in the moonlight and pray for greater skill in sewing. It was also the custom to air books and clothes in the sun during the day.
4. The crescent moon. "Half a mirror" hints at a story of parted lovers who each kept half a mirror as a love-token.
5. See *Su Xiao-xiao's Tomb*, below.

### Passing by the Hua-qing Palace
*5-character: 1 rhyme*

This deserted winter palace, famous for its hot springs, had been one of the resorts of Emperor Xuan-zong (*regnet* 712–56) and his ill-starred favourite, the beautiful Yan Guei-fei (d. 756).

1. The jewelled, red nets stretched across the windows to keep out insects and dust.
2. Mosses.
3. The palace contained many shrines to various deities. Since the bowls are full of dew (rain) the roof must be leaking. They should have held sacrificial wine. "Silk" refers to silk screens.
4. During the rebellion of An Lu-shan (755–63), Emperor Xuan-zong fled to Shu, in southwest China. Hence he was known derisively as the "Prince of Shu."
5. The famous hot-springs are so deserted that no one comes there even to pluck parsley.

### Song: Seeing off Shen Ya-zhi (Together with an Introduction)
*7-character: 4 rhymes*

1. Shen Ya-zhi was not only a fine poet but had also gained fame as a writer of tales of the supernatural.
2. Hu-zhou, in Zhejiang, was Shen's home.
3. The bamboo was for use as a whip.
4. To Zhejiang.
5. Officials attached to the Department of Rites, who conducted the *ju* examinations.
6. A small boat. This section describes Shen's coming to Chang-an for the examinations.
7. Guan Zhong (d. 654 B.C.), prime minister to Duke Huan of Chi, once confessed he had run away from battle three times, for the sake of his old mother.
8. Each month of the year was allotted a certain note on the pitch-pipes. Since the examinations were held in autumn, Shen would return then.

### Expressing My Feelings
*5-character: 1 rhyme*

1. Si-ma Xiang-ru (179–117 B.C.), styled Chang-qing, is mentioned several times in He's poems, always with admiration. Xiang-ru was the finest writer of rhyme-prose of his time—probably the finest in Chinese literary history. He eloped with Wen-jun, daughter of a local millionaire. Later he took service under Emperor Wu

(r. 141–87 B.C.). He retired to Mao-ling (Xing-ping county, Shanxi) and died there of diabetes after many years of illness. In this poem He is comparing the dying poet's plight with his own.

2. This is quite untrue. Both rulers had shown Xiang-yu great favours. He is simply projecting his own situation on to the ancient poet.

3. "Liquid gold" was a mixture of gold and mercury. The document in question, which dealt with the imperial sacrifices, was handed over to the Emperor after Xiang-yu's death.

4. His hair has turned prematurely white.

5. He cannot wear the turban, that symbol of life of ease, because he is so hard at work.

6. Bitter-cork is a mountain tree, the bitter yellow bark of which is used as a drug and a dye. In early folksongs, it is a symbol of suffering. Hence the line means not only that Li He is out of office and dressed like a commoner—for during Tang all the common people had to wear yellow clothes—but also that he had suffered a great deal.

### Written after the Style of a Poem by Liu Yun
*5-character: 2 rhymes*

Liu Yun was governor of Wu-xing during the Liang dynasty (502–57). He wrote a famous *yue-fu* ballad, which begins:
> "On an islet I gather white duckweed,
> Sunset, spring south of the River."

1. For paulownia from Shu, see the poem, *Song: Li Ping at the Vertical Harp*, above.

2. Where a singing-girl lived.

3. Two lovers.

### Song of the Sword of the Collator in the Spring Office
*7-character: 1 rhyme*

His twelfth elder cousin held the post of Collator in the Spring Office (Secretariat) of the household of the Crown Prince.

1. "Elder" was a term used by second-degree graduates when addressing those who had taken their doctorates.

2. A reference to Zhou Chu (Jin dynasty), who dived into a lake to kill a dragon that was plaguing his district.

3. The finest swords had hilts of shark skin.

4. Jing Ke was the epitome of the knight-errant, a hero who tried to assassinate the detested First Emperor of Qin. He's cousin, Qin, should never bring the sword into the Crown Prince's office since it is the heart of a regicide.

5. Lan-tian (Indigo-field), in Shanxi, was famous for its "jade" which was actually a green-and-white marble.

6. Liu Bang, founder of the Han dynasty, once killed a huge snake which lay across his path. That night an old woman appeared to him in a dream, lamenting loudly, and told him that the snake was the son of the White King of the West.

### Song: A Nobleman at the End of the Night

1. Aloeswood was the most popular aromatic of Tang.

2. A girl sits alone in her room waiting for her lord to return? Or possibly, a nobleman, not yet in bed after a night's hard drinking, waits for the dawn which must summon him to court.

### Ballad of the Grand Warden of Goose Gate
*7-character: 2 rhymes*

The title is that of an old *yue-fu* ballad. Grand Warden (*tai-shou*) was a rank roughly equivalent to Governor. Yan-men ("Goose Gate") commandery was in Shanxi. Ostensibly the poem deals with the defeat of a Chinese army during the Later Han.

1. During the Warring States period King Zhao of Yan, anxious to attract to his court all the finest men of his time, offered a thousand pieces of gold to those who came to have audience with him in this tower and were subsequently accepted into his service. The ruins of this tower stood eighteen *li* southeast of the river Yi.

2. "Jade Dragon" was a favourite name for a sword during Tang times.

### Song: Great Dike
*Irregular: 3 rhymes*

A girl from Hen-tang, near Nanjing, is begging her love not to linger in the gay quarters of Ta-ti ("Great Dike") but to come home quickly. Ta-ti, near Xiang-yang, in south Hubei, was famous for its wine and its brothels. Hen-tang was also noted for its singing-girls, one of whom is here begging her lover to stay away from her rivals.

1. "Bright moons"—pearls.
2. Great delicacies for the gourmet. The girls are tempting their clients with the promise of such delicacies.

### Music for Strings from Shu
*5-character: 2 rhymes*

Name of a type of *yue-fu* ballad.
1. Lotuses on calm water.
2. The Zhuo-jin river in Sichuan (Shu).
3. She weeps tears of blood at the thought of the dangers her lover must endure while journeying downriver through the terrifying Qu-tang Gorge, Sichuan.

### Su Xiao Xiao's Tomb
*Irregular: 3 rhymes*

Su Xiao-xiao was a renowned singing-girl from Qian-tang (Hangzhou) who lived during the Southern Qi dynasty (479–502). A tomb, said to be hers, in Jia-xing county, north Zhejiang, was destroyed by fanatical Red Guards during the Cultural Revolution. The Tang writer, Li Shen, recounts the story that sounds of music and singing could be heard coming from the tomb on stormy nights.
1. Singing-girls rode in carriages with varnished sides. Su's carriage may well have been buried with her.
2. The will-o'-the-wisps are like candles lit for the lovers who will never come. After burning for over 300 years, they seem faint and feeble.
3. In spite of the legend that her lovers visited her on stormy nights, she is waiting in vain. The Western Grave-mound (Xi-ling) was near Hangzhou.

### A Dream of Heaven
*7-character: 2 rhymes*

The first four lines describe the moon; the next two the Islands of the Immortals; the last two describe the earth, all as seen from heaven.
1. Animals in the moon.
2. "Cloud Towers"—the Jade Towers of the moon.
3. Fairy-maidens in the moon ride in carriages jingling with simurgh-bells,

their girdle-gems tinkling. The roads are cassia-scented because of the cassia tree there.

4. Three Islands of the Immortals endure throughout geological epochs of time, while the seas cover what was once land, then recede again.

5. An allusion to the nine provinces of the empire. The last lines suggest a famous passage in *Zhuang-zi*, XVII.

### Song for the Boy Tang
### Song of Du, Duke of Bin
*7-character: 1 rhyme*

This boy, Tang-er, was a young son of Du Huang-tang, Duke of Bin. His mother was a princess of the reigning house.

1. A vessel used in the Imperial Temple.

2. The horse's tail is formed from bamboo leaves.

3. "Eastern neighbour's daughter" is a stock expression for a pretty girl. Chinese often write characters with the forefinger, either in the air or on the palm of the hand.

### Sealing up Green Prayers
### A Sacrifice Performed at Night by the Taoist Master, Wu
*7-character: 4 rhymes*

The Sealing up of the Green Prayers was a Taoist rite. The sacrifice described in this poem was presumably to drive away the demons of plague and drought.

1. The Jade Dog was one of the guardians of Heaven.

2. The girls were handmaidens of the spirits.

3. The Father of the Primal Unity, or Emperor of Heaven.

4. Chang-an had six main highways. Droughts and plague were wreaking havoc among the people.

5. Jin Mi-di (134–86 B.C.) was a foreigner whose family acquired great wealth and power during the Former Han.

6. Yang Xiung (53–18 B.C.) was a literary man of the same period, who was so poor he once served as a common soldier. He is contrasting the affluence of the *nouveau-riche* foreigners (Uighurs and Tibetans) in the capital with his own plight. These lines mean: "Even if the rich die in this plague, they will have enjoyed life. Yet poor scholars like me will die filled with resentment."

7. When calling up a ghost it was customary to use some article which the dead man had handled frequently and would recognize. Hence to summon Yang Xiung the medium would employ an antique halberd, a weapon Yang had once carried.

## Twelve Lyrics for Music on the Theme of the Twelve Months of the Year (together with an Intercalary Month) Composed While Taking the Examinations in Henan-fu.

These poems were written in 809 when He was a candidate for the district examination of Henan-fu. They were almost certainly intended to demonstrate his poetic gifts to the examiners before the actual examination.

### First Moon
*7-character: 3 rhymes*

1. One version reads: "In the first month we climb a tower to welcome spring's return."
2. The clepsydra, or water-clock.
3. Perhaps a reference to the cutting of willow-branches at the Cold Food Festival, held in early April.
4. When the leaves can be tied spring will really have arrived.

### Second Moon
*7-character: 2 rhymes*

1. A ford in Henan.
2. The northern swallow is noted for its loud cry.
3. Nobody seems quite sure what this line means. A Japanese commentator translates: "In the rose-bush curtains the mist is caught and green dust is produced." Presumably the picnic-spot is screened by roses, very much as the Japanese still curtain their cherry-viewing picnics (*hanami*).
4. At sunset the party ends.

### Third Moon
*7-character: 3 rhymes*

1. A wind that blows when the sun comes out after rain.

2. "They brush on their eyebrows fashionably close to their eyes."
3. A walled road ran from the women's apartments in the palace down to the Serpentine.
4. The Serpentine was a winding lake in the grounds of the palace.
5. For the palace-maidens who have been left behind, spring seems as melancholy as autumn, while the fallen pear-blossoms look like withered leaves.

### Fourth Moon
*7-character: 3 rhymes*

1. The rain is scented because of the blossoms. The green haze refers to the leaves.

### Fifth Moon
*5-character: 2 rhymes*

1. The finest wells were lined with lead. One commentator says that water drawn at break of day was known as "flowering water." Another believes the term referred to water used for putting on cosmetics.
2. Symbols of love.
3. The sleeves or skirts of the palace dancers look like whirling snow.
4. "Sweet dew" and "fragrant sweat" refer to the perspiration of the dancers in the summer heat. The last line means that the dancers' bodies are beaded with sweat which looks like seeds of grain.

### Sixth Moon
*Irregular: 2 rhymes*

1. The raw silk used for their robes looks as though it has been dusted with frost. The speckled bamboo makes mats as cool as jade feels in autumn.
2. The Scarlet Emperor is Zhu Rong, guardian-spirit of the South.

### Seventh Moon
*3-character: 1 rhyme*

1. The Milky Way.
2. The plate was put out to catch the dew.

3. Hibiscus.
4. A cloud formation which looks like terraces of white jade.

### Eighth Moon
*5-character: 1 rhyme*

1. This couplet has the style of an old *yue fu* ballad.
2. This could refer either to the cricket, whose cry sounds like the reeling of silk, or to the spider.
3. "Lamp-flowers": a peculiar twisting of the snuff of the wick, thought to be lucky.

### Ninth Moon
*7-character: 4 rhymes*

1. "Pu-shou": brass animal-heads into which the rings of the knockers were set.
2. "Flowers of dew": dewdrops about to freeze.
3. "Kingfisher brocades": autumn leaves.
4. "Cock-herald": a term used for the palace watchmen who announced the dawn each day.
5. The kolanut tree is a symbol of autumn.

### Tenth Moon
*7-character: 3 rhymes*

1. The water in the palace clepsydra is close to freezing.
2. The snuff of the wick forms a flower as the lamp burns: since this is a lucky omen, the lamp is said to smile. Yet it is so cold that the light the lamp gives, burning there unmoving, seems to be frozen too, as are its motionless shadows.
3. Candles in dragon-shaped holders.
4. The corridors linking the women's apartments with the main palace were built high off the ground: hence "winged."
5. She is melancholy as the crescent moon of winter. Clearly, the poem is concerned with one of the emperor's neglected favourites.

### Eleventh Moon
*7-character: 3 rhymes*

1. Or: "Go coiling into the distance, shivering."

2. Snow.
3. Wine from Zhong-shan would make one drunk for a thousand days.
4. Both these places were in Lin-qiong county, Sichuan.

### Twelfth Moon
*7-character: 1 rhyme*

1. The feet of the sun-crow.

### Intercalary Month
*Irregular: 2 rhymes*

This was an extra month added from time to time to make the lunar year agree with the solar year.

1. A lunar year was composed of seventy-two periods of five days each.
2. To keep track of the months, the court astronomer would set twelve pitch-pipes on a tube and fill them with bullrush-ash. The ashes were blown from the tube when the appropriate month arrived. Since there was no tube for the intercalary month, He is clearly implying that the calendar is in disorder. This was a grave accusation since it constituted an attack on the emperor himself, who was held to regulate the seasons and the calendar through his virtuous behaviour.
3. "Western Mother"—Xi Wang Mu (the Mother who is Queen in the West) was ranked among the chief Taoist deities. The peaches of the Mother ripen only once every six thousand years and confer immortal life on all who eat them. This is another reference to the emperor's preoccupation with the elixir of life to the neglect of his duties.
4. Xi and He were originally the charioteers of the sun. Later they were historicized as the first Directors of astronomy under the legendary sage-king, Yao. The *Shu-jing* (Classic of History) relates that in 2159 B.C. Zhong Kang punished Xi and He for neglecting their duties and letting the calendar fall into disorder. So the last line of our poem criticizes the dereliction of duty evidenced by the imperial minister—another thrust at the emperor. This poem, unlike the others, could not have been written in connection with He's candidacy for the doctoral degree as its inclusion would have ensured his immediate failure.

## A Ballad of Heaven
*7-character: 4 rhymes*

This poem is another satire directed against Emperor Xian-zong, who had commanded all the Taoist adepts of the empire to appear at his court with recipes for immortal life. These are the real Immortals. He is saying, how can we hope to imitate them?

1. The "Silver Bank" is part of the "River of Heaven" (the Milky Way).
2. The Palace of Jade, the Cassia Tree, and the fairy maidens are all found in the moon.
3. Lung-yu, daughter of Duke Mu of Qin, married the Immortal Wang Zi Qiao (the "King's son" of line seven).
4. The jade pipes of his *sheng* (mouth organ) were shaped like goose-quills.
5. "Jade Grass": a mythical plant.
6. A legendary island in the Eastern Seas, abode of the Immortal Maidens.
7. Gods and Immortals can afford to be careless of the passing of time. To them whole epochs, during which land rises out of the sea and sinks back beneath it again, are as nothing.

## A Wild Song
*7-character: 6 rhymes*

1. In the immense stretches of time that have elapsed since the world came into being (a Buddhist insight) the wind has levelled the mountains to the plain.
2. Tian Wu, god of the waters, turns sea into dry land over geological epochs of time.
3. The peaches of the Mother who is Queen in the West ripen only once every six thousand years. During the passing of these millennia Grandfather Peng (the Chinese Methusaleh) and Wizard Xian (a doctor during the reign of Yao who became a spirit and so knew the date of every man's death) will themselves have died countless times. For He, the so-called Immortals have a life-span as ephemeral as a gnat's in comparison with the eons of time that the universe has endured.
4. The great Hindu master, Śri Ramana Maharshi, made this question the basis of his system of meditation. The answer is: "The Self" (*ātman*).

5. Song Wu-di sent Ding Wu to recover the body of his son-in-law who had fallen in battle. Later, during the reign of Song Xiao Wu-di (r. 453–64) a mournful *yue-fu* ballad appeared based on this event in which the words "Governor Ding" figured in a chorus. Li He is remembering this song.

6. The Lord of Ping-yuan (3rd century B.C.) was famous for his munificence in supporting large numbers of retainers. He regrets that there is now no one who would employ him as the Lord of Ping-yuan would have done.

7. He is mistaken here. The Lord of Ping-yuan ruled in Zhao but was not buried there, so the libation could not have been poured on his grave.

8. The jade toad in the water-dock, which caught the drops in its mouth.

9. Perhaps the girl with the zither who was coaxing him to drink?

10. A difficult line: it might mean "The autumn scene changes before one's eyes to a fresh green" or "In an instant black eyebrows change to autumnal white."

11. Why must young men waste their precious youth in a dreary scramble to become the servants of others?

## Coming of Autumn
### *7-character: 2 rhymes*

1. The cricket is called "the spinner," since its cry sounds like the reeling of silk.

2. Before the invention of paper early in the second century A.D., books were written on slips of green bamboo which had been burnt to remove the oily outer layer. Here He is referring to his own verse, which no one will ever read.

3. Most commentators think this refers to a "bookworm."

4. Perhaps "a dead girl's spirit."

5. The "Graveyard Lament" (*Dai Hao-li Xing*) of the fifth-century poet, Bao Zhao. He is comparing himself to Bao Zhao.

6. *Zhuang-zi*, XXVI, "Chang-hong died in Shu (*circa* 500 B.C.). Chang-hong had been unjustly put to death. Three years after his burial his blood had turned to emerald jade." I think this means that the resentment He felt, embodied in the poem she has written (metaphorically) with his very blood, will turn into precious jade with the passage of time.

## Song to the Goddess
*7-character: 2 rhymes*

Probably the daughters of Emperor Yao, the spirits of the river Xiang. This poem is a comment on the death of Xian-zong's mother in the autumn of 816. This event was accompanied by destructive floods, which were taken as a sign of heaven's displeasure with the Emperor. He is once again satirizing Xian-zong's futile quest for the elixir of life—futile, since in spite of all his own efforts he could not save his mother.

1. An allusion to the inefficacy of the drugs which should have cured the empress. Calamus plant was thought to confer immortality.
2. A minor water-spirit of great beauty.

## The King of Qin Drinks Wine
*7-character: 5 rhymes*

The poem is a hymn of praise to Emperor De-zong (*regnet* 779–805), who had died when He was only a boy of fourteen, not a eulogy of the First Emperor of Qin.

1. The eight points of the compass.
2. The military prowess of the Emperor was manifest everywhere.
3. Xi and He were charioteers of the sun.
4. A kalpa was an Indian (later Buddhist) unit of measure. A cosmic cycle of 4,320 million years constituted one kalpa. At the end of each kalpa came a great dissolution (Mahāpralaya), when the universe was reduced to ashes. The reign of De-zong, He is saying, was a time of unexampled prosperity, a new era rising out of the ashes of the old.
5. A large wine-vessel shaped like a dragon spouted wine from its mouth for its guests.
6. The zithers (*pi pa*) had golden grooves on their bridges for the strings.
7. A line that has led to a good deal of speculation on the part of the commentators. Literally it reads: "Dong-ting rain feet come blow mouth organ." The line is a complex one, fusing many images together: but the basic allusion is to the music played for the Yellow Emperor on Dong-ting lake in northern Hunan (see *Zhuang-zi*, XIV), which sounds like raindrops on water.
8. The phoenix is not a musical instrument, but a singer.
9. The dancers were clad in ocean-pongee (*hai-shao*), a rare and costly

fabric said to be woven by the mermen or shark people who lived under the sea off the coast of Champa.

10. "Beautiful girls with yellow make-up."
11. Literally: "Immortal candle-trees." This could denote either candles decorated with paintings of Immortals or candlesticks in the shape of Immortals.
12. This refers to the palace beauties.

### Pearl—A Luo-yang Beauty
*7-character: 5 rhymes*

1. Like a fairy.
2. Hair-ornaments.
3. Music from her *Zheng* which had reddish brass strings.
4. "Moths" and "willows" were synonyms for the arched, painted eyebrows of a Chinese lady. The girl is drunk, trying to forget her loneliness.
5. A reference to Mount Wu, in Shu, where a Prince Xiang made love to a goddess. "A Shu-mountain dream is a dream" about love-making.
6. The goddess of Mount Wu controlled the clouds and the rain. Hence mist (clouds and rain) here mean "an amorous dream."
7. The last four lines are spoken by the girl herself who is contrasting her own loneliness (bird in a gilded cage!) with the lively life she once enjoyed as a singing-girl.
8. "Clouds" and "snow" stand for a man's robes. Lu Yu was notorious for his love of wine and women.

### The Lady Li
*7-character: 3 rhymes*

Lady Li was a favourite of Emperor Wu of Han (*regnet* 141–87 B.C.) whose premature death plunged the Emperor into despair. He's poems would appear to be an elegy for some favourite or other of the reigning Emperor.

1. The Purple Emperor is one of the three highest divinities dwelling in the Nine Palaces of the Great Purity.
2. Here the lonely simurgh stands for the Emperor. *Shang* was the note of the pentatonic scale associated with autumn and sadness.
3. See the poem *Singing-girls in the Brazen Bird Tower*, below.
4. The Jade Toad was a clepsydra made in the shape of that animal.

For the Cock-herald, see "Ninth Moon", note 4, above.

5. I suspect this line is a hint to the Emperor that though his favourite is dead, there are still many other beautiful women at his command.

### Song of the Horseman
*5-character: 1 rhyme*

An allusion to the story of a certain Shu-li Mu-gong who once slew a man to avenge his father and then flew to the hills. Here he was awakened one night by the whinnying of a supernatural horse, which warned him he was in danger. This is a poem about revenge and Shu-li Mu-gong himself is supposed to be speaking.

1. During the Six Dynasties period, Xiang-yang, in Hebei, was famous for its warriors.
2. The blade was clean and cold because he had not yet slain his enemy.

### The Royal Ladies of the Xiang
*7-character: 2 rhymes*

Legend had it that when Emperor Shun died his two wives, the daughters of Yao, buried him on Mount Cang-wu in Hunan. They wept so bitterly that their tears of blood left stains on all the bamboos of this region. They then threw themselves into the River Xiang, were changed into spirits, and became wives of the River God.

1. Possibly female shamans summoning the two goddesses.
2. Nine Doubts Mountain is another name for Mount Cang-wu. "Red flowers": the red-speckled bamboos of this region.
3. This alludes to the deaths of Shun and his wives. The line also suggests the meaning: "…among mist-hung kolanut trees." "Departure of Simurgh" and "Farewell of Phoenix" were tunes played on the Chinese lute (Qin).
4. "Clouds and rain"; generally a symbol of love.
5. This region was famous for its maples.

### Thirteen Poems from My Southern Garden
*7-character: 1 rhyme*

Poems written in He's home in Chang-gu, while he was making up his mind to take office in Lu-zhou in 814.

1. Xi Shi, most renowned of all Chinese beauties, came from Yue.
2. No respectable Chinese girl would ever get married without a go-between or match-maker.
3. The ruined Fu-chang palace in Chang-gu.
4. This refers to a type of silkworm that produced as much as eight ordinary silkworms.
5. No commentator has explained this line satisfactorily.
6. The gardener came from Yue, in southeast China.
7. Shi-ji, LV, biography of Zhang Liang (d. 189 B.C.) recounts how Zhang met a poorly dressed old man on a bridge. The old man tested him by dropping his shoe under the bridge and then ordering Zhang to pick it up. Later, after testing his patience still further, the old man presented him with a book on the art of war which brought him to success.
8. Wu-gou (Hook of Wu) was the name of a famous type of sword used by the southern aborigines.
9. Over fifty Chinese districts in Henan and Hebei were in the hands of tribal peoples at this time.
10. The portraits found in the Ling-yan pavilion were those of military men who had aided Tang Tai-zong in his struggle for power.
11. Literally: "... a marquis of ten thousand households."
12. He has been studying all night, perfecting his literary style. ("Carving grubs" was a contemptuous expression for writing verse.) There is no point to all this, since a country incessantly at war has little use for poets. The quickest way to gain renown is to fight on some distant frontier.
13. When the poet Si-ma Xiang-ru returned home after eloping with Wen-jun, he found his house in ruins.
14. The Han statesman and philosopher Dong-fang Shuo (154–93 B.C.), styled Man-qian, was noted for his sense of humour—a trait which enabled him to criticize the Emperor yet remain in office.
15. A river in Zhejiang, famous for its copper. Ou-ye Zi cast swords there.
16. An old man who changed into a white monkey to elude his girl-opponent. This is another poem about the futility of a literary career.
17. Magnolias and pepper gave fragrance to the wine.
18. Bian Rang (*floruit* late 2nd-early 3rd centuries A.D.) was a brilliant young man who was given high office when still a youth, thanks to the sponsorship of Cai Yong (133–92), an outstanding poet and writer of the Later Han. Here He is referring to his relationship

with Han Yu—a shade ironically perhaps, since he himself had not achieved office.

19. He will use the bamboos for fishing rods, rather than write poems on them.

20. A reference to the poet Xi Kang (223–62), who here stands for He himself.

21. Pine Stream and Cassia Cave were places in Chang-gu. Dragons always lived in deep, black water. Wang says the eggs were lizard eggs.

22. A name for purified sodium sulphate (Glauber's salt).

23. Yu Qing (Warring States period) wrote the *Yu-shi Chun-qiu* when in great misery.

24. The "Wheat-rain season" begins on 20 April.

### Song of the Brazen Immortal Bidding Farewell to Han
*7-character: 3 rhymes*

Yao interprets this poem as a protest against Xian-zong's extravagance in building two new palaces and constructing an ornamental lake, the Dragon-head Pool. All these activities, He is saying, areas futile as the quest for immortality. Han Wu-di also sought for eternal life, surrounding himself with every luxury. Yet where is he now? Nothing remains of all his glory. Even his Brazen Immortal fell into the hands of others. The latter was a statue which Wu-di had set up on top of his Shen-ming tower. "It was placed high on a metal column, holding a bowl to catch the dew; reaching beyond the vile, clogging dust of the world to obtain the limpid elixir of the pure, translucent ether." Wu-di was accustomed to collect the dew from this vessel and drink it, mixed with powdered jade, in the hope that this would make him immortal. Over three hundred years later, Emperor Ming tried to have the statue brought to his capital. But it proved too heavy to transport over such a distance; so it was eventually left forlornly standing on the banks of the river Ba, in Shanxi, with its dew-plate broken from its hands.

1. Han Wu-di (whose surname was Liu) was buried in the Mao-ling tomb in Xing-ping county, 80 *li* northwest of Chang-an. "Guest of the autumn wind" is a reference to Wu-di's having written a song called *Autumn Wind*, about the brevity of life. It also suggests that his life was as brief as summer; that he is now one with the dead leaves of autumn; that instead of wine and singing-girls, he now has only the cold wind of autumn to entertain him as it whistles through his bones.

2. Cassia trees are growing among the ruins of balustrades.
3. The thirty-six palaces of Chang-an. "Earth-flowers" means moss.
4. The statue still looks on the moon as belonging to Han, though everything else has been usurped by Wei.
5. Xian-yang was the ancient capital of Qin.
6. A famous line.
7. Wei-cheng was the name given by Han to the district around Xian-yang. The change of names suggests the passing of the dynasties.

### Ballad: Time Goes on Forever
*5-character: 1 rhyme*

1. "Jasper blossom"—the moon? Or perhaps "dark blue clouds at night"?
2. Qin Shi Huang-di tried to build a bridge across the sea, to reach the islands of immortality, only to have it pulled down by spirits.
3. "Pillars of bronze": both the pillar on which the Brazen Immortal of Han Wu-di stood and those pillars, 3,000 *li* in circumference, which held up the sky over Mount Kun-lun.

### The Young Man with a Yellow Hat
*Irregular: 3 rhymes*

A boatman.
1. "South shore" suggests parting.
2. See above, the poem *The Royal Ladies of the Xiang*.
3. "Zither"—actually a *se*, a zither with twenty-five strings.
4. "Yellow arrowroot" is also the name of a ballad.
5. Lotus blooms in early summer, deer parsley in autumn. She has waited in vain for her husband's return all these months.
6. Incense-burners in the form of ducks, symbols of conjugal love.

### Twenty-Three Poems about Horses

These poems, though ostensibly concerned with horses, are in fact about the neglect and misuse of men of genius. Since He was born in the Year of the Horse (890), he saw himself as a thoroughbred, ill-treated and unrecognized. He's patron Han Yu frequently employed this very metaphor, insisting that though there were "thousand league horses" in plenty, nobody had the wit to recognize them.

1. Suffering bitter hardship, the poor scholar finds still more misery in store.
2. The Emperor of Zhou, at least, knew a thoroughbred when he saw one.
3. The constellation Fang was said to be composed of four horses.
4. A reference to the sand-dunes.
5. Mount Yan-ran, now known as Mount Hang-ai, in Mongolia.
6. Another vivid picture of He at the end of his tether.
7. Mu Gong, or the Eastern King, is the male principle of the air, while the Mother who is Queen in the West is the female. From these two principles heaven and earth are formed.
8. High-king Mu of Zhou was said to have feasted with the Mother who is Queen in the West and the Eastern King at the Peach Blossom Banquet, which takes place at the side of the Jade Lake and is attended by all classes of Immortals. He was driven to their palace in the Kun-lun mountain by his eight famous horses. He's prince would be unable to do this since his horses are worthless. This poem is a thrust at rulers who (a) spend their time seeking immortality, and (b) employ only third-rate men. This poem is a protest against the Emperor's appointment of a eunuch, as Commander-in-Chief of the forces attacking Wang Cheng-zong.
9. Russet Hare was a renowned horse ridden by the hero Lü Bu, during the period of the Three Kingdoms.
10. "Fruit-tree ponies" were dwarf ponies from Korea.
11. Legend has it that a descendant of Shu An of Liao, called Dong-fu, could tame dragons.
12. Xiang Yu, defeated by the founder of the Han dynasty in the struggle for the empire, gave away his steed, Dapple, to the man who had ferried him across the river Wu. Shortly afterwards, he killed himself.
13. Another protest against wanton neglect of genius. Bo-luo, a famous judge of horseflesh, came across a magnificent horse dragging a load of salt up a steep hill.
14. A description of a newborn colt. Peach-blossom markings were the sign of a fine horse.
15. Since there are no connoisseurs of horseflesh left, the young man in question can only present the bones of a fine horse to King Xiang's spirit; for since King Xiang has the power to dream of horses, perhaps he at least will know a fine horse when he sees one.
16. A satire on some rich, successful, and worthless young man?
17. Duke Huan of Qi (685–643 B.C.) had a piebald horse so fierce it frightened off tigers.

18. A genius labors under heavy disabilities. But when it comes to the test, he will outstrip all others.
19. Pampered horses are fed on cereals, not grass.
20. Long teeth were the sign of a horse that could run 1000 leagues in one day. The poem means that those in power are afraid of men of genius.
21. Bo-luo Sun Yang of Qin, a famous judge of horseflesh. A horse with whorls of hair on its belly was said to be capable of covering 1000 leagues a day.
22. Legend has it that the first Buddhist scriptures were brought to China on the back of a white horse.
23. Zhang-tai street, in Chang-an, was located in the quarter where the singing-girls lived.
24. "Fish-gut": name of a famous sword.
25. A young prince wearing a belt and sword needs a fine horse. So a ruler needs a talented man around him if he is to establish a reputation.
26. Why does the emperor dismiss his patient officials simply because the empire is temporarily at peace? Gao-zhou was a malarial region in Guangdong to which many officials were banished.
27. The blood-sweating horses of Ferghana were famous throughout antiquity.
28. Bells adorned the bits of horses.
29. Li Shao-chun was an Immortal who was seen riding a black mule in Pu-ban, over three months after his supposed death.
30. Emperor Wu of Han dabbled in alchemy, trying to make gold by smelting cinnabar.
31. Emperor Wu invaded Ferghana to seize its blood-sweating horses; but even they were not truly divine.

### Song: Bearded Shen Playing His Tartar Horn
*5-character: 1 rhyme*

Type of flageolet.
1. Li Dao-zong was Prince of Jian-xia.
2. Tao Yuan-ming (365–427) and Xie Ling-yun (385–433) were the greatest poets of the pre-Tang period.
3. A reed instrument with nine holes and a mouthpiece like the Tartar horn.
4. Ju Yin, of the Jin dynasty, was so poor that in the summer he

studied by the light of fireflies which he caught himself. His host, though poor, was an assiduous student.

## Song of the Old Jade-Hunter
*7-character: 3 rhymes*

A ballad of social protest, very much in the style made popular by Bo Ju-yi, Yuan Zhen and others.

1. One of the most sought-after types of jade during Tang.
2. A woman's hair-ornament which shook as the wearer walked.
3. Indigo Field (Lan-tian) among the mountains of Shaanxi provided the finest "jade," actually a type of green-and-white marble.
4. During the summer the cuckoo—believed to be the soul of a banished emperor—cried day and night, so the story went, until its mouth ran with blood.
5. Their ghosts hate the officials whose depredations drove them to their death while hunting for jade.
6. A type of creeper also called "think-of-your-children." "Ancient terraces" means "mountains" here.

## Ballad of an Aching Heart
*5-character: 1 rhyme*

1. *The Songs of Chu.*
2. The spirit, weary of journeying through endless reincarnations, lodges for a while in the body.

## Song: On the Lake
*7-character: 3 rhymes*

1. The plum-breeze is the wind that blows down the plums in the fifth lunar month. A singing-fan was used to screen the face when singing.
2. Crown Prince Shi of Yue was sent as a hostage to the King of An-yang. The king's daughter, Mei-zhu, fell in love with him and yielded herself to him.
3. Shu produced a very fine writing-paper. The expression rendered as "a delicate letter" reads literally "a letter in small characters." The fineness of the calligraphy was a mark of the good breeding of her lover.

### The Caves of the Yellow Clan
*7-character: 2 rhymes*

The region of south Guangxi and west Guangdong was inhabited by aborigines called the Yellow Cave Natives who were for long a nuisance to the imperial government. In the winter of 816 they staged a large-scale uprising.

1. Bronze drums were the finest artifacts of aboriginal culture.
2. Their war-paint was evidently reddish-purple, like the flowers of the arrowroot.
3. The alligator was said to "make a noise like a drum and sound the watches of the night."
4. The bamboo-viper was particularly venomous. "Flying crawlers" are "flying hairy caterpillars." The *you* was a fabulous beast said to spit sand onto the shadows of people, who then sickened and died.
5. "Bamboo-horse" can only have been the name of some type of vehicle, since horses could not survive in the jungles of the south.
6. While the aborigines quietly go home with their plunder, the government armies wreak vengeance on the harmless inhabitants of Rong-zhou, in order to lay claim to a resounding victory.

### Song: The Screen
*7-character: 1 rhyme*

A poem about a newly married couple whose bed is surrounded by an elaborate screen.

1. The hinges of the screen look like glass coins.
2. There were twelve screens arranged in pairs across the bed.
3. Gold cicada-shaped hairpins.
4. A type of incense.
5. The tying of wine-goblets with a sash was part of the wedding ceremonies.

### Walking through the South Mountain Fields
*Irregular: 2 rhymes*

"*Xing*" here does not mean "Ballad."

1. White was the colour assigned to autumn, being the colour of mourning.
2. Note the synaesthesia in this remarkable image.

3. The will-o'-the-wisps burn as feebly and as sinisterly as the black lacquer lamps placed in tombs.

### Joys of a Princess Travelling in Battle Array
*7-character: 4 rhymes*

A satire directed against a princess of the time going out to a banquet in He-yang accompanied by her retinue, many of whom are her own handmaids accoutered for war to act as her bodyguard. Alternatively, a satire on a eunuch-general, here ridiculed as a "princess."
1. "Purple Swallow"—name of a famous thoroughbred of the early Han. He-yang was renowned for its flowers.
2. A serrated pennon stood before the tent of the commanding officer. Though the general herself has not yet risen, brocade clothes are bestowed on the ladies of her retinue.

### "After a Drinking Party" Zhang-Che, My Elder, Once Presented Me with a Poem on This Theme. At That Time Zhang Wa Serving as Adviser in Lu-Zhou.
*7-character: 3 rhymes*

Zhang Che (d. 821) was one of He's closest friends.
1. "Dragon-head" was a sobriquet applied to the foremost of a group of friends.
2. Zhang was a descendant of the Princess Ning-qin. Bamboo tablets decorated with fish-barbs were part of the insignia of the highest officials.
3. Officials of the sixth and seventh ranks wore green robes. Hence the line means: "As you crossed the Tai-hang range to take up your first post, your (commoner's) robes turned green."
4. The Golden Horse Portals and the Stone Culvert Pavilion both stood in the capital during Han times. Here they denote high office.
5. The *zhi* (loosely rendered "unicorn") was used as a symbol on the caps worn by the President and Vice-President of the Tribunal of Censors when they were preferring charges. Great officers of state had to put cloves in their mouths to sweeten their breath when they addressed reports to the emperor.
6. He, whose style was Chang-ji, came from Long-xi commandery in Gansu.
7. In Shanxi.

### Verses on Being Presented with a Length of Summer Cloth by the Mountaineer of Luo-fu.
*7-character: 2 rhymes*

Summer-cloth was a light fabric woven from the *ke* plant (*pueraria thunbergiana*). The Mountaineer was a Taoist Immortal living on Mount Luo-fu in Guangdong.

1. On the Orchid Terrace of King Xiang of Chu, every breeze was delightful.
2. Another name for Luo-fu.
3. The demons cry out because the precious cloth they have woven has been given away.
4. In July the heat is so great that snakes lose their venom and fish burrow into the sand of the river-bed.
5. The cloth is brilliant as the sky.
6. Wu was renowned for its steel.

### A Few Remarks Addressed to Huang-Fu Shih from the Jen-ho Quarter
*7-character: 5 rhymes*

This poem was written in the winter of 810, when He was setting off to Chang-an to take his Selection examination, after having failed to qualify for the doctorate. Huang-fu Shi was a patron of He's. The Ren-he quarter of Luo-yang was a pleasant, sparsely settled district near the Chang-xia gate.

1. A reference to Huang-fu's debacle in an examination scandal which led him to lose his official position.
2. Officials of the seventh grade and upwards wore white writing-brushes in their hair.
3. He was also affected by the disgrace of his patron.
4. A reference to his failure to qualify for the doctorate examination.
5. Dao Jian and Ding Jun-du were renowned as judges of horses. Here He is referring to his patrons, the great poet Han Yu and Huang-fu Shi.
6. This suggests a nervous breakdown consequent on the shock of his rejection.
7. The Office of Heaven was a name for the Ministry of Civil Office. Clearly, He was going to sit for another examination.

8. Candidates for the Selection examination were supposed to be in Chang-an by the twentieth day of the tenth month.

## Song of a Palace Beauty
### *7-character: 4 rhymes*

The summer of 813 was marked by severe floods, alleged to be due to a predominance of the Yin (female) element. The Emperor therefore sent three hundred of his harem back to their homes. This poem depicts the plight of a girl who was not sent back.

1. The candle-light is seen through the gauze of her bed-curtains.
2. "Palace-wardens" was a name given to geckos, which were fed on cinnabar until they turned red. They were then pounded up in mortars, the resulting paste being used to mark the bodies of the Emperor's concubines. It was believed that such spots would not disappear until the woman had sexual intercourse. Thus a check could be kept on the behavior of the women of the harem—hence the name "palace-wardens." The girl lies awake listening to the noise of the mortars, reflecting bitterly that she will never have need of the palace-wardens again.
3. Incense-braziers were often made in the form of animals, generally ducks or elephants.
4. The seven stars of the Dipper.
5. A net stretched across the edge of the eaves. See above, the poem *Passing by the Hua-qing Palace*.
6. Lady Zhen was a discarded favourite of Emperor Wen of Wei (*regnet* 220–26). She was eventually forced to commit suicide.
7. Long Island (Chang-zhou) was the old name of a county in Jiangsu, in the ancient territory of Wu. Like the Lady Zhen, the girl came from Suzhou, a place famous for its beautiful girls. The Long River (the Milky Way) seems to curve down the sky in the direction of Chang-zhou, forming a watery pathway which could lead her home.

## Hall After Hall
### *Irregular: 1 rhyme*

He is once again visiting the ruins of Hua Qin palace (see above, the poem *Passing by the Hua-qing Palace*).

1. When a temple in Shao-xing dedicated to the legendary emperor Yu was being repaired, during the Liang dynasty (A.D. 502–57), a beam of plum-tree wood was said to have come magically flying to the site.
2. For these springs, see the poem *Passing by the Hua-qing Palace* above. The stone in question is arsenolite, a poisonous substance used for accelerating the growth of silk worms.
3. "White phoenixes"—the emperor's ladies.

### Be Sure to Take Care of Yourself
### Two Poems Written When I Escorted Young Li on
### His Way to Mount Lu.
*5-character: 1 rhyme (Poem 1)*
*Irregular: 4 rhymes (Poem 2)*

He's younger brother was going to Mount Lu, the famous Buddhist centre in Jiangxi.

1. No ceremonial farewell meal for the traveller.
2. One of the peaks of Mount Lu.
3. The famous Nine Rivers of Chu.
4. The Stone Mirror stood on the summit of Pine Gate Mountain, north of Xin-jian in Jiangxi. It was a natural rock-formation, so smooth and polished it looked like a mirror.
5. It was customary to say farewell under a willow.
6. Literally: "The warp of the threads in my spirit-tower is as raveled as the hanging silk of spring (silkworms)." "Spirit-tower" simply means "heart."
7. He is describing the dilapidation of his house.
8. The horns blown at sunset when the gates were shut.

### Let Wine Be Brought In!
*7-character: 2 rhymes*

1. Zhu-fu Yan (d. 127 B.C.) was a scholar from Qi, who wandered around for many years seeking employment in vain. He was not given a post until he sent up a particularly brilliant memorial. This allusion would imply that Li He had not yet found employment.
2. His family had been leaning against the willows, waiting for him to return, for so long that they had finally broken the tree down!

3. Ma Zhou (601–48) was a retainer of Chang He's, but this was in Chang-an, not Xin-feng (Shaanxi). In Xin-feng he had astonished an innkeeper by his capacity to drink. In Chang-an, in 631, he wrote a memorial to the emperor on Chang's behalf which so impressed Tai-zong that he summoned Ma to court.

### Long Songs After Short Songs
*5-character: 2 rhymes*

"Long song" and "Short song" were the names of *Yue-fu* ballads, both of which had for their theme the shortness of man's life. The story goes that He wrote this poem when he was only seven years old. This is, of course, quite untrue. Our poet is ill and grieving over his failure in the examination.

1. His hair was cut short because of his illness.
2. At this time Emperor Xian-zong had retired to Qin; hence the allusion.
3. One commentator plausibly equates the moon with the Emperor and the high rocks which bar Li He from the moon with the powerful officials of the court.

### Song: Do Not Dance, Sir!
*7-character: 4 rhymes*

Shi-ji, VII, biography of Xiang Yu, relates the story of the struggle for empire between Xiang-yu of Chu and Liu Bang, Lord of Pei, who afterwards became the first Han emperor. Liu Bang's forces had been the first to enter the Qin capital, Xian-yang, and take possession of the strategic Han-gu Pass. Enraged at this, Xiang Yu was about to attack Liu's forces when he was visited by his rival in his camp at Hong-men. At the feast that followed, Fan Zeng signalled to Xiang Yu with his girdle-pendant, silently asking permission to have Liu killed. When Xiang did not reply, Fan ordered Xiang Zhuang to perform a sword-dance in the course of which he was to kill Liu where he sat. However, as Xiang Zhuang was dancing, Xiang Bo, an uncle of Yu's, leapt up with his sword and joined in the dance, "protecting Liu with his body so that Xiang Zhuang could not smite him." At this juncture Liu's carriage-guard, Fan Kuai, strode into the hall, shouldering aside the sentries, and denounced Yu for attempting to kill his master. Thanks to the intervention of these two men, Liu was able to escape.

This episode, as recounted by the historian Si-ma Qian, became so popular that it figured widely in both folk-tales and plays.

1. The lute (*Zheng*), symbol of Chinese culture, could not survive in that barbarous, southern atmosphere.
2. Xiang Yu was still not drunk enough to kill Liu Pei.
3. *Shi-ji*, VI, biography of Liu Bang, says he was begotten by a red dragon.
4. See ibid. The history recounts how the First Emperor of Qin heard that "there was an emanation characteristic of a Son of Heaven in the southwest," and set out to destroy Liu Bang who fled and hid himself among the swamps and rocks of Mang and Tang. His wife, however, was able to track him down because wherever he went he was followed by the auspicious cloud mentioned above. Mang was in the old state of Pei, in Henan. Tang was in ancient Liang, in Jiangsu.
5. These lines describe Liu Bang's capture of the Qin capital.
6. He has put these words in Fan Guai's mouth, for the *Shi-ji* does not record them. Cutting off the kneecaps and disembowelling were ancient punishments.

### Four Poems about New Bamboo-Shoots in My North Garden at Chang-gu.
#### *7-character: 1 rhyme*

1. Bamboo-shoots are called *long-sun*—"dragon's grandchildren."
2. A highly ambiguous line. It could mean: (a) "On this unfeeling bamboo, I, who am full of bitterness at my lot, write my verse"; (b) "I have no one to love me, so full of bitterness I write my verse"; or (c) "I write verses, some of them beyond passion, some of them full of resentment." The bamboo as it grows will carry his verse into the air, far out of the reach of men.
3. The poet hacks away at the green skin of the bamboo until the white under-surface is exposed. On this he writes his verses. The commentators take the "Songs of Chu" to refer to He's own poems, which he frequently compares to the *Chu Ci*.
4. "Purple path"—either a path in the garden or else the road itself.
5. To make fishing-rods.
6. The poet Si-ma Xiang-ru retired to Mao-ling, Shaanxi, when he fell ill.
7. *Shi-ji*, CXXIX, biography of Huo Zhi, says: "A man with a thousand arpents (*mou*) of bamboos is on a level with the marquis with a fief of ten thousand households." (6.6 *mou* is approximately one acre.)

8. Or: "When the wind blows among my thousand arpents of bamboos, I greet the rain with a whistle."

### She Steals My Heart
*5-character: 1 rhyme*

Presumably a poem celebrating the beauty of some singing-girl or other, with whom He had become involved. My translation of this highly allusive and obscure piece of verse is in several places at best tentative.

1. Sung Yu, a poet who seems to have lived at the court of King Qing-Xiang of Chu (*regnet* 298–265 B.C.), is the supposed author of the *Jiu Bien* (The Nine Arguments) of the Chu Ci. Tradition has it that he was a romantic and dissolute fellow, much given to philandering.

2. Incense was burnt in a censer.

3. The magpie was a common motif on mirrors. This alludes to an old story about a husband and wife who broke a mirror in two on parting, each keeping one half. When the wife proved unfaithful, her half of the mirror changed into a magpie and flew off to tell the husband.

4. Probably ornaments made from the iridescent elytra of the gold-and-turquoise *chrysochroa* beetle.

5. The cardamom flower symbolized love. For cardamoms, see Schafer, *Golden Peaches*, pp. 184–85. "Lotus" (*liǎn*) and "love" (*liěn*) were pronounced rather alike in Ancient Chinese, both in the level tone. Here the lotus symbolizes affection.

6. The Pearl Game, in which a plateful of pearls was skillfully juggled, as a professional entertainer's act, just the sort of diversion a singing-girl would put on for her clients.

7. The red nets were to catch birds, the green to catch fish.

8. A satirical touch! The mother of the Han Emperor, Ling-di (*regnet* 168–89), the Empress Dowager Yong-luo, was so greedy for food and money that she became the butt of a popular ballad, from which He is quoting.

9. She instructs her maids to keep the household accounts and asks her servant-lad about what medicines she should buy. Then she undresses, retires to bed, and dreams of bearing a son.

10. "Geese" jewellery worn on the temples. To dream of bears was an omen of a baby boy, as snakes were omens of a baby girl.

11. She is hopelessly in love with someone who has left her to pine

away like a fading rainbow. Her efforts to forget her love are as vain as those of the *qing-wei* bird that tried to fill in the Eastern Sea or Master Simple of North Mountain who set out to remove Mount Tai-lang and Mount Wangwu. Alternatively, the lines might well refer to He's efforts to gain her love, which though seemingly hopeless were finally crowned with success.

12. Lovesickness has wasted her away, so that her bones stick out like the "dragon-bones" found in an apothecary's shop.

13. Maple-leaves fall on the spot where she has been drinking.

14. The day-lily was also known as *yi-nan*, "should-have-a-son." The lanes of Chu were the streets in the Golden Wall quarter in the northwest of Luo-yang, where the singing-girls lived.

15. The screen was set with jade patterned like tortoise-shell.

16. Wei Huan (220–91) was a celebrated calligrapher of the Jin dynasty, renowned for the elegance of his draft script. The girl is writing a letter in a hand as vigorous as that in which Wei Huan transcribed the *Yellow Courtyard Classic* (*Huang-ting jing*), a well-known Taoist work.

17. There are several versions of the Han Peng legend, the most usual of which relates that Han Peng, a minister of the state of Song, had a beautiful wife. His lord, King Kang, threw him into prison where he died, and then seized the girl, who thwarted his designs by killing herself. Furious at being thus frustrated, the king had the two bodies buried in separate graves: but from each of these there sprouted a tree, in the branches of which, interlaced over the tombs, two birds came to sing. Thus, the Han Peng birds are symbols of undying love. For another version of the legend, see A. Waley, *Ballads and Stories from Tun-huang* (London, 1960), pp. 56–64.

18. The fragrant candles have burnt out.

19. Xin-feng was the suburb of Chang-an where wine was made.

20. Her jade-pendant bore a pattern of millet.

21. Euphemisms for love-making.

22. Wen Qiao (288–329), a minister of the Jin dynasty, sent his beautiful cousin a betrothal present of a vanity mirror.

23. Jia Chung (217–82), a prime minister of the Jin dynasty, had a daughter who was having an affair with a handsome retainer of his called Han Shou. Chung noticed that Shou's clothes bore the scent of a rare perfume his daughter used, and so discovered who her lover was.

24. During the Six Dynasties, certain words acquired special connotations in love poetry. "Lotus-root" is a symbol for girl, while "fish" stands for pleasure. In the second line, "stone-lotus" stands for

lover, and "man" stands for woman. The secret meaning of the lines is thus: "Pleasure was born beneath the girl's body. The woman was tightly held by the man's hands."

25. It was the custom for a singing-girl to spray the mane of her lover's horse with water when he left. This was probably a magical practice designed to ensure the lover's return. An alternative translation, based on the older commentaries, runs:

> "She knits her blue eyebrow, eyes full of tears,
> On the tower she sprays her hair, a horse's mane."

26. *Shi-jun* was a Han dynasty title meaning "Governor." The line is probably a reference to the Han Ballad *The Mulberries by the Path*. See J. D. Frodsham, *An Anthology of Chinese Verse* (Oxford, 1967), pp. 4–6.

27. The poet Si-ma Xiang-ru was said to have held the office of Custodian of the Royal Tomb. Presumably these two lines are spoken by the girl, who is comparing herself to the modest Luo-fu of *The Mulberries by the Path* and her lover (Li He?) to this romantic poet. The Governor would then be a rejected admirer.

28. The Wang family of Lang-ye, Shandong, was one of the most powerful of the Six Dynasties period. He is referring either to Wang Xian-zhi (344–88), a scion of this clan, who is said to have had a concubine called Peach Leaves to whom he wrote poems or to Wang Zi Qiao, the Immortal.

29. The beautiful and talented concubine of the great minister Xie An (320–85).

30. "The Three Stars": Orion. Carriages of influential people gather in the street of the Bronze Camel in Luo-yang. Another reference to *The Mulberries by the Path*: "Lord Governor came from the South country. His team of five stood waiting there." This may well mean that the girl had rejected the advances of an influential admirer in favour of Li He.

31. Rhinoceros horn was taken in powdered form during Tang, especially as an antidote to poison. It was not used as an aphrodisiac at that time. Mercury was among the most important Chinese *materia medica*. The girl was probably taking "silver tallow," an amalgam of silver, tin and mercury commonly used as a sedative.

32. "Royal hour" means "auspicious time." On the seventh night of the seventh month, stars known as the Herd-boy and the Weaving Lady met.

33. Heaven was said to have three palaces. Hence this line must refer to

He's post in the Court of Imperial Sacrifices. The fortune-teller is predicting that on the seventh night of the seventh month Li He and the girl will meet, like the Herd-boy and the Weaving Lady.

34. Mica was one of the "superior drugs" of the Chinese pharmacopoeia. It was said to lighten the body and lengthen life.

35. Li He is wending his way home just before dawn after spending the night with this girl.

### Five Exhortations
*5-character: 3 rhymes (Poem 1)*
*5-character: 1 rhyme (Poems 2–5)*

A satire on rapacious officials. Since the middle of the eighth century, China had agreed to take as many horses from the Uighurs as the latter cared to send them. Since each horse cost fifty pieces of silk this placed a tremendous burden upon the silk-industry. In 809 Bo Ju-yi wrote a memorial estimating that some 500,000 pieces of silk had been used to buy such horses. Bo Ju-yi and other poets all wrote poems sympathizing with the peasant women who had to work themselves to exhaustion to supply the tax-collectors with silk.

1. During the Later Han dynasty, He-pu county, Guangdong, was stripped of the pearls it produced by its local officials. Long-yang, Henan, was where Li Meng (early 3rd century A.D.), of the kingdom of Wu, planted a thousand orange trees, telling his children on his deathbed that they now had a thousand wooden slaves to produce wealth for them.

2. This was a tax notice.

3. He is arguing—from personal experience—that geniuses, who do what they must (while talent does what it can), find youth has passed them by while they were immersed in their work. They are so impatient to reap success, which will only come with the years, that for them time seems to crawl along. Yeats thought much the same, as is evident from his poem, "What then?" See *Collected Poems* (London, 1952), p. 347.

4. A sign of high office.

5. Jia Yi (201–168 B.C.) was a brilliant, young writer who lost favour with Emperor Wen when he was slandered by his envious contemporaries and later died tragically. "Bluebottles" could stand for "slan-

derers," as in Song 219. Alternatively, it could mean that bluebottles, whining round the corpse, were the only mourners for Jia Yi.

6. The Cold Food Festival was held on the 105th day after the winter solstice, just before the Qing-ming Festival. He visits Jia Yi's grave during the Qing-ming Festival, as was the custom, and sees the landscape mirror his mood.

7. Emperor Wen, who was stupid enough to listen to the calumnies of fools.

8. Mount Zhung-nan was the site of many graveyards.

9. Some editions read: "Spring's beauty ages under the wind's shears."

10. Yao believes this is a reference to Shun-zong's accession.

11. "Lacquer torches"—will-o'-the-wisps, generally called "ghost fires." "Newcomers"—those newly buried.

12. Yen Zun, styled Jun-ping, was said to have been Lao-zi's teacher. He lived in Cheng-du, Sichuan, where he told fortunes in the marketplace for a living, always shutting up shop for the day when he had gained a hundred cash.

13. He meant to refer not to Han Bai, styled Kang-bai (332–80), of the Eastern Jin dynasty, but to Han Kang, styled Bai-Xiu, of the Later Han. He sold medicines in the marketplace at Chang-an, gaining such a reputation for honesty that the Emperor himself finally sent for him. Kang, however, managed to escape.

14. Outstanding men have fled from the workday world, leaving only a crowd of noisy nonentities behind them.

15. A toad was supposed to live in the moon.

16. Chang-e, goddess of the moon with her cassia tree.

17. Or perhaps:
    "The fairy maid watches her dewy cassia,
    The lowering clouds gradually descend."

18. A scholar-hermit of the Later Han. He is referring to his own loneliness and poverty.

### In the Third Month I Pass by the Imperial Travelling Lodge
*7-character: 1 rhyme*

When Emperor Xuan-zong stayed at the lodge, several girls had been brought in to spend the night with him. After his departure, the girls were commanded to remain immured in the lodge for the rest of their lives though the emperor would never return there.

1. Or: "The palace is surrounded by a moat where prince's feather and artemisia grow."

### Following the Theme of He and Xie: Singing-Girls in the Brazen Bird Tower
*5-character: 1 rhyme*

The Brazen Bird Tower in Ye (Lin-zhang county, Henan) had been built by Cao Cao, first Emperor of the Wei dynasty, in A.D. 210. When he died, he left instructions to his sons that all his concubines were to be immured for life in the mausoleum tower. Morning and evening, the girls had to bring food and wine to his bed, which stood with drawn curtains upon the topmost story. On the first and fifteenth days of every month, the girls had to dance and sing before his bed, just as though he were still alive.

1. Stone horses lined the path to the royal tombs, which lay west of the tower.
2. Because the girls are so numerous.
3. A sacrificial table on which offerings to Cao's spirit were laid.

### Seeing Off the Banquet Officer Qin on His Military Expedition to the North
*5-character: 1 rhyme*

Qin's identity is unknown. He held a post in the Office of Imperial Banquets.

1. Glue for sticking together the sections of composite-bows was made in autumn, when the nomads attacked.
2. The river Ba flows through Shaanxi, east of Chang-an.
3. During the Former Han, Zhou Ya-fu (d. 143 B.C.) had encamped at Xi-liu (Little Willow), northwest of Chang-an, while on a punitive expedition against the nomads.
4. Comets were portents of war.
5. Elms planted along the Great Wall.
6. Jade Gate is a strategic point in Gansu, west of Dun-huang.
7. Towards the end of the Later Han dynasty, the corpse of the rebel Dong Zhuo (d. 192) was left in the marketplace with a fire burning in the fat of its belly. Hence our line reads literally "...planted fire in Dong Zhuo's navel."

8. Tai-chang—an officer of the Court of Imperial Sacrifices.
9. Peach-blossom markings were a sign of a fine horse.
10. A reference to the farewell banquet given to him by the emperor, in connection with his new appointment.
11. All these were presents bestowed on him by the emperor. "Fish-gut" was the name of a famous sword of antiquity. Sticks of incense were burnt to mark the watches of the night. Falcons were kept awake at night to make them hungry and fierce.
12. The last ten lines have vexed the commentators into disagreement. Presumably this couplet means that he parted from his wife when he set out for Yellow Dragon Fort in Liao-dong, and on the way took a concubine at Qing-meng (Green Grave) in Inner Mongolia, south of present day Huhehot. A broken, bronze mirror is the symbol of the parting of husband and wife. "Sunny Terrace" refers to a line from the *Gao Tang fu*, a poem attributed to Sung Yu, where the goddess with whom the king has spent the night mentions this spot on Mount Wu. Hence our line may allude to a clandestine love-affair. It is possible, however, that the line simply means that Qin was thinking of his wife while on his journey.
13. While he defeats the nomads ("slays the dragon"), his wife laments his absence. Hou Tiao was supposed to have invented the vertical harp at the instigation of Han Wu-di.
14. Presumably a reference to his taking his sons with him. But some commentators believe this refers to singing-girls from Qian-tang, a city famous for its courtesans. This poem has defeated all the commentators, for it is either incomplete or else full of mistakes.
15. One commentator believes this refers to the story in *Huai-nan-zi* about Ci Fei slaying the water-dragon. Another thinks it refers to Zhou Chu, who slew a dragon at Long Bridge.

### Written in Reply
*7-character: 1 rhyme*

1. Officials of the third degree and upwards wore golden-fish purses at their belts.
2. Perfume made and given to him by a palace lady.
3. "Yong-chou": the district round the capital.
4. The night-heron was commonly kept as a pet since its presence was supposed to avert fires.

### On a Painting of the Walls of Yong-dong
*5-character: 1 rhyme*

Yong-dong is a well-known port in Zhejiang. Since both a dawn scene and a night scene are depicted, He may be describing two paintings.
1. Sea-spray ("water-flowers") wets the head-bands of the soldiers, who are welcoming the spirits of the tide with banners and drums.

### Bachelor Xie Had a Concubine by the Name of Gao-Lian Who Deserted Him for Another Man. Xie Tried to Make Her Stay with Him, but was Unsuccessful. Later She Grew Sentimental about Him. Those of Our Party Wrote Poems Satirizing and Vilifying Her. Later I Added Four Poems of My Own.
*5-character: 1 rhyme*

1. "Mud" stands for the girl; "clouds" for her first husband.
2. "Elder sister": the girl in question, who was, of course, no relative of He's.
3. Insignia of high office.
4. One commentator believes that "simurgh" here stands for the girl. It is more likely that her vanity-mirror was cast in the form of a simurgh.
5. A cosmetic made from the safflower.
6. A prince who had a concubine by the name of Emerald Jade was so infatuated with her that he wrote her a *yue-fu* beginning: "When Emerald Jade split the melon...." The expression *po-gua* ("to split a melon"), when used of a girl, means "to reach her sixteenth year," since the character for "melon" can be split up into two characters which look like the graph for "eight." But in the strongly satirical context of our poem, the phrase also suggests the expressions *po-shen* and *po-zhen*, both of which mean "to be deflowered." The next line of the couplet carries on this suggestion.
7. Because the rank of her new master was so exalted. But the line might also mean: "What man dare she look in the face (after such infamous conduct)?" This poem has been brilliantly translated by Schafer, *The Golden Peaches of Samarkand* (Berkeley and Los Angeles, 1963), p. 116.
8. She is thinking of her former husband with as much ardour as the bee shows when honey-gathering.

9. Aromatic candles were popular in well-to-do households. But since the lady already has a lamp in her room (line 5), the incense-stick here was presumably for sweetness rather than light.

10. See Schafer, *Golden Peaches*, pp. 115–16, for a discussion of the *chrysochroa* beetle, whose wing-cases were used as ladies' hair-ornaments and love-talismans.

11. Mandarin ducks—ironically in this context—are a symbol of faithful love.

12. The sound of the pounding of washing-blocks with batons had reminded her of the days of her poverty and so prevented her from sleeping. It was not so much the noise as her conscience that was troubling her!

13. Sung Yu here stands for Bachelor Xie.

14. Wen Shu, pet-name Wen-ying, son of Wen Qin of Wei dynasty, was a general at eighteen. Gao-lian had obviously married a military man.

15. The tops of the frames which held musical stones, drums, and so on were often shaped by the handles of halberds. The uprights of such stands were ornamented with dragons.

16. A "cassia window" is a window with a cassia tree growing across it.

17. To welcome guests in such a way was the height of vulgarity.

18. On the beams, customarily ornamented with dragons and phoenixes, she sees only a crow, symbol of her present husband.

### While Studying in Chang-gu, I Showed This Poem To My Servant-Lad from Ba
*5-character: 1 rhyme*

Ba was the name of the ancient state which occupied present-day Ba county, Sichuan. The boy, who belonged to the Lao people, may have been the lad who accompanied He when he wandered round the countryside writing poems.

1. Disappointed and ailing after failing to obtain his doctorate, He sees himself as a defeated fighting-cock, nursing its wounds.

### The Servant-Lad from Ba Replies

2. An allusion to He's "new *yue-fu*" criticizing the government and the times. He seems to be hinting that writing these ballads has ruined his career.

### I Take Cui's Place in Seeing Off a Traveler
*5-character: 1 rhyme*

1. The mist is so thick that the slightest movement of their horses will make them lose sight of each other.

### Leaving the City
*5-character: 1 rhyme*

This poem was written in 810, after He had been refused his doctorate.
1. The Han-gu Pass.
2. The wind was blowing him in the direction of Chang-an.
3. He had no official position.
4. "Qing-qing" would refer to a mistress rather than a wife. There is no indication that He was married.

### Plant No Trees
*5-character: 1 rhyme*

1. Several versions read "...the moon over my southern couch." This seems inferior.

### Setting Out
*5-character: 1 rhyme*

### Four Poems Written After Looking at a Painting of the Jiang-tan Park
*5-character: 1 rhyme*

1. The Jiang-tan Park, 20 *li* southeast of present Nanjing, had been established by Emperor Wu of Liang in A.D. 543. Anciently, this territory had belonged to the state of Wu.
2. The Tai-cheng palace was built by Emperor Cheng of Chin in A.D. 332. It stood near the Ji-ming temple in modern Nanjing.
3. The imperial carriage was decorated with kingfishers' wings.
4. King Xiang of Chu was notorious for his love of women and pleasure. This line is perhaps a thrust at Xian-zong.
5. This poem continues the description of the palace ladies, who are wearing red-flowered slips under yellow gowns.
6. Money shaped like knives was used in parts of Northeast China in ancient times.

7. Bows were decorated with horn.
8. The ladies have been weeping because the emperor did not spend the night with them. In spite of their gorgeous attire, they are all deeply unhappy. Another thrust at the emperor?
9. In this *vignette* the palace-ladies are seen as austringers hunting hares, pheasants, and partridges with goshawks. "Scissored wings" is puzzling. I suggest their wings look like the open blades of scissors. Jesses are straps fixed to the hawk's feet. They are attached to the leash by a swivel.
10. These were black and white hounds known as "Song magpies."
11. Black Dragon Mountain stood very close to Nanjing.
12. The ladies have dismounted to search for their arrows.
13. Emperor Wu of the Southern Qi dynasty (*regnet* 482–93) found that his harem could not hear the palace drum which told the hours, so he set up a bell in the Jing-yang tower to let them know when it was time to get up.

**While Recovering from a Drinking-Bout in the Elder Zhang's House in Lu-zhou, I Sent This Poem to My Fourteenth Elder Male Cousin through the Agency of a River Messenger.**
*5-character: 1 rhyme*

Li He wrote this poem at the end of his life, while he was staying with his friend Zhang Che in Lu-zhou. At this time hostilities had been recommenced against the rebel general, Wang Cheng-zong. This explains the presence of the River Messenger, a military courier who travelled in the region south of the Yangzi bearing urgent messages.
1. Zhao-kuan was in the south, Lu-zhou was up north, in the ancient territory of Zhao. Hence the marked difference in climate.
2. A traditional name given to urgent military despatches.
3. The battlements were white with mist.
4. A reference to the military situation.
5. His "turban" was a night-cap.
6. "Silver": perhaps traces of frost. Perhaps the remains of a picture done with silver paint.
7. "Coins": round patches of moss, looking like copper coins covered with verdigris, were growing on the steps of the artificial hill in the garden.
8. "Traveller's wine": the wine he had been drinking while travelling. Note the allusion to his lung complaint.

9. A little evergreen bush often found growing on the roofs of old Chinese houses, where it finds a footing in the dirt that accumulates between the ridge-shaped tiles, is known as "roof-pine." The "tile-animals" were highly coloured ceramic beasts placed on roofs to ward off evil influences.

10. Yan was the old name for the territory in the north next to Zhao. It was famous for its horses.

11. Zhao-guan was in former Chu territory.

12. Wine flavoured with pepper or cinnamon was a southern delicacy, as were perch and bream.

13. Island in the Yangzi, i.e., in the south. He is half-playfully asking his cousin whether the delights of the south are going to prevent their reunion.

### Song: Hard to Forget
*5-character: 1 rhyme*

1. During Tang, high officials planted halberds before their gates.

2. The blinds resemble flutes which, when gilded by the sun, "blow the sun's colours."

3. Cloves stand for love. The indiscriminate interlacing of branches here suggests the promiscuity of the men of this rich family. Hence the lady, neglected, "turns to the sunset."

### The Noble Son-in-Law of Jia Gong-lü
*5-character: 3 rhymes*

For the story of Jia Chung, styled Gong-lü, who married off his errant daughter to Han Shou, see above. This poem is evidently pure satire. A rich, young man, tired of his well-born wife, is to spend the day with a singing-girl.

1. A coral pillow was the height of luxury. The perfume that sickened our hero must have been the rare scent used by his wife, with whom he shared the pillow.

2. Literally: "A sunny male-rainbow...." The rainbow was a sexual symbol for the Chinese. The line means that the man was closeted with the girl.

3. Pan Yue (d. A.D. 300) was so good-looking that women found him irresistible. He once held the rank of Governor of He-yang county.

### Song: Drinking All Night, Asleep All Morning
*7-character: 2 rhymes*

This ballad is probably a satire on the marriage of the Princess of Pu-ning, daughter of Xian-zong (*regnet* 805–20), to Ji-you, dissolute son of the powerful Yu Ti. This alliance was contracted in spite of the protests of many of the more upright officials of the court. He is obviously hinting that the princess will be corrupted by her husband's licentious behaviour.

1.  The warmth of her face, heated by wine, brings out all the fragrance of the powder.
2.  Literally: "silk from Chu," an allusion to her marriage with the son of a governor of a circuit in this region.

### Written by the Tomb of Wang Jun
*5-character: 1 rhyme*

Wang Jun (206–85) played a major part in helping the Jin dynasty overcome the kingdom of Wu in A.D. 280 and thus briefly unify China. He was buried in his native place on Mount Bai-gu, Shaanxi, in a magnificent tomb surrounded by a wall fifteen miles long, with four entrances flanked by lines of funereal pine and cypress.

1.  "Little Dong" was Wang Jun's pet-name. A popular song about Little Dong said that he:

    > "Did not fear the tigers on the shore
    > But only feared the dragons in the water."

    This led the Prime Minister to give Wang high office.
2.  The writing on the funeral inscription has worn away, while Wang's sword, buried with him, has rusted.
3.  The tomb and the ground around it have been ploughed over.
4.  The fields south of the tomb.

### The Traveller
*5-character: 1 rhyme*

1.  Probably Mount Zhung-nan, near Chang-an.
2.  The name used during the Han dynasty for the place where high officials stayed while awaiting audience with the emperor.
3.  See note above. Lu-Zhou was situated in the ancient territory of Zhao. The Lord of Ping Yuan, Zhao Sheng, was the son of a feudal lord of Zhao.

4. During the Warring States period, Feng Xuan, a retainer of Lord Meng Chang of Qi, expressed his dissatisfaction with his lot by beating time with his sword and singing: "Long sword, why don't we go home?"
5. Letters were sometimes written on strips of silk.

### After Days of Rain in the Chong-yi District
*5-character: 1 rhyme*

This poem was written between 811 and 814, when He was working in the Office of Rites. The Chung-yi district was the second street east of Vermilion Bird Gate, in the ninth sector of Chang-an.
1. A reference to the Department of State Affairs (the Southern Palace), which was responsible for the examination. These two lines must be understood as criticizing the blindness and stupidity of the examiners who had refused to let him sit for his doctorate.
2. Chang-gu lay to the east of Chang-an.
3. Once again He is hinting that he would like to give up scholarship and gain fame as a soldier.

### Feng Hsiao-lien
*5-character: 1 rhyme*

Feng Xiao-lian was a skillful *pi-pa* (lute) player and dancer who rose from being a bondmaid to become the favourite of Hou-Zhu (*regnet* 566–77) of the Northern Qi dynasty. After the fall of the dynasty, she fled and hid herself among the common people. But Emperor Wu (*regnet* 560–78) of the Northern Zhou dynasty captured her and gave her to one of his princes. This poem must describe her plight while in hiding.
1. Or possibly: "For dispelling the spring-wind (love) melancholy of others, how much have I earned since this morning?" This rendering has the girl herself speaking these lines.
2. A belt with a bamboo-leaf pattern.
3. This almost certainly refers to her *pi-pa*.

### Presented to Chen Shang
*5-character: 3 rhymes*

Chen Shang, styled Shu-sheng, was a fifth-generation descendant of the royal house of the Chen Dynasty (*regnet* 557–89).

1. The *Laṅkāvatāra-sūtra* is one of the most important classics of the Chan (Zen) sect.
2. Literally: "you hoe among the sacrificial dishes." The line means Chen is undergoing great hardship while studying rites and music.
3. Chen was an enthusiastic partisan of Han Yu's *gu-wen* movement, which aimed at driving out parallel prose and replacing it by a more classical style. Chen seems to have carried this to such lengths that even Han Yu complained that his style was too antique for clarity.
4. Mount Tai-hua, used as a symbol for Chen Shang, is one of the five sacred mountains of China.
5. Two constellations.
6. Literally: "...into a *pu-su*." This is the big-leaf oak, a tree considered useless for any purpose.
7. Straw dogs were used for sacrificial purposes and then discarded.
8. During Tang, only officials of the fifth degree were authorized to wear black belts. He must be referring to a Han dynasty practice.
9. Ancient swords were believed to have magical powers, among them those of flying in the air and roaring like tigers. He sees Chen and himself, with their talents unused, as priceless swords locked away forever in a box, forgotten by all.

### Fishing
*5-character: 1 rhyme*

1. A canal red either with silt from the fields or with flowers.
2. The *Zie-xian zhuan* tells the story of one Ling-yang Zi-ming who caught a white dragon while out fishing. He was so frightened that he promptly let it go; whereupon, in gratitude, it let him catch a white fish, in whose belly he found a silken letter which contained the recipe for the elixir of life.
3. "Lone cocoon": silk from a single cocoon.
4. "Wild paddy": Indian rice (*zizania aquatica*).
5. One commentator thinks both the newt and the frog were used as bait.
6. Zhan He, a character of the time of the Warring States who is mentioned in *Lie-zi*, was an expert fisherman, who could catch a fish as large as a cart with a single strand of silk, half a grain, and a hook made from a beard of wheat. See A. C. Graham, *The Book of Lie-zi*, p. 105.
7. The Zhan-guo ce carries the story of the Lord of Long-yang, a handsome favourite of the King of Wei, who caught a dozen or so

fish while out fishing, only to burst into tears. He was afraid that, just as he had wanted to throw away the first fish he had caught once he had caught even bigger ones, so the king would one day wish to discard him.

8. His own momentary disappointment at his failure to catch anything—symbol of his failure to achieve his ambitions—vanishes at the sight of the weeping girl, whose sorrows are greater than his.

### Poem Presented to My Second Elder Cousin (Its Rhymes Harmonizing with a Poem of His) When He Stopped Being a Messenger, Sent Back His Horse, and Went Home to Yan-Chou
*5-character: 1 rhyme*

Yan-Zhou lay some 210 miles northeast of Chang-an. He wrote this poem to console his cousin at his loss of office.

1. His talents were not used. Wang Yuan, of the Later Han dynasty, once offered "to block up the Han-gu Pass with a ball of mud."
2. For the Long-tou song, see J. D. Frodsham, *An Anthology of Chinese Verse*, p. 106.
3. Lime-water was dropped into heated wine to clear it. This was called "ash-wine."
4. His cousin no longer goes hunting wearing his official robes, but watches cock-fights at home.
5. "To return to Wu" means "to retire from office." "To enter Ying" (ancient capital of Chu) means "to assume office again."
6. A reference to the saying: "Peach-tree, plum-tree do not say a word, yet people beat a path beneath them." Though he is living in retirement, his brilliance will make people seek him out.

### Presented in Reply
*5-character: 1 rhyme*

Probably He wrote this poem to commemorate his friend's acquisition of a new concubine.

1. Zhang Fang, Marquis of Fu-ping, used to accompany Emperor Cheng of Han (*regnet* 33–37 B.C.) when the latter roamed around in disguise.
2. In A.D. 359, a Fairy called Lü-hua ("Green Flower") is said to have visited the house of one Yang Quan and presented him with a poem.

3. Si-ma Xiang-ru once sold wine for a living. Later, tradition asserts that he built himself a Lute Tower. Presumably Green Flower had just become the concubine of He's friend, who has got drunk (the jade tree sprawled among the goblets) to celebrate the event.

### Written on the Wall of Zhao's House
*5-character: 1 rhyme*

Zhao seems to have been a friend of He's who was living pleasantly in retirement.
1. One cooks, while the other pounds rice to make flour.
2. The Wu edition reads "stone well."
3. Zhao's skin was a healthy, peach-blossom colour.

### Spring Melancholy
*5-character: 1 rhyme*

1. A man who supported his widowed mother by weaving nets and making sandals. He supported his widowed mother by what he considered menial employment.
2. In A.D. 465, a Liu Song emperor cast irregular shaped and unpolished coins worth one-twelfth of a tael. Even the elms remind He of his poverty.
3. It was an ancient custom to welcome the returning swallows in the second month of spring with a sacrifice to the tutelary spirit of births and marriages.
4. A reference to a custom about which the commentators know nothing. We may interpret "flying silk" as "gossamer." Since the shrike was a bird of ill-omen, it is not surprising to find it chased away.
5. "Northern lute" (*hu-qin*) here refers not to the modern *hu-qin* but to an instrument like the *pi-pa*. This was made of red sanderswood studded with mother-of-pearl.

### Immortals
*5-character: 1 rhyme*

1. Yao believes this poem is a satire on the self-styled Immortals who thronged Xian-zong's court, all promising him eternal life.

He is pointing out that no real immortals would ever come to court, for their place is far from the haunts of men. During Han Wu-di's reign, those who came to court claiming that they knew that the Magic Peaches of the Mother who is Queen in the West were ready to ripen were legion. Yet they were clearly frauds, for these peaches ripen only every six thousand years.

### Song of He-yang
*Irregular: 3 rhymes*

I understand this as a poem about two singing-girls whom He had evidently met some years previously while passing through He-yang county, Henan. He may well have written this poem while on his way to Lu-zhou in 814.

1. "Autumn blue" is a blue-black colour. Perhaps the lines mean that He considers himself too old for a love-affair with a young girl.
2. The poet Si-ma Xiang-ru fell in love with his future wife while in Linqiong, Sichuan.
3. In He-yang.
4. This might refer to Yan Hui, the favourite disciple of Confucius, whose hair turned white while he was still young. Some commentators refer to Yan Si, who was asked by Emperor Wu of Han why he still held the junior post of Gentleman though his hair was white. Yan explained that he had failed to find favour with either Emperor Wen (*regnet* 180–157 B.C.) or Emperor Jing (*regnet* 156–141 B.C.). Emperor Wu, touched by his story, finally promoted him. He sees himself as old before his time, a white-haired menial.
5. A licensed singing-girl wore a silver plaque at her belt, inscribed with her name.
6. Probably a reference to their hair-styles, rather than to their goblets.
7. The host sat on the east side of the room.
8. Or: "Wet mouths red on the flagons."

### Song: An Outing among Blossoms
*5-character: 1 rhyme*

"Blossoms" refer to the girls as well as the flowers.

1. The Cold Food Day, when nothing hot was eaten and no fires were lighted, fell on the eve of the Qing-ming Festival at the end of the

second or beginning of the third lunar month, in early spring.

2. Willows are traditionally connected with the Qing-ming Festival.
3. Because of the cold.

## Spring Morning
*Irregular: 1 rhyme*

Lines 1 to 10 describe spring in the palace; lines 11 and 12 describe spring among the nobility; lines 13 to 16 describe spring among the people.

1. "Vermilion City"—the palace.
2. A reference to an old ballad which tells how the First Emperor of Qin rolled up clothes which he presented to the palace beauties.
3. Flying Swallow of Zhao (Chao Fei-yan), a famous beauty.
4. During the Han dynasty, the Princess of Ping-yang built a famous rockery in her garden.
5. Pan Yue (d. A.D. 300), when Magistrate of He-yang in Henan, planted flowers and fruit-trees everywhere in the country.
6. Placing stones on the base of their looms to keep them steady.

## The Palace of Peace and Joy
*5-character: 1 rhyme*

An old ballad of this title dates from the sixth century. The An-le Palace ("Palace of Peace and Joy"), built in A.D. 223 by the Emperor of Wu, stood in Hubei, southeast of Chang-an. It was pulled down in A.D. 250 to provide material for building palaces in the capital. The commentators differ widely in their interpretations of this poem.

1. The Wardrobers (*shang-fu*) were ladies in charge of the royal ward robes.
2. Xiao Lun, Prince of Shao-ling (*circa* 507–51), was a son of Emperor Wu of Liang. Some commentators believe these lines should read: "Shao-ling melons, not yet washed, are swaying in the long, azure waves of the jars."
3. Zuo Guan was a high-ranking official during the reign of Emperor Huan of Later Han (*regnet* 146-68) and hence could never have seen this palace. The line simply means: "Even high-ranking palace officials were happy to serve in a menial capacity just to be present at these banquets."
4. "Wormwood" is beach wormwood. Mountain dogwood was

planted near wells so that its leaves could fall into the water. This was held to keep the water fresh and pure.

### Butterflies Dancing
*7-character: 2 rhymes*

1. A young girl peers from behind her screen at the young man on his white horse.

### A Young Nobleman of Liang
*5-character: 1 rhyme*

Probably a satire on some young general of noble birth, notorious for devoting his time to singing-girls, rather than to military matters. The nobleman in question may have been a descendant of the royal house of Liang (502–57). It is possible, however, that he was a member of the Tang royal house. If so, He would be availing himself of a literary convention to protect himself from a charge of *lèse-majesté*.

1. Xiao was the surname borne by the house of Liang. While pregnant with Emperor Wu of Liang (*regnet* 502–49), his mother had a vision of a supernaturally beautiful bullrush flower, which she promptly swallowed.
2. A veiled allusion to his love-affair.
3. A type of expensive, ornamental paper, mottled with silver.
4. During the Jin dynasty, the great general Tao Kan (259–334) planted willows all over Wu-chang district, Hubei. The camp was presumably in this locality. The reference to Tao Kan is highly ironic. Our young fop playing at soldiers is contrasted with one of China's finest soldier-statesmen, a man noted for his integrity and austerity.
5. Literally: "The girl from the Guan-wa palace" (in Wu). Here the expression means simply, "a beautiful girl."

### Song: Planting Tree-Peonies
*7-character: 3 rhymes*

1. Chinese thoroughwort (*eupatorium chinense*) and *du-heng* (*asarun blumei*).
2. During Tang, tree-peonies were greatly prized and very costly. The gold is for buying these flowers.

3. One commentator thinks this line means: "The two singing-girls named Liang and Wang have grown old and departed but Silk Robes (another singing-girl) is still here." This is forced and quite unconvincing. He has several poems which mention a "Prince of Liang"—here he is clearly referring to some nobleman or other who was fond of peonies. Perhaps "Prince of Liang" was the name of a variety of peony. If so, the line would be intentionally ambiguous. "Sendal robes" would then mean both "silk clad dancing girls" and "peony leaves."

4. Name of a ballad. Note how the peonies are seen as dancing girls—expensive beauties whose loveliness is all too fleeting.

5. The embroidered awnings, which were probably used to shade the peonies, were made of patterned silk from Shu.

6. The poet Pan Yue, whose minor name (*xiao-zi*) was Tan-nu, is another of He's favorite characters. The Xie girl is not the fourth-century poetess Xie Dao-yun, but the renowned singing-girl who belonged to the great statesman Xie An (320–85).

### Song: Digging a Well in the Back Gardens
*Irregular: 2 rhymes*

The title is taken from an old ballad, dating from the Jin dynasty, whose theme is much the same as this. Love between husband and wife must be deep and inexhaustible as the well which is being dug in the back gardens of the palace.

1. Xun Can, styled Feng-qian (*floruit* 3rd century A.D.), married General Cao Hong's daughter because he admired her for her beauty alone, paying no attention to her character. Yet when she died he pinned away from grief in just over a year. The girl wants a husband like this.

### Song: Throwing Off My Sadness Written under Mount Hua
*7-character: 3 rhymes*

1. Mount Tai-hua in Hua-yin county, Shanxi, between Xi-an and Luo-yang.

2. We may date this poem at A.D. 810. The line would thus refer to He's rejection as a *jin-shi* candidate.

3. *Xun-zi*, XIX, p. 22b. "Zi Xia was so poor his clothes were (like the

feathers of) a hanging quail. Someone said: 'Why doesn't he look for an official post?' He said: 'The feudal lords look down on me, so I cannot become a minister.'"

4.  It was said of Zhu Zhen of the Later Han that he was so poor "his carriage was like a bird's nest, his horse like a hound."

5.  The "beflagged pavilion" here refers to a tavern, not to the market-place, as some commentators would have it.

6.  Yi-yang was the old name for the county where Li He's family lived. It lay about 120 miles east of Mount Hua.

7.  One commentator thinks this refers to the story of the Immortal Shi Cun who jumped into a wine-pot, made it his universe, and called it "the winepot of Heaven." Another interprets this as a reference to the story of Fei Chang-fang of the Later Han who met an old man with a magic wine-jar, from which the two of them could drink all day without emptying it. Fei followed the old man into the jar and learnt the arts of immortality.

8.  One commentator interprets "to cultivate heart and bones" as meaning "to cultivate mental energy."

## Qin Gong
### 7-character: 5 rhymes

1.  For Liang Ji see note 4, below. Feng Zi-du was the favourite slave of the Han general, He Guang (d. 68 B.C.). See the poem attributed to Xin Yan-nian in J. D. Frodsham, *An Anthology of Chinese Verse*, p. 14. After He's death, Feng took his late master's wife as his mistress.

2.  "Scented mist"—incense-smoke.

3.  Tallies were used at drinking-parties to keep track of how many cups each person had drunk, so nobody could refuse another goblet on the grounds that he had already had too many.

4.  Liang Ji had a private zoo in his garden. Hence it would have been Qin's duty, as Steward of the Household, to supervise the rearing of these animals.

5.  Deer were supposed to turn white when they reached 1,500 years old.

6.  "Eternal galleries"—long galleries in the imperial palace. Liang Ji had free access to the palace.

7.  "Yellow River"—a river of gold from the imperial treasury.

8.  Jin-shu, XII, records that in A.D. 292, 303, and 361 "the sky split open, due to a deficiency of the Yang element." This meant that women were playing too great a role in the government.

9. A reference to Qin's intimacy with his master's wife, Sun Shou—whose comb he takes as a love-token.

### "Ballad on the Boys by the Walls of Ancient Yeh"
### An Imitation of Wang Can's Satire on Cao Cao
*3-character: 4 rhymes*

Ye (in Henan) was the capital set up by Cao Cao.

1. *Han-shu*, XCV, Biography of Yin Shang: "In Chang-an...gangs of young men from the villages killed officials. They were bribed to avenge grievances and held meetings at which they drew lots with pellets. Those who drew red pellets killed military officials, those who drew black pellets killed civil officials, those who drew white pellets looked after the funeral ceremonies (for those of their number who were slain). Within the walls dust rose at evening. People surged about, robbing and looting. Dead and wounded lay around the streets." In 815 rebellious generals sent assassins to Chang-an who had murdered the Chief Minister, Wu Yuan-heng. This poem probably refers to the murder.
2. *Lie-zi*, V, mentions a sword which could cut jade as if it were mud, which the Western Rong presented to King Mu of Zhou. *Huai-nan-zi*, VIII, tells of the bow with which the legendary archer Yi shot down nine suns.
3. Just as the Chief Minister Cao Cao gained power at the expense of the Emperor, so men like Huang-fu Bo gained power at the expense of Xian-zong.

### Singing of Yang's Purple Inkstone with a Green Pattern
*7-character: 2 rhymes*

The mountains of Duan-zhou, in Guangdong, produced a famous purplish stone, veined with green, used for making fine inkstones. We do not know who Yang was.

1. The green stains on the stone remind the poet of Chang-hong's blood, which turned to emerald jade.
2. Ink was often made with pine-soot mixed with musk.
3. Chinese ink is in block form and has to be rubbed on the stone, which must therefore be firm enough to cope with all types of ink.
4. An inkstone, said to have belonged to Confucius, was preserved in the sage's tomb-temple in Shandong.

### Thoughts in Her Chamber
*5-character: 2 rhymes*

Ostensibly the poem deals with a lady, lying awake in her room alone and neglected, as her husband sets out on a long journey. These verses may be comment on Li He's own unhappy position.

1. Literally: "New cassia like moth-eyebrows." The line also means: "The lady's moth-eyebrows are like new cassia."
2. Bells in the form of the mythical simurgh were attached to horses' bridles.
3. "Crickets": *holochlora brevifissa.*

### Dawn in Shih-cheng
*Irregular: 3 rhymes*

The whole atmosphere of this poem suggests a *ci*. Mo-chou, heroine of many a southern folksong, lived in Shi-cheng, Hubei.

1. Perhaps the Great Dike mentioned above.
2. "Crimson spheres": flowers.
3. At dawn on the seventh night of the seventh lunar month, the Weaving Lady and the Herd-boy must part again, after their brief tryst.
4. Older commentators believed this referred to the story of a guest of King Zhuang of Chu, who was imprudent enough to dally with one of the King's ladies when the candles blew out during a banquet and had his cap-strings torn off. The King then ordered all his other guests to tear off their capstrings before the candles were lighted again, so as not to disgrace the man. But this story surely has nothing to do with the poem. The girl's lover, leaving her at dawn, has given the girl his scent-sachet as a keepsake.
5. "Spring curtains": curtains aglow with spring sunlight.

### Lament That the Days Are So Short
*Irregular: 3 rhymes*

1. Sun and moon.
2. Bears' paws were a rich man's delicacy; frogs were eaten by the poor.
3. The Spirit Lady was worshipped by Han Wu-ti. The Great Unity was the supreme deity of the Taoist pantheon.

4. The Ruo tree is a mythical tree in the far west (not the east), the foliage of which gives off a red glow at sunset.
5. Chu-ci, *The Heavenly Questions*, p. 49: "What land does the sun not reach to? How does the Torch Dragon light it?"
6. Perhaps the feet of the dragon that drew the chariot of the sun?
7. Elixirs of life.
8. Not the Ren Kung-tzu of *Zhuang-zi* XXVI, but some other unidentifiable Immortal.
9. Emperor Wu of Han, an assiduous seeker after immortality, was buried in Mao-ling tomb. Liu was his family name, Che his personal name.
10. Ying Zheng, another ardent searcher for immortal life, was the notorious First Emperor of Qin. He died while on a journey, so his attendants, anxious to conceal his death until they returned to the capital, filled the carriages with abalone to hide the smell of the corpse.

### Second Year of Chang-ho
*Irregular: 4 rhymes*

The title of the poem is from the title of an old ballad. The second year of the *Zhang-he* period (A.D. 88) was an unusually prosperous one. This poem is an idyllic picture of peasant life, so far removed from the brutal realities of He's own time that I suspect his intent was satirical.

1. "Coiled clouds": auspicious five-coloured clouds.
2. The seeds on the panicled millet (*shu*) are as numerous as those one finds on ordinary millet (*su*).
3. A characteristically disturbing image which one would have difficulty in finding in any other Chinese poet. The Seven Stars (the Plough) and the Moon Goddess (here called Heng-e) will perish in their turn. He's cosmology is markedly Buddhist.

### Returning to Chang-gu in Spring
*5-character: 3 rhymes*

This poem, written when He had returned to Chang-gu after his examination failure, falls into three sections. The first deals with his life in Chang-an; the second with his journey home; the third with his sojourn in Chang-gu. Stylistically, the poem is very close to some of Han Yu's verses.

1. Literally: "… when my hair was bound up."
2. During the reign of Emperor Wu of the Former Han, Zhang Jun became an official at the early age of eighteen—just the age when He failed to enter the bureaucracy. Yan Hui, a disciple of Confucius, found his hair had turned white when he was still young. Hence the couplet means: "Before I had a chance to become an official at eighteen, my hair had turned prematurely white."
3. "Net of Heaven": the examination system.
4. He must have lingered on in the capital till the spring of 810, probably recovering from his sickness. Then a spell of unseasonably hot weather drove him to seek the shelter of his home, in the cool of the countryside.
5. Mount Li lay east of Chang-an.
6. The terraces of the Qing-hua palace, on the slopes of Mount Li.
7. Wealthy travellers hasten down the road, their perfume scenting the breeze.
8. Mount Tai-hua was famous for its cypresses, stretching in a row for eleven *li*.
9. "Hides" and "wings": the bark and leaves of the cypress trees.
10. Or: "…shrouded the distant borders."
11. A reference to the story of a black panther which stayed up among the rain and clouds of Mount South for seven days without coming down for food, in order to soak its fur and pattern it. He is no tiger fighting his way savagely through an official career, but a literary panther, willing to suffer solitude and privation on his Mount South (the hill near his family estate) for the sake of his verse.
12. Officials have to go north (like the bird of Han), or south (like the dace in the Xiang) during the course of their career. All of them are caught in the snares of the world, from which He has escaped.

### Chang-gu
### (A Poem Written on the Twenty-Seventh Day of the Fifth Month)
*5-character: 1 rhyme*

This poem was written two months after the previous poem, sometime in late June. He is describing the country around his home, where the Chang-gu river flows past the foot of Mount Nü-ji (Maiden's Table).

1. A reference to Mount Nü-ji.
2. An obscure line. Another translation reads: "Caves in the coign of the mountain rise up in stories around me."
3. "Yellow arrowroot": so called because it yields a yellow dye.
4. A much-disputed line. The shadows of the horses on the waters resemble the ancient Chinese character for "horse."
5. Most commentators think this means the road to the Temple of the Divine Maiden of Orchid Fragrance, the tutelary deity of Mount Nü-ji. One disagrees, believing that the road led to a shrine dedicated to Chi-ying, Princess of Yu-zhen (Jade Purity), daughter of Emperor Rui-zong (*regnet* 662–90 and 710–12), who was a well-known Taoist deity. In that case "Spirit Maiden" would refer to Yu-zhen, not to the tutelary deity of the mountain.
6. Min is the old name for Fujian province, where the speech of the aborigines was thought to sound like the song of birds.
7. A description of the Fu-chang palace, originally built by the Sui (589–618) and rebuilt in 657, the ruins of which lay to the east of the valleys. As was customary, its inner rooms had once been painted with a paint containing oil of pepper.
8. The hair of young children was braided into horns.
9. Bamboo-slips were an ancient writing material.
10. The poet Tao Qian (365–427) was a renowned toper.
11. The favourite concubine of the great statesman Xie An (320–85).
12. "Pale-moths": the reflections of the peaks. Some commentators gloss as "the moon."
13. During the reign of Emperor He of the Later Han (*regnet* 88–106) two imperial envoys, travelling in disguise to Sichuan, stopped for the night at the house of a certain Li He (not to be confused with our poet) and were astonished to discover that he knew who they were. He explained that two "envoy-stars" (shooting-stars) had just appeared over Sichuan, hence he was expecting them. Cheng-du, Sichuan, is called "City of Brocade" because of the beauty of its surroundings. Our line means simply:
    "The fire-flies are like the envoys in the story and Chang-gu is as beautiful as Cheng-du."
14. The Li family came from Cheng-ji county, Gansu.
15. "Master Wine-sack skin" (Chi-yi Zi-pi) was the name taken by the great statesman Fan Li (*floruit* 5th century B.C.) when he retired to Qi after helping Yue defeat Wu. He means he should like to retire to Chang-gu—but only after achieving high office.

### Lament of the Brazen Camels
*5-character: 3 rhymes*

Brazen Camel Street in Luo-yang derived its name from two small bronze camels placed on either side of the street. Since these animals are mentioned in a late third-century work, they must have been standing there for several hundred years by He's time. The point of this poem, I think, is that while men generally lament the shortness of life, conventionally symbolized by spring blossoms, immortal beings like the camels find life intolerable because it repeats itself endlessly. This is yet another of He's anti-Taoist poems. Another layer of meaning may perhaps be uncovered beneath this. The *Jin-shu* relates that Suo Jing (239–303), realizing that rebellion was about to overthrow the dynasty at any moment, pointed to these camels and prophesied that they would soon be overgrown with thorn-thickets. He may well be hinting that unless the power of the eunuchs is checked, the same fate will befall the camels once more. This would be another reason for weeping.

1. For "eastern neighbour" see above.
2. The Tian-jin bridge. A fashionable quarter.
3. Actually Bei-mang, a hill north of Luo-yang, which was used as a burial ground.
4. In Chinese temples today one sees candles set in bowls to protect them from draughts.

### I Journey from Chang-gu and
### Arrive at Luo-yang through Rear Gate
*5-character: 1 rhyme*

He must have written this poem in 811, while on his way to take up his post in Chang-an. On his way there, he stopped for a while at his house in Luoyang and consulted a fortune-teller.

1. The frost and ice on the bamboos look like congealed venom, drawn from the snakes by the cold.
2. Xian Liao was an officer of the state of Jin during the Spring and Autumn period, who prophesized good fortune for a man threatened with disaster.
3. An allusion to Ruan Xiu (270–311), an eccentric character whose biography states that he always carried a hundred cash tied to his staff when he went out, so that he could go and get drunk in any wine-shop.

4. Both King Xiang of Chu and Emperor Wu of Han were noted for their love of literature.
5. "Since literary merit no longer counts for much, what sort of menial position will I be given in Chang-an?" "To carry firewood" also means "to suffer poverty."

## On the First Day of the Seventh Month at Dawn
### I Enter the Tai-Hang Mountains
*5-character: 1 rhyme*

This poem was probably written in 814, when He was on his way to Lu-zhou. Autumn began on the first day of the seventh lunar month.
1. A much-disputed line. It may also mean: "The reeds are suddenly wet with fragrant dew."
2. "Bridges": actually plank roads laid up the side of a mountain.
3. Chang-gu lay southwest of Luo-yang.
4. "Rock's breath": mist and clouds, believed to emanate from mountains.

## Autumn Cold:
### A Poem Sent to My Twelfth Elder Cousin, the Collator
*5-character: 1 rhyme*

See the poem, *On the First Day of the Seventh Month at Dawn I Enter the Tai-Hang Mountains*, above.
1. Officials below the ninth grade wore blue robes.

## Moving Grass and Setting Our Nets
*Irregular: 4 rhymes*

This was the title of one of the eighteen *Drum, Flute, and Bell Songs of Han*.
1. Qi was famous for its silk.
2. The nets were camouflaged with leaves.

## Music Rising to the Clouds
*Irregular: 2 rhymes*

This poem deals with a celebration in the palace on the first day of the eighth month.

1. Presumably the smoke of incense rising to the clouds.
2. The *se* had fifty strings.
3. Ying was the clan name of the Qin royal house. The girls are likened to the Weaving Lady from the Milky Way (the Heavenly River).

### Mo To Lou Tzu
*5-character: 3 rhymes*

The title is untranslatable. This was originally a non-Chinese ballad.
1. From Jade Gate, Gansu, to the territory around Karanor, where in 120 B.C. the Han general He Qu-bing (145–177 B.C.) captured the Golden Man, an image worshipped by a local tribe.
2. The Liao river in Liao-dong.
3. The Long-tou river is in Shaanxi, nowhere near Liao-dong. The reference here is to the old ballad Long-tou Song, which begins:
    "The flowing waters of Long-tuo,
    Come pouring down from the mountains,
    I brood upon my loneliness,
    Blown by the wind through this wilderness."

### Ballad of the Savage Tiger
*4-character: 1 rhyme*

A satire on oppressive government, of which the tiger was the symbol. Caught between the Central Government and the warlords, the people are harassed as though by tigers.
1. Huang, of Dong-hai, had magical powers which enabled him to control snakes and tigers. Unfortunately for him, he lost these powers through drinking to excess and was eventually killed by a tiger.
2. The *zhou-yu* was a white tiger with black markings which appeared only when a state was perfectly governed. It would not tread on grain nor eat living things. Niu Ai was a duke turned were-tiger, who ate his own elder brother. He is pointing out that some tigers are worse than others.
3. Confucius found a woman weeping at the foot of Mount Tai. Though her whole family had been killed by tigers she refused to leave the district, because there was no oppressive government there. This caused Confucius to remark that an oppressive government was more savage than any tiger.

### Ballad of the Rising Sun
*Irregular: 3 rhymes*

1. A mythical mountain in the extreme west of China, said to be the gateway to heaven.
2. The sunflower, which follows the sun (a symbol for the emperor) in its course, is an emblem of loyalty.
3. The valley where the sun rises.
4. A mythical tree in the far west, whose branches give out a red glow in the evening.
5. When the ten suns of the Fu-sang tree, which the sun climbs as it rises, came out together during the reign of Yao, Yi, the Archer, shot down nine of them, so saving the earth from conflagration.
6. Adopting the version found in *Wen-yüan ying-hua* (Taipei, 1965), III, p.1194.

### Bitter Bamboos: A Diao-xiao Ballad
*Irregular: 2 rhymes*

This poem does not have the form of a Tang ballad so the title may be a misnomer. The bitter bamboo (*phyllostachys bambusoides*) was used for making flutes.

1. Xuan-yuan—the personal name of Gong-sun Xuan-yuan, the legendary Yellow Emperor, supposed to have ascended the throne in 2697 B.C. and to have reigned for a century.
2. Legend says the Yellow Emperor sent his minister Ling Lun to a valley north of the Kun-lun mountains. Here he cut the bamboos from which the twelve pitchpipes were made, thus creating music and regulating the cosmos.
3. During the reign of Emperor Zhang of the Later Han (*regnet* 75–88), a scholar named Ji Jing found a white jade pipe under the shrine of the legendary Emperor Shun in Leng-dao (east of Ning-yuan county, Hunan).

### Lyric for the Duster Dance
*Irregular: 5 rhymes*

The duster-dance, which originated in Wu during the period of the Three Kingdoms (220–80), was performed with a feather-duster or a fly-whisk. He's lyric is another satire on Emperor Xian-zong's quest for immortality.

1. A famous wine from Wu-xing county, Zhejiang.
2. The Shen-ming tower where the Brazen Immortal stood.
3. The text is corrupt here.
4. The shell of the turtle was supposed to have been the original source of the eight trigrams of *The Classic of Changes*.

### Song: Sitting through the Night
*7-character: 2 rhymes*

Title of a ballad first written by the fifth-century poet, Bao Zhao. A woman waits in vain through the night for her lover to come.

1. "Leaden flowers": face-powder.
2. Lu Yu, styled Gan-yu, was a well-known poet of the Chen dynasty (*regnet* 557–89).

### Song for Vertical Harp
*Irregular: 1 rhyme*

This song is based on a ballad of depressing banality which runs as follows:
> "Sir, do not ford the river!
> Now you've gone and forded the river!
> Into the water you've sunk and drowned—
> What are we to do?"

He has improved on this considerably by using the device found in *The Summons of the Soul* (*Zhao Hun*) in the *Chu Ci*, where a sick man is recalled to health by reminding him of the joys of life. Even so, our poem seems singularly uninspired.

1. Qu Ping—Qu Yuan, the reputed author of the *Li Sao*, is said to have drowned himself in the river Mi-luo, a tributary of the Xiang, in 278 B.C.
2. Mentioned as having drowned himself by walking into the sea carrying a stone.

### Mount Wu is High
*Irregular: 1 rhyme*

One of the eighteen *Drum, Flute and Bell Songs of Han* bears this title. Mount Wu, a famous twelve-peaked range, rises up on the northern banks of the Yangzi and stretches from Sichuan to Hubei. It was on this mountain that Jade Beauty, daughter of the legendary Scarlet Emperor, was buried, thus becoming its tutelary deity. King Huai of Chu (*floruit* 3rd century B.C.) once spent the night with her, not knowing who she was. When she left him she told him that in the morning she took the form of clouds on Mount Wu, in the evening she marshalled the rain. Huai's son, King Xiang, had the same experience.

### Under the Walls of Ping City
*5-character: 4 rhymes*

Ping-cheng was a northern border outpost in present Ta-tong county, Shanxi, close to the Great Wall. The Han settlement of this name lay east of the Tang fort. In 200 B.C. Emperor Gao-zu of the Former Han was besieged in Ping-cheng, which became the scene of the great battle.
1. "Farewell swords"—swords presented as parting mementoes.
2. Literally "Sea-wind"; but "Sea" here stands for the Gobi, a desert being a sea of sand.
3. The Han-gu Pass was regarded as the gateway to China.
4. The bodies of men who had died on active service were sent back home for burial, wrapped in horsehides. The final line is so subversive that many commentators have sought to amend it, as for example, Suzuki Torao, who renders it as: "We do not mind going home as bundled corpses. This is better than dying as traitors." The line as it stands speaks of mutiny or suicide.

### Pleasures South of the Yangzi
*7-character: 2 rhymes*

1. Sunset clouds.
2. The moon.

### Joys of the Rich
*7-character: 10 rhymes*

Though actually directed at some contemporary of He's, this poem is ostensibly a satire on the infamous Liang Ji (d. A.D. 159), one of the richest and most powerful men in China during the closing decades of the Later Han. Liang owed his rise largely to the fact that his sister was the Consort of Emperor Shun (*regnet* 125–44). After Shun's death,

Liang poisoned his successor and put the government in the hands of his sister as Regent. Not until 159 did the young Emperor Huan (*regnet* 146–68) become powerful enough to overthrow Liang and his party in a coup that resulted in the execution of dozens of Liang's adherents and the dismissal from office of over three hundred high officials. Prior to this, Liang had been emperor in all but name for close on fourteen years. He and his wife, Sun Shou, lived in splendour in Luo-yang, vying with each other, so we are told, in vice and luxury. See Liang's biography in *Hou Han-shu*, XXXIV, pp. 14b–25a.

1. Liang's biography described him as "a man with an owl's shoulders and a wolf's eyes." Both are symbols of cruelty and oppression.
2. "Pepper Apartments": the palace of the Empress, his sister.
3. Highly unorthodox dress, especially when worn at court, indicating Liang's contempt for Confucian propriety.
4. Han-dan (Heibei), the capital of the ancient state of Zhao, was famous for its singing-girls.
5. "Cinnabar Hill": a place mentioned in the compendium of travellers' tales, the *Shan-hai jing*, as the haunt of the phoenix. To eat one of these auspicious birds would be the height of barbarism and vulgar opulence. Compare the proverb: "To burn a lute to cook a crane."
6. Literally: "Macaques as big as a fist were not worth eating." Macaques were a Sichuan delicacy.
7. "Blossom-rain": heavy downpours that strip the blossom from the trees at the end of spring. They were too busy carousing to notice the rain.
8. Master Hong Yai was an Immortal who had once been known as Ling Lun. He was said to have cut the bamboos from which the Yellow Emperor made the twenty-four musical pitch-pipes. See note above.
9. Liang had a collection of rabbits in his park which he guarded zealously. Over ten people were put to death for having killed some of these animals, in ignorance of the prohibition.
10. Throughout this poem He has followed Liang's biography in the *Hou Han-shu*. Only this last line makes it clear that this is not just a historical exercise but a satire.

### Let's Drink Wine
*Irregular: 3 rhymes*

1. The charioteer of the sun.
2. A three-legged crow lived in the sun. Yan-zi was a mountain where the sunset.

3. Legend said that a peach-tree with roots 3,000 *li* long grew on the summit of Mount Tao-du. On top of the tree was a golden cock which sang when the sun shone on it.
4. Ru Shou is the spirit of autumn. The Green Emperor is the spirit of spring.
5. "Tattoo gold": fine gold from the south where the tattooed aborigines lived.
6. Why worry about the future?
7. One reads: "Carriages come to Chang-an in an endless stream." Since both Liang Ji and Shi Chung lived in Luo-yang, not Chang-an, our version is clearly preferable.
8. For Liang Ji, see note 1 above.
9. Shi Chung (249–300) was a millionaire infamous for his extravagance and cruelty. His estate, Golden Valley Garden, lay just outside Luo-yang. Li He is obviously thrusting at some of his degenerate contemporaries, perhaps at officials and eunuchs notorious for their rapacity.

## Delights of the Jasper Flower
### *Irregular: 3 rhymes*

1. "Dragon-decoys": heavenly horses, believed to be related to dragons, which their presence would attract.
2. *Lie-zi*, III, recounts the story of High-king Mu of Zhou, who drove his team of eight famous horses round the world. When he came to the Kun-lun mountains, the Mother who is Queen in the West feasted him by the Jasper Pool.
3. The Five Emperors who govern the Five Regions of the universe and reside in the Five Planets.
4. Literally: "The Pool of Yu," where the sun bathed after it had set.
5. Metal was the element associated with autumn in the Han system of correspondences. Hence the "metal wind" is the west wind.
6. The sweet dew sent down by Heaven to reward a king of great virtue (*de*).
7. Second-class elixirs of life.

## Cold up North
### *1-character: 2 rhymes*

One commentator believes this is a satire on the Armies of the Divine Plan, which had grown so used to soft living under their eunuch commanders that they had no chance of standing up to the Tibetan invasion of 812, when the barbarian armies staged a winter campaign in Gansu. All this seems rather farfetched.

## Reflections on the Ancient Terrace of Liang
### *7-character: 3 rhymes*

During the Former Han, Prince Xiao of Liang constructed a magnificent palace and a park for his pleasure in Sui-yang, Henan. In the park, which extended for several hundred *li*, stood the Yao-hua palace and the Goose Pool. This poem is yet another example of He's obsession with the theme of the inexorability of time. The prince could not stay the course of the years for all his wealth. Now nothing is left of his palace but ruins; it has dissolved into air as suddenly as it seemed to spring out of it.

1. The Milky Way seems to pour down on to the terrace, whose ruins stand out starkly against the night sky.
2. A stock example of impious behaviour, taken from a legend about an early emperor who shot at a skin bag filled with blood and hung on high, claiming he was shooting at Heaven. There is of course no record of the Prince of Liang having behaved in this way. The bells were musical instruments.
3. His fur robes were embroidered with golden tigers.

## Do Not Go out of Your Gate, Sir!
### *Irregular: 2 rhymes*

An enigmatic poem. The point of the title, I think, is that the official career has become so dangerous that one is safest in retirement. This poem may have something to do with Han Yu, whose strict principles were always involving him in trouble. The difficulty is that it is impossible to translate the poem correctly without knowing what it is about. My very tentative interpretation is as follows: "One of He's friends (Han Yu?) is menaced by vicious enemies. All his troubles will end with his death, which will paradoxically enough be his real reward. (This is a very un-Chinese idea, neither Confucian nor yet Taoist, which reveals Buddhist influence on He's thought.) Our poet himself is in a similar plight, being menaced by dangers from every side. Like Yan Hui, his hair has turned white while he is still young. Is he to meet with the same fate as Bao Jiao, a man of strictest principles who came to a miserable end? Yet we must not despair at seeing virtue so shabbily treated.

What looks to us like an undeserved death is in fact Heaven's way of sparing the good from further suffering. If you doubt the truth of my words, think of Qu Yuan, who found inspiration in his despair."

1. The "bears and serpents" of our test is almost certainly a variant of the "nine-headed serpent" of the *Chu Ci, Zhao Hun*, p. 104:

> "And the great Nine-headed Serpent who darts
> Swiftly this way and that

And swallows men as a sweet relish."

2. A reference to his friend's enemies.
3. "Orchid girdle": a symbol of the virtuous.
4. According to the *Huai-nan zi*, Li-yang commandery in Anhui turned into a lake in one night. Is He referring to some sudden calamity which had overtaken him?
5. The roaring of the dragons sounds like brazen rings being shaken.
6. The *ya-yu* (loosely rendered "griffon") was a fabulous beast with the head of a dragon, tail of a horse, and claws of a tiger. It ate only the wicked.
7. Bao Jiao was a recluse of Chou times who set himself such exaggerated standards of conduct that he starved himself to death.
8. Yan Hui, the favourite disciple of Confucius, had white hair before he was thirty. Like He, he died young.
9. Qu Yuan, unjustly slandered and banished, was supposed to have been inspired to write *The Heavenly Questions* by the frescoes that he saw in the ancestral temples of the kings of Chu. In his despair he scrawled questions on the temple walls seeking to know the meaning of life before drowning himself.

### Song of the Magic Strings
*7-character: 2 rhymes*

A female shaman exorcises evil spirits. A ballad of this title existed as early as the 3rd century A.D. It originated in the south, long the home of shamanistic culture.

1. The god arrives, riding the whirlwind.
2. The shaman dances.
3. The spirit brings the wind.
4. Both animals were greatly feared by the Chinese.
5. "Horned dragon": painted on the wall of the shrine.
6. Owls were considered unlucky. Forest demons (*mu mei*) were four-legged beasts with human faces.

## Magic Strings
*7-character: 2 rhymes*

1. This is synaesthesia, sound and scent blending into one.
2. Paper money is burnt at Chinese funerals. Here it is used as an offering to the spirit.
3. Wood of a tree mentioned in the *Zhan-guo ce*. Planted on the grave of a wife who had died while her husband was away on a campaign, its branches would turn towards the quarter where he happened to be.
4. A mountain range which stretches for over 800 *li* across Central China.
5. Or perhaps: "The Spirit lingers long between Something and Nothing."

## Farewell Song of Magic Strings
*7-character: 2 rhymes*

1. For the goddess of Mount Wu, see poem above. This is the shaman's farewell song to the departing goddess.
2. This must refer to the goddess and not to the shaman.
3. The Yangzi flows at the foot of Mount Wu.
4. "Fallen orchid": a boat.
5. Mount Zhung-nan, near Luo-yang, perhaps.
6. The cassia flowers in spring and autumn. The last line hints that this may also be a love poem. Perhaps Li He himself is the cassia-tree of the penultimate line.

## Song of Green Water
*5-character: 2 rhymes*

A poem of Emperor Wu Liang (*regnet* 502–49) refers to A-hou ("poor Hou") as the child of the singing-girl Mo-chou ("Never Sorrow"). We do not know whether A-hou was originally supposed to be a girl or a boy: but Late Tang writers thought A-hou was a girl. The last four lines of this poem have produced endless speculation among commentators.

1. Presumably no one will marry her on account of her profession as a singing-girl.

### Song: Sandy Road
*7-character: 3 rhymes*

During Tang, on the appointment of a new Prime Minister, sand was strewn along the road from his private residence to the eastern quarter of the city. Our poem celebrates the appointment of a Prime Minister, seen riding to audience at dawn.

1. The tamarisk, thought to bear a resemblance to a human figure, was called "man-willow" (*ren-liu*). The trees look half-asleep at this early hour.
2. Smoke from incense-burners.
3. To the court of the Son of Heaven.
4. Dragons were carved on the nine gates of the palace.
5. Since the government is a good one, the macrocosm responds to the order displayed by the microcosm. So there are no droughts or other calamities. All this is due to the virtue of the Prime Minister.

### The Emperor Returns
*7-character: 3 rhymes*

The fourteenth of the *Han Cymbal Songs* bears the title "The Emperor Goes to Hui." This originally referred to Han Wu-di's visit to Hui-zhung. He misunderstood this, so I have translated accordingly.

1. Zhuan Xu, a legendary ruler, had a magic sword which could leap from its case to subdue his enemies.
2. Chi You—a rebel defeated by the Yellow Emperor.
3. The text is very corrupt here. I have followed the Wu edition. The usual text reads: "From high heaven auspicious clouds (thunder?) fall everywhere to earth. (Within) the (four) seas for a thousand leagues, earth displays no smoke (from warning beacons) to frighten us."

### The Grand Official Carriage Comes on a Visit.
### Written at the Command of Assistant Secretary Han Yu and Censor Huang-fu Shi When They Visited Me.
*Irregular: 3 rhymes*

We may safely discount the story that He wrote this poem when he was seven. Han Yu was appointed Assistant Secretary to the Board of

Prisons in the sixth month of 809, becoming Magistrate of Henan the following year. Huang-fu Shi became Censor in the Court of General Affairs in 808. We may therefore conclude that this poem was written in 809, probably just before the examination held to select the doctoral candidates from Henan-fu.

### Lady of the Cowrie Palace
*7-character: 1 rhyme*

We have no idea who this goddess was. Some commentators believe her to be the Dragon Lady, others a Sea Spirit. The poem describes her image standing in her temple.

1. The mermaids are her handmaidens.
2. Though the goddess should rightfully occupy the Six Palaces or Chambers of an Empress, she must remain alone in her shrine.
3. Commentators quote the story of a king of Kashmir who caught a simurgh and caged it, only to find it would not sing. His wife pointed out that simurghs only sang when they saw their own kind, so he deceived the bird by putting a mirror in its cage. The bird then sang a mournful song and died. The goddess, rare and beautiful as a simurgh (and like this bird, mirrored in the silver sign above her) is unlike the simurgh in being immortal and free of all passions.

### The Temple of the Goddess of Orchid Fragrance
*5-character: 1 rhyme*

This goddess was probably the tutelary spirit of Mount Shen. See the poem *Delights of the Jasper Flower* above. This poem was written in the third month of the year in which He wrote the *Chang-gu* poem. The first ten lines describe the environs of the temple; the next four describe either the goddess herself or a shamaness dancing; the remaining lines describe the wanderings of the goddess.

1. The Jade Lady—traditionally associated with clouds and rain—was the tutelary spirit of Mount Wu. The River Lord was the husband of the Ladies of the Xiang.
2. The Fairy, Wei Shu-qing, used to ride a white deer, while Qin Gao rode a red bream.
3. "Caves of pearl" is glossed as "dimples."
4. The ducks were incense-burners which have grown cold in her absence.

### I Escort Wei Ren-shi and His Brother to the Pass
*5-character: 1 rhyme*

Wei Ren-shi is mentioned as addressing a remonstrance to the throne in A.D. 824. Apart from this, nothing is known of him. When He wrote this poem, Wei and his brother were probably going to Chang-an to sit for their examinations.

1. They are all too sorrowful to get drunk.
2. Hinting at success in the coming examinations.
3. The hill south of He's house in Chang-gu.

### Outside the Walls of Luo-yang, I Take Leave of Huang-fu shi
*5-character: 1 rhyme*

Huang-fu Shi, a pupil of Han Yu's, was a patron of various writers of the time, among them Li He. Though rude, arrogant, bad-tempered, and something of a drunkard, he enjoyed a great reputation for learning among his contemporaries. Since three other poems of He's are concerned with Huang-fu Shi, the two would appear to have been close friends.

1. Dragon Gate (Long-men shan) was one of the two mountains that formed the Yi Pass, a few miles south of Luo-yang.
2. During He's time, officials of the sixth and seventh grades wore green robes.

### A Cold Gorge at Twilight
*1-character: 1 rhyme*

1. Foxes had supernatural powers. Shrines to white foxes are common even today in Japan.
2. The Eastern Bean Goose.
3. The bitter bamboo is generally used for making flutes.

### The Official Has Not Come
### A Poem Written in the Office of My Senior, Huang-Fu Shi
*Irregular: 1 rhyme*

1. All commentators agree that this poem was probably written when Huang-fu Shi was Chief of Staff in Lü-hun.

## Song of an Arrowhead from Chang-ping
*7-character: 3 rhymes*

Chang-ping, seven miles west of Gao-ping county, was the site of an ancient battle field. Here, in 260 B.C., the forces of Qin were said to have captured and then buried alive 400,000 men of Zhao. Farmers were still turning up relics of the massacre in He's day, over a thousand years later. He may have written this poem in 814, when he was on his way to Lu-chou, which is not far from Chang-ping.

1. "Three spines": the triangular arrow-head.
2. The dead were crying out with hunger, since they had not been buried with proper rites nor offered libations.
3. Curds and mutton are the food of the northern nomads, not of the Chinese.
4. "Ghost fires": will-o'-the-wisps.
5. The money from the sale of the relic was to be used for buying a basket in which to offer sacrifices to appease the spirits of the fallen. Older commentators understood this line as meaning: "Urged me to take my money and buy bamboo to make a new arrow-stem." This is erroneous.

## Song: The Mansion by the River
*7-character: 4 rhymes*

1. A wife is thinking of her husband who has gone off to Jiang-ling, in Hubei, a busy commercial centre.
2. "Carp-wind": the wind of late autumn.
3. The crocodile's cry presaged rain. "Plum-rain" fell in summer, when the plums were ripe. Her husband has been gone for several months already.
4. Taverns flew linen flags which were changed when the rainy season began.
5. "Little Jade": a name used for serving-girls during Tang. The mountains on the screen make the wife recall her absent husband.

## Song: Beyond the Frontiers
*5-character: 3 rhymes*

1. "Thistle Gate": another name for Su county, Hebei, near present Beijing. The moonlit desert is dazzling white.
2. "Green Sea": the Kokonor.

3. Sentries beat metal drums to mark the night-watches.
4. Green Grave is the name of the place in Central Asia where Wang Zhao-jun, the Chinese princess who married a Han chieftain, is buried. The horses of the nomads who have massed for the attack have eaten all the grass round the spot and stripped it white as the desert sands.
5. "Banner Head": the constellation Mao, which roughly corresponds to the Pleiades. The flickering of these stars was said to augur trouble on the northern frontiers.
6. The Yellow River.

### Dyed Silk on the Loom in Spring
*7-character: 4 rhymes*

Peach-Leaves (Tao-ye) was the name of a beautiful concubine of Wang Xian-zhi.

### Song of the Young Five-Grain Pine
*7-character: 2 rhymes*

Several interpretations of this poem are proposed by the commentators. My translation is eclectic. The fruit of the five-grain pine was said to be an elixir of longevity which drove off the Three Worms that attack one's life. In this poem the pine laments that its owners are too busy and their associates too uncouth for them to appreciate its rare qualities.

1. A Fairy mentioned in the *Shen-xian zhuan*. See poem above.
2. This may mean that the pine was a dwarf-tree (*bonsai*). It is more likely that the leaves were cut for eating.
3. The maps indicate that the owners were busy local officials: the scholars were presumably their subordinates and their colleagues. The implications that Xie and Du were unable to appreciate the pine are just a pleasantry among friends.
4. "Pointed stones" (*shi-sun*)—needle-like pieces of granite used for decorating gardens, but here metonymy for He's home in Chang-gu.

### Song: By the Pool
*5-character: 1 rhyme*

A poem of this title was written by one of the wives of Emperor Wen of Wei before her execution. This quatrain of He's is perhaps a lament for a concubine of the Crown Prince, who was put to death in the eighth month of 809.

1. "Duck" is the only reading that fits the above interpretation. There is no drake in the pool.

### Song: General Lü
*Irregular: 7 rhymes*

Lü Bu (d. A.D. 198), the great warrior of the Later Han, here stands for some Tang general whom He admired, left idle at home while eunuchs mismanaged the imperial armies. This general probably bore the surname Lü.

1. Lü Bu's famous steed.
2. Chang-an.
3. The tomb of the Tang Emperor Xuan (*regnet* 712–56), ten miles northeast of Pu-cheng. The general, who may have been Commander of the Guards of the Imperial Mausoleum, is weeping over the fallen glories of the dynasty.
4. Eunuchs and women prevent the General from explaining the gravity of the situation to the emperor.
5. During Tang, the handles of official seals were shaped like fish. During Han times the seals had tortoise-shaped handles. Only high officials could wear silver seals.
6. The commander is a eunuch, probably the hated Tu-tu Cheng-cui.
7. Mount Heng, in Hebei, was in territory controlled by the rebel general Wang Cheng-zong.
8. He is once again using his favourite horse metaphor. Good men are left to starve while parasites prey on the court.
9. At Scarlet Hill (Chi-jin shan) in Guei-ji, Zhejiang, Ou-ye Zi once forged swords with copper from the He-ye stream and tin from the mountains.
10. The "green-eyed general" was certainly not a Chinese.

### Don't Wash Red Cloth!
*Irregular: 1 rhyme*

A wife laments her husband's absence at the wars. Her beauty will fade as quickly as red cloth which has been washed too often.

1. Place unidentifiable.

### Song in the Wilds
*7-character: 2 rhymes*

1. The finest bows were made from mountain mulberry.
2. Geese were said to carry reeds in their beaks to defend themselves against arrows when they flew back north in spring, since they were too fat to be able to fly at a safe height.
3. Earlier commentators understood these lines as referring to the goose or the hunter. But second-degree graduates (e.g. Li He) during Tang had to wear linen clothes.
4. A man's lot in life may not be easy: but if he is talented enough he may yet bring good fortune for himself, as surely as a skillful hunter can shoot a goose. The winter of his poverty may yet turn to spring.

### Let Wine Be Bought In!
*Irregular: 2 rhymes*

1. "Amber" is metonymy for wine.
2. "Perfumed airs": the singing-girls and dancers.
3. The line refers to the shortness of the season, not to the time of day.
4. Liu Ling (221?–300?), a noted toper, was so fond of drink that he had flasks of wine buried with him. Yet his grave is now untended and no wine is ever poured on it as a libation.

### Song: A Lovely Girl Combing Her Hair
*7-character: 6 rhymes*

1. Xi-shi who came from Yue (Zhejiang) during the Warring States period was the most renowned of all Chinese beauties. Her name stands for any beautiful woman.
2. The girl is wearing her hair in a "falling-from-your-horse chignon," a chignon set on one side of the forehead, like a rider slipping from the saddle. This style, which originated during Han times, persisted well into the nineteenth century. Half the perfume of her hair is aloes and sandalwood, the rest, her natural fragrance.
3. The back of the mirror was decorated with simurghs.

## A Shining Wet Moon
*Irregular: 3 rhymes*

1. Palace ladies, out in boats on a moonlit night, are picking water chestnuts.
2. Geese are flying low, just above the autumn mist.
3. Stone Sail is a mountain in Guei-chi, Zhejiang. Mirror Lake lies south of Shan-yin, Zhejiang.
4. "New reds": probably lotus flowers.
5. "Slime-silver": a glistening material, colour of a snail's track.

## The Capital
*5-character: 1 rhyme*

## Drums in the Street of the Officials
*7-character: 1 rhyme*

During Tang, drums sounded throughout Chang-an to announce the closing of the city gates at dusk and opening at dawn.

1. "City of Han": the palace in Chang-an. "New blinds" refers to the empress's apartments.
2. Flying Swallow: Zhao Fei-yan, the notorious and beautiful consort of Emperor Cheng of the Former Han (*regnet* 33–37 B.C.).
3. Emperor Wu of the Former Han and the First Emperor of Qin were both known for their frenzied pursuit of immortality. Our poem is clearly another attack on Xian-zong's unavailing search for the elixir of life.

## A Song for Xu's Lady, Zheng
## (She Having Asked Me to Write This When I Was in Her Garden)
*7-character: 6 rhymes*

Zheng was a singing-girl who had come to Luo-yang, found fame and fortune there, and succeeded in establishing herself as the favourite of one of the scions of the Hsü family, maternal relatives of the Han emperors.

1. Zheng Xiu was the favourite of King Huai of Chu (Warring States period).
2. The southeast gate of Luo-yang.
3. Peonies were used to arrange assignations during Tang.

4. Never Sorrow, the famous courtesan from Shi-cheng, here stands for Miss Zheng.

5. The pillow was made of "Night-shining Jade," probably chlorophane, a luminescent variety of fluorite.

6. Wang Zhao-jun (later known as Ming-jun to avoid the taboo name of Emperor Wen of Jin, 211–65) was the concubine of Emperor Yuan of the Former Han (*regnet* 48–33 B.C.). He gave her to the ruler of the Xiongnu as a bride. This line could also mean: "A long piece of Shu paper with a portrait of Wang Zhao-jun on it is rolled up into a scroll."

7. Since Si-ma Xiang-ru is dead, Li He is the only great poet of love remaining. Cao Zhi (192–232) was one of the finest poets of the pre-Tang period. Like He, he was a scion of a royal house.

### Song: A New Summer
*7-character: 4 rhymes*

1. The silkworm-thorn resembles the mulberry, its leaves being used to feed early silkworms.

### On the Theme of "Dreaming I Was Back at Home"
*5-character: 1 rhyme*

1. A fish sleeps with its eyes open. He is studying so hard he has no time to sleep.

### Passing through Sandy Park
*5-character: 1 rhyme*

Sandy Park was a large imperial preserve of some 800 square miles in Shanxi. It was used for rearing horses and other domestic animals needed for the palace. Yao believes that this poem refers to the floods which devastated the district around the capital in the spring of 812.

1. A reference to the floods which have ruined the official residence of the Superintendent of the Park; or a reference to the ruins of the Xing-de palace, which stood to the south of the park.

2. The park is almost completely deserted, only a few animals having survived the floods.

3. Like a goose which wants to return north in spring, He is unable to go home.

## On Leaving the City and Parting from Chang You-xin
## I Pledge Li Han with Wine
*5-character: 5 rhymes*

Zhang You-xin won his doctorate in 814. Li Han was a descendant of Li Dao-ming, Prince of Huai-yang, of the Tang royal house. He was a pupil of Han Yu, whose daughter he married. This poem was written in 814, when He was leaving Chang-an to return to Chang-gu.

1. The drums that announced the closing of the city gates at nightfall.
2. Zhao Yi, of the Later Han dynasty, was a talented man whose over bearing manner frequently got him into serious trouble. He was obviously aware of the trouble his own haughtiness had brought on him.
3. Ma-ching: Si-ma Xiang-ru, a poet to whom He frequently compares himself.
4. Because the land was uncultivated.
5. Su Qin, a character mentioned in the *Zhan-guo ce*, once remarked that in Chu food was dearer than jade, and firewood more costly than cassia. He is complaining of the cost of living in Chang-an.
6. Halberds were set before the gates of noblemen and high officials, the number varying according to rank.
7. Literally: "pour out the water-beetle's mother." An allusion to the belief that if the blood of the mother-beetle is smeared on one string of eighty-one cash and the blood of its offspring on another string the two lots of money will always seek each other out. Hence the expression means "to have an inexhaustible supply of money."
8. Meng Zong of Wu studied under a certain Li Su. His mother made him a quilt twelve times as wide as normal so he could share it with other scholars who stayed overnight while visiting his master.
9. During Han, official seals had knobs in the shape of tortoises. During Tang, these knobs were shaped like fish. Once again He is using a Han symbol to refer to Tang. The line means that the officials of the time were not doing their jobs properly.
10. An allusion to the Confucian belief that name and thing must be in perfect accord if a state was to be properly governed.
11. The six commanderies of Long-xi, Tian-shui, An-ding, Bei-di, Shang-jun, and Xi-he were noted for their brave men during Han times.

12. For Song Yang (Bo Lo) see above, *Twenty-three Poems about Horses*. You Wu-zheng was another famous judge of horses.
13. Zhejiang (Yue) had long been famous for its kerchiefs.

### My Southern Garden
*7-character: 1 rhyme*

A description of late spring in Chang-gu.
1. He is wearing Confucian dress as he walks in his garden. Guo Tai (128–69) set the fashion for wearing hats with one corner bent, after his own got caught in the rain.
2. Mount South in Chang-gu.
3. Zheng Xuan (127–200) was one of the greatest commentators on the Confucian classics. He is complimenting the people of Chang-gu by implying that they are as observant of the Confucian precepts as if they came from Zheng's own village in Shandong.
4. *The Summons of the Soul (Zhao Hun)* is one of the poems in the Chu Ci, pp. 101–9.

### Song: Imitating the Singing of Dragons
*Irregular (4- and 7- character): 3 rhymes*

As a young man, Fang Guan (697–763), who later became Prime Minister, was studying in a valley of Mount Zhung-nan when he heard strange cries coming from the mountain. An old man told him that this was the singing of dragons, a sound always followed by rain. Later he came across a Buddhist monk who had succeeded in imitating a dragon's cry perfectly by striking a copper bowl in a certain way. Jiao-ran then wrote a poem called *Striking the Copper Bowl to Imitate a Singing Dragon*. He is modelling himself on this. Our poem, however, is undoubtedly satirical. Men are frightened of real dragons (geniuses) and chase them away, but like to try to imitate their song nevertheless. This otherwise fine poem is marred by its rather precious diction.
1. *Han Wu Nei-zhuan* lists the lungs of a white phoenix and the blood of a blue simurgh as exotic drugs. The cry of the true dragon, here contrasted with the faint sound of the bowl, is as terrifying as the shriek of these slaughtered birds. So the cry of the true poet—that rarest of creatures—is one of agony.

2. The dragon brought wind and rain, which made the cassia seeds fall.
3. Like the Western Mother, the dragon has gained immortality.
4. For the River Ladies, see above, *The Royal Ladies of the Xiang*. The Ladies are weeping over the dragons' departure.
5. A reference to the Blue (or White) Lotus-flower Dragon-king.
6. Iron—a metal of which dragons were terrified—had been dropped into the water to drive them away.

### Song: A Modest Maiden in the Spring Sunshine
*7-character: 1 rhyme*

This poem and the next one were not found in the earliest edition of He's work, but are attributed to him in the Song anthology, the *Yue-fu shi-ji* of Guo Mao-qian. On this account, the commentators have been wary about assigning authorship of these works to He. I can see no reason why these should not be from his own hand.

7. "Clouds of dawn": her hair.
8. "Hills of brocade": the quilts.
9. "Icy cave": the girl's room.

### Joys of Youth
*7-character: 1 rhyme*

10. Wang Ji (Sui dynasty) wrote the *Record of the Land of Drunkenness*.
11. "The girl from Wu": a conventional expression for a beautiful woman.
12. "Master Lu": see above poem.

### Six Satires
*5-character: 1 rhyme*

1. Another variant on the "bird in a gilded cage." A singing-girl, though patronized by princes, is desperately unhappy because her true love—who is presumably poor—is far away.
2. The second poem is perhaps a satire on the marriage of a Chinese princess of the imperial house to the Uighur Khan. Wang Zhao-jun came from Shu.
3. There are at least three places of this name. The one referred to here is probably in Mongolia.
4. A deadly attack on a eunuch general—probably Tu-tu Cheng-cui himself—who was conducting the campaign against the rebel gover-

nor Wang Cheng-zong. The appointment of a "lady-general" aroused such a storm of criticism that the emperor was compelled to dismiss him. He's verses must have played their part in this. The whole poem rings with a savage indignation rarely found in Chinese verse.

5. A satire on a rich, young man, son of some general or other, who has risen to wealth and eminence through his father's influence. "Green Gate": the eastern gates of Chang-an.

6. Ban Jie-yu (*floruit* 48–6 B.C.) was for many years the favourite of Han Cheng-di (*regnet* 33–7 B.C.). Towards the end of her life, seeing herself ousted by a younger favourite, she withdrew to the Palace of Eternal Trust, where she lived out the rest of her days. She is best known for a poem supposed to have been written on a round fan which she sent to the Emperor after her loss of favour.

7. As Ban did, when invited to ride with the Emperor. She refused on the grounds that only degenerate rulers allowed women to accompany them on their outings.

8. Paper money, burnt at funerals, flutters around the graveyard pines.

9. A party is going on in a wealthy household.

10. A reference to the legend about ten suns once appearing on the Fu-sang tree. The line means: (a) the entrance court was bright with candles, (b) the sun never set on their merrymaking.

11. "White fishes": culters. The fish are attracted by the music.

12. Whistling was a form of entertainment.

13. Because Mount South is eternal, while man's life is ephemeral.

### Song: Never Sorrow
*5-character: 2 rhymes*

Songs about a singing-girl called Mo-chou (whose name means "Never Sorrow") date back to the Six Dynasties period, probably to the early fifth century or so. They belong to that rather languid yet passionate tradition of southern love-songs which was later to assert itself anew in that genre known as the *ci*.

1. A pool near Jiang-ling. North of it stood the Fishing Tower of King Zhuang of Chu.

2. The fishes were painted on the prow of the boat, which she need-ed for gathering lotuses.

3. For aloeswood, see above Poem.

4· She was playing a *se*, see Poem 1 from *Six Satires* above.

5. Or possibly: "A sliver of waning moon, like a curtain-hook."

### Pleasure Comes at Night
*7-character: 2 rhymes*

A fashionable singing-girl, with a wealthy clientele, entertains her guest.

1. A pattern of carp was carved onto the candelabra.
2. Gibbons were so fond of wine that they were generally captured by making them drunk. Hence wine-jars were often shaped like gibbons.
3. Literally: "A smile from A-hou…" A-hou was a name used for singing girls, deriving from a poem of Emperor Wu of Liang.
4. Dawn has come and her guest is departing for the court.
5. Where high officials stayed while awaiting audience with the emperor.

### Deriding the Snow
*5-character: 1 rhyme*

A girl is deriding the snow because its promise of the joy of spring is false, since her soldier husband is still away from home.

1. Cong-ling mountains: mountains in the Himalayas, north of Nepal.
2. "Orchid isles": perhaps gardens of rich families in Chang-an.
3. "Dragon Sands": the desert beyond the Great Wall.
4. Ding Ling-wei, from Liao-dong (on the Korean border), was a Taoist who could change himself into a crane. He returned home after an absence of a thousand years to find all his friends long dead. The girl is comparing her husband, now feathered white with the snow that is falling beyond the Great Wall, to an aging crane that has flown off to Liao-dong never to return. We could also translate thus: "It's been long since the snow parted from the crane on the walls of Liao. The feather-robe by now must have grown sere."

### Ballad: Spring Longings
*7-character: 1 rhyme*

A courtesan, alone at night, is dreaming of her lover.

1. She is playing her *pi-pa*, which is decorated with a pattern of phoenixes and fairies, with a plectrum, whose guard was made of gold. So: "Strumming with a plectrum tipped with gold, she plays 'Fiery Phoenix.'"
2. "Clouds": her hair.

3. Dragon-brain was a name given to Borneo camphor, a highly prized aromatic.
4. "A-hou": see "Pleasure Comes at Night" above.
5. Zhou Yu (175–210) was noted for his bravery and good looks.

### Ballad of the White Tiger
*7-character: 6 rhymes*

Commentators generally maintain this poem couldn't have been written by He. While agreeing that this poem is markedly inferior in style to the rest of He's work, I feel that since arguments based on stylistic grounds alone are rather dubious, its exclusion from this collection would be unjustifiable. The white tiger stands for the Qin dynasty, which conquered the last of the feudal kingdoms in 221 B.C., thus bringing about the formation of a centralized state. White was the symbolic colour assigned to Qin; the tiger was the symbol of oppressive government. The King of Qin, who reigned as First Emperor of Qin (Qin Shi Huang-di) from 221 to 210, was a ruthless innovator, a great destroyer of tradition, who earned for himself the undying execration of the Confucian literati.

1. The fire-bird was the symbol of the Zhou dynasty. When King Wu of Zhou was on his way to destroy the Shang dynasty, fire fell from heaven upon his house and then took on the form of a red crow with a melodious song.
2. Li Si, Qin Shi Huang-di's minister, persuaded his master to order that all histories of the feudal states (with the exception of those of Qin) should be burnt, as well as *The Classic of Poetry*, *The Classic of History*, and the philosophical works of the Hundred Schools.
3. The expression *pei jue* "to wear a jade ring at the belt," also means by a play on words, "to act decisively." The government was militaristic and ruthless.
4. Qin Shi Huang-di is said to have sent the magician Xu Shi on an expedition to search for the three magic islands of the Immortals which were supposed to lie in the Eastern Sea. On his return, Xu Shi excused his failure by claiming that a great fish had prevented him from reaching the islands. He went on to ask that an archer with a multiple-firing crossbow should accompany him on his next trip to deal with the fish. The Emperor then ordered that all fishermen and sailors should take arms against this fish.

5. Nobody could enlist the aid of Heaven to destroy Qin. "Sky River": the Milky Way.
6. Literally: "Who suffered most, who suffered most?"
7. Jing Ke, also known as Jing Qing, was a man from Wei who eventually became a retainer of Prince Dan, the heir-apparent of the state of Yan. He was something of a drunkard, spending his days sprawled in the marketplace with his friend Gao Jian-li, who was a skilled performer on the five-stringed zhu-lute, singing and drinking wine. In 227 B.C., when Yan was menaced by Qin, he volunteered to set off on a suicidal mission to assassinate the King of Qin. The attempt failed and Jing was cut to pieces. Gao Jian-li then tried to avenge Jing's death by filling his lute with lead and attacking the King of Qin with it. This attempt was also unsuccessful.
8. Liu Bang, the founder of Han, called himself the son of the Scarlet Emperor. Hence the Han banners were scarlet.

### Someone I Love
*Irregular: 5 rhymes*

Here the poet is speaking through the person of Wen-jun, wife of the poet Si-ma Xiang-ru. She is waiting for him to return from his journey to Shu.
1. Sichuan.
2. Literally: "the wind of the second lunar month." This can fall any time between the end of February and mid-April.
3. As did the tears of the two wives of Shun, which fell upon the bamboos near the river Xiang and made them speckled.
4. The Milky Way.
5. The *yi-yuan*, a fifth-century collection of tales of the supernatural, carries the story of a certain Tao Kan, who pulled up a shuttle while out fishing. After he had taken this home and hung it up on a wall, it changed into a red dragon and flew away. Presumably shuttles were sometimes carved in the shape of dragons to commemorate this story.
6. The Weaving Lady and the Herd-boy, lovers separated by the river of the Milky Way, are fated only to meet on the seventh day of the seventh month, when the wings of magpies form a bridge for them to cross the waters which divide them. Since the west wind, the harbinger of autumn, has not yet risen, the seventh month is a long way off.
7. The moon.
8. Pieces of jade arranged so that they would tinkle musically when the wind blew, were hung by the windows of well-to-do houses.

9. To consult the omens so that she might know when her husband would return. One version reads "south of the Wall..."

### Ridiculing a Young Man
*7-character: 6 rhymes*

1. As Han Yan, companion of Emperor Wu, did during the Former Han dynasty, losing a dozen a day.
2. Either "I have never been under obligation to anyone," or "I have never travelled."
3. An allusion to a passage in a Buddhist sutra which warns: "When the hair grows white and the face turns haggard, death is near." This poem is surely too superficial and vulgar to be anything but a forgery.

### A Private Road in Eastern Kao-ping County
*5-character: 1 rhyme*

This poem was probably written when He was visiting Zhang Che in Lu zhou. Gao-ping county is in Shanxi.
1. *Ternstroemia japonica.*

### Ballad of the Immortals
*7-character: 2 rhymes*

1. On the magic islands of the Immortals in the Eastern Sea.

### Song: Dragons at Midnight
*7-character: 5 rhymes*

1. *Gong* and *zhi* are the first and fourth notes of the pentatonic scale.
2. Images evoked by the music.
3. The sound of silk being beaten on the fulling-blocks in autumn, to make winter clothes, is a familiar symbol of parting and sorrow.

### The Kun-lun Envoy
*7-character: 2 rhymes*

Emperor Wu of Han sent Zhang Qian as an envoy to the far west, where he came upon the source of the Yellow River, in a range of mountains he dubbed "Kun-lun." Though this poem appears to be a satire on the insatiable ambitions of Emperor Wu, who was always eager to enlarge his empire, it is actually an attack on Emperor Xian-zong.

1. Emperor Wu was already buried in the Mao-ling tomb before Zhang returned.
2. No Taoist recipes could give the Emperor the secret of eternal life. For the brazen bowls see the poem "Songs of the Brazen Immortal Bidding Farewell to Han" above.
3. Stone unicorns (*qi-lin*) and carved dragons around the mausoleum are weathering with time.

### Tang-ji of Han Sings as the Wine is Drunk
*5-character: 2 rhymes*

In the ninth month of A.D. 189 Dong-zhuo forced the boy-emperor, Liu Bian (Shao-di), to abdicate after a reign of only a few months. In the first month of the following year Zhuo ordered Li Ru, one of his officers, to force the Emperor to drink a poisoned draught. The Emperor then held a farewell banquet at which his wife, Tang-ji, sang and danced for him. When this was over, he drank the poison and died. Afterwards Tang-ji returned to her native town to live in seclusion, refusing to marry.

1. Since the Emperor was not imprisoned at Yun-yang (Shanxi), one commentator believes this is an allusion to Cheng Miao, who was said to have invented the form of writing known as *li-shu* (clerkly script) while in prison at Yun-yang. Hence Yun-yang here is simply a literary term for "gaol." Since the Emperor was on the verge of death he is styled a "ghost."
2. The usual text reads:
   "Grasping swords as bright as autumn water,
   Evil powers often threatened the emperor."
3. The expression "a mountain of jade about to topple" was used to describe the poet Xi Kang (223–62) when drunk.
4. The Emperor will not be buried with imperial honours.
5. "Zhao-yang": the name of the palace of the Han Empress Zhao Fei-yan. Here it means the palace where Tang-ji had lived.
6. "Southern road": the busy road to the south. Tang-ji will live in seclusion.

## Song: Listening to Master Ying Playing the Lute
### 7-character: 4 rhymes

Ying was evidently a celebrated performer on the *qin*. Han Yu also wrote a poem to him with the same title.

1. The clouds drift towards the Milky Way leaving the moon ("the isle of cassia flowers") shining serenely.
2. "Two phoenixes": Ying's hands.
3. The lute sounds like the singing of the goddess of Mount Tianmu (in Xin-chang county, Zhejiang), which was once heard by a King of Yue.
4. "Hidden" because worn inside the garments.
5. See the poem *Song of the Sword of the Collator in the Spring Office* above, for the story of Zhou Chu.
6. Zhang Xu, a contemporary of Li He's, was famous for his calligraphy in the draft script. When drunk he would rush wildly around shouting, then soak his long hair in ink and use it to write down huge characters. When sober, he could remember nothing of this, swearing he must have been possessed by a spirit.
7. Master Ying must have resembled a Buddhist monk.
8. This was the great lute (*da qin*) which was eight feet one inch in length.
9. Literally: "Not the grandson of a kolanut tree." Mount Yi-yang, in Jiangsu, was renowned for its kolanut trees, which were prized for lute-making. The small branches which were generally used were called "grandsons." He remarks that this particular lute is so big it must have taken a whole tree to make it, not just a branch.
10. A mat of dragon's-beard or Baltic rush.

## Ballad of the World
### 5-character: 1 rhyme

A young girl, brought up in the Imperial palace, leaves it to become a singing-girl.
1. "Shang-lin park": the Imperial park.
2. "Pomegranate skirt": the pomegranate-coloured skirt of a singing-girl.

# Select Bibliography

❦

The following editions of Li He's poems were among those consulted:

CHINESE EDITIONS
*San Jia Ping Zhu Li Chang-ji Ge Shi*. Shanghai, 1959.
*Li He Shi Ji*. Edited by Ye Cong-qi. Peking, 1959.
*Li Chang-ji Wen Ji*. Taibei, 1967.
*Li He Ge Shi Bian*. Taibei, 1971.
*Tang Li He Xie Lü Gou Yuan*. Hong Kong, 1973.

JAPANESE EDITIONS
*Ri Ga*. Edited by Arai Ken. Tokyo, 1959.
*Ri Chūkichi Kashishū*. Edited by Suzuki Torao, 2 vols. Tokyo, 1961.
*Ri Ga*. Edited by Saitō Shō. Tokyo, 1967.

Among secondary works consulted were the following:

ENGLISH
Chen, David. "Li Ho and Keats: A Comparative Study of Two Poets."
    Unpublished dissertation, Indiana University, Bloomington, 1962.
Du Guo-jing. "The Poetry of Li Ho (790–816)." Unpublished disserta-
    tion, Stanford University, 1974.
Fish, Michael B. "Mythological Themes in the Poetry of Li Ho (791–817)."
    Unpublished dissertation, Indiana University, Bloomington, 1973.
Robertson, Maureen A. "Poetic Diction in the Works of Li Ho (791–817)."
    Unpublished dissertation, University of Washington, Seattle, 1970.
South, Margaret T. *Li Ho: A Scholar-official of the Yuan-ho period (806–821)*. Adelaide, 1967.

CHINESE
Ai Wen-bo (Robert L. Frick). *Li He Shi Yin De (A Concordance to the Poems of Li Ho 790–816)*. Taibei, 1969.
Hu Yun-yi. *Tang Shi Yan Jiu*. Shanghai, n.d.
Qian Zhong-shu. *Tan Yi Lu*. Shanghai, 1937.

Zhou Cheng-zhen. *Li He Lun.* Hong Kong, 1972.
Zhou Lang-feng. *She Ren Li He.* Shanghai, n.d.

JAPANESE
Harada Kenyu. "Ri Chōkichi o megutte,"
*Hō Kō* nos. 1–6 (March 1953–September 1956).
"Ri Ga no shōki,"*Hō Kō*, no. 10 (July 1963); no. 13 (October 1966): also in
   *Kyōto Joshi Daigaku Jinbun Ronsō*, nos. 7, 8 and 14–18 (November
   1962–June 1970). Ri Ga Kenkyu (January 1971–).
Kusamori Shinichi "Suisho no kyaku—Ri Chōkichi den," 41 chapters in
   *Gendai-shi techō* vol. 8 no. 9 and vol. 16 no. 4.

For a complete bibliography see my *The Poems of Li Ho* (Oxford, 1970),
   pp. 284–89.

# Index of Poems